MANAGING
CHANGE
IN ORGANIZATIONS

Stefan Sveningsson & Nadja Sörgärde

MANAGING CHANGE
IN ORGANIZATIONS

Los Angeles | London | New Delhi
Singapore | Washington DC | Melbourne

Los Angeles | London | New Delhi
Singapore | Washington DC | Melbourne

SAGE Publications Ltd
1 Oliver's Yard
55 City Road
London EC1Y 1SP

SAGE Publications Inc.
2455 Teller Road
Thousand Oaks, California 91320

SAGE Publications India Pvt Ltd
B 1/I 1 Mohan Cooperative Industrial Area
Mathura Road
New Delhi 110 044

SAGE Publications Asia-Pacific Pte Ltd
3 Church Street
#10-04 Samsung Hub
Singapore 049483

Editor: Ruth Stitt
Assistant editor: Martha Cunneen
Production editor: Imogen Roome
Marketing manager: Lucia Sweet
Cover design: Francis Kenney
Typeset by: C&M Digitals (P) Ltd, Chennai, India
Printed in the UK

Library of Congress Control Number: 2019943573

British Library Cataloguing in Publication data

A catalogue record for this book is available from
the British Library

ISBN 978-1-5264-6443-9
ISBN 978-1-5264-6444-6 (pbk)

At SAGE we take sustainability seriously. Most of our products are printed in the UK using responsibly sourced papers and
boards. When we print overseas we ensure sustainable papers are used as measured by the PREPS grading system. We
undertake an annual audit to monitor our sustainability.

For Agneta and for Line and Tim

CONTENTS

LIST OF FIGURES AND TABLES

FIGURES

TABLES

ABOUT THE AUTHORS

Stefan Sveningsson is Professor of Business Administration at the School of Economics and Management, Lund University. He has been visiting researcher at Cardiff Business School, Melbourne University, University of Sydney and Auckland Business School. His research includes leadership, managerial work, strategic and organizational change, and the organization of knowledge-intensive work. He has published several books and journal articles. Recent books include *Changing Organizational Culture* (2nd edition, Routledge, 2015, with Mats Alvesson), *Managerial Lives: Leadership and Identity in an Imperfect World* (Cambridge University Press, 2016, with Mats. Alvesson), and *Reflexive Leadership* (Sage, 2017, with Mats Alvesson and Martin Blom).

Nadja Sörgärde is a senior lecturer in Business Administration at the School of Economics and Management, Lund University. She has been a visiting scholar at the University of Queensland and University of Technology Sydney. Her research focus is organizational change, culture and identity, and she has studied change processes in the private as well as the third sector. She is a respected lecturer and has received a prize for her teaching and pedagogical work.

PREFACE

Organizational change is one of the most written about areas in modern leadership – and organizational literature. Despite all this literature with advice and recommendations, most organizations don't succeed in their efforts to change. Why is there a need for yet another book on the subject? Well, our hope is that we will be able to contribute something outside the standard recipes for change. It's about deepening our understanding of processes of change and problematizing the current view of change as something necessary. We believe that a technical perspective of change – *how* you do it – is not sufficient. Understanding *what* change means for those engaged is crucial, and what social dynamics – relations and interactions – characterize processes of change. The ambition is also to put forward a more critical view on *why* change today is perceived as something normal. Is change always needed and what does it mean to develop a more sceptical approach to it?

The book is the result of a longstanding research and teaching collaboration between the authors, within and with the support of the research group LUMOS (Lund University Management & Organization Studies) at Lund University School of Economics and Management. We want to give a special thanks to Mats Alvesson for his support and encouragement to the project and also to Tony Huzzard, Dan Kärreman and Jens Rennstam for reading and commenting on a previous version of this script. We would also like to thank the Foundation of Handelsbanken and the Knut and Alice Wallenberg Foundation for research grants that have made the studies and the work behind this book possible.

Lund, October 2019
Stefan Sveningsson and Nadja Sörgärde

ONLINE RESOURCES

Head online to https://study.sagepub.com/sveningsson to access a range of online resources that will aid study and support teaching. *Managing Change in Organizations* is accompanied by:

FOR LECTURERS

- PowerPoint slides, featuring tables and figures from each chapter, which can be adapted and edited to suit your own teaching needs.
- A selection of SAGE Business Cases relating to the key topics and concepts of the book.

FOR STUDENTS

- Read Free SAGE Journal Articles related to each chapter, to extend your knowledge and support your assignments.
- Test your understanding and prepare for exams with interactive Multiple Choice Questions.
- Watch Online Videos from SAGE Video and YouTube to discover more about the key concepts discussed in the book.

INTRODUCTION

In contemporary society, organizational change is often seen as a natural part of everyday organizational life – as something as inescapable as income taxes and death. Organizations are increasingly faced with demands and expectations to engage in organizational changes in order to keep up with ever changing markets and customer preferences, technological development, globalization, institutional and political changes, demographic and cultural shifts and fashionable management ideas and recipes. Thus, the external environmental forces of organizational change in current society are numerous. In addition, these forces are also mutually influencing each other in complex ways that often make them vague and ambiguous rather than something that provides clear guidance on how to cope with them in terms of managing change. Moreover, organizational change is also often driven by internal organizational forces such as when organizations that emphasize innovation rely on a creative workforce for strategic change and development. Internally-driven change can also be the result of managerial actions to reduce costs and improve efficiency in order to enhance competitiveness. But regardless of whether it is triggered by largely external or internal forces, change is something that organizations are significantly challenged by, and consequently is something that is becoming increasingly important to understand and manage.

A company that seems to understand environmental forces well and is able to turn these insights into productive managerial actions is the American company Amazon, which seem to thrive on organizational change more or less continuously.

MINI CASE 1.1

Organizational change at Amazon

Being one of the most successful global companies of the 21st century, Amazon shows that organizational change can be an inherent part of the way an organization is managed and developed. Established in 1994 by Jeff Bezos as a digital platform for selling books, it has become a leading digital platform offering a wide variety of different products and services – music, film, toys, tools, food, clothes, streaming-services, cloud-services, etc. – on a global level. In 2018 Amazon represented 4% of the total retail commerce in the US and 44% of the e-commerce market. It is characterized as a company that is obsessed with customer orientation and that has managed to create an extremely well-oiled machine that strives for efficiency in all parts of the value chain in order to rapidly provide customers with low-priced products. As Amazon states:

Amazon is guided by four principles: customer obsession rather than competitor focus, passion for invention, commitment to operational excellence, and long-term thinking. (HUI Research Council, 2018)

Regarded from an organizational change perspective, Amazon offers several valuable insights. The company's revenues have expanded by approximately 29% a year since 2003 and it has been profitable since 2002. The steady growth has been possible by its constant reinvestment of profits in its operations in order to provide for innovation through a substantial research and development focus. In 2017 Amazon invested $16.1 billion in R&D, which makes it one of the largest companies investing in operations. It is important to note how Amazon has very successfully exploited a variety of external developments in society, such as technological development (digital media, cloud-services), the globalization of markets, changing customer preferences (e-commerce), etc. However Amazon is also driven by internal forces, in particular by a strong culture of innovation and feedback systems, which encourage learning and continuous development and change (HUI Research Council, 2018). For instance they have invented new forms of logistics, which facilitate efficient and fast deliveries. This culture is supported by the long-term oriented practice of reinvesting profits in the organization.

Netflix is another example of an organization that has successfully been drawing on changing customer preferences and technological development, and has accomplished continuous growth in its innovative streaming services. Starting out as an online DVD rental company in 1998, Netflix a few years later realized the potential in streaming services and began a change process that made them the largest streaming company in the world with close to 140 million subscribers as of 2018 (BBC News, 2018; Lawrence, 2018; Statista, 2019). Part of the success of Netflix is often said to be their culture of change, where people are encouraged to be critical of the status quo and to be honest about business prospects even if it means antagonising others (Taylor, 2018). Both Amazon and Netflix illustrate the value of a culture that triggers innovative change by drawing on market and technological forces. In addition to these organizations one should also mention some of other classic consumer-product companies, such as Coca-Cola Co., Procter & Gamble Co., and Carlsberg Breweries, which adapt to constantly changing customer preferences by organizational changes that maintain strategic development in terms of new products.

Organizational changes that necessarily follow from acquisitions and mergers are often seen as being particularly challenging, but here too we find some telling illustrations that seem to counter conventional wisdom. For example, while there are some well-known cases of failed mergers within the car industry – Daimler & Chrysler, General Motors & Saab, Ford & Jaguar – there are also encouraging illustrations that suggest that the organizational changes following a merger can be productive for organizational change and strategic development. When Zhejiang Geely Holding Group acquired Volvo Cars from Ford Motors in 2010, many observers were afraid that the Chinese owners would transform Volvo's high-quality brand into a low-cost image. In contrast, however, Geely facilitated Volvo's engagement in technological development and maintained its reputation as an innovative producer of high-quality cars, partly by establishing a new innovation centre aimed at increased digitalization and the development of the self-driving car. As a member of Volvo's management team, Lex Kerssemakers, commented when talking about Geely and its founder, Li Shufu, the man behind the acquisition of Volvo: 'He gave us balls again' (Gruley & Butters, 2018).

There is no shortage of illustrations of successful organizational and strategic change. A number of examples can be found in the business press. These examples can be inspirational and provide change agents with encouragement and optimism about the possibility to accomplish the often complex and multifaceted task of formulating and implementing organizational change. They can also provide us with some clues and insights about what needs to be considered when engaging in change. In addition to that, critical reflection upon the actual need to change is also important. In some situations, cherishing and strengthening the established business with its core competences, and thus not embarking upon radical change, could be a wise choice. This book takes as its starting point the huge interest in organizational change in modern organizations and looks at it from different angels. The broad aim is to provide a qualified overview and review of ideas, models and concepts – the language of organizational change – in order to facilitate a critical understanding of change as well as support managerially driven efforts to formulate and implement change.

The rest of this introductory chapter will be structured as follows. We continue by discussing the background of this book in more depth. In particular, we will stress the importance of developing a varied view of organizational change, where its importance as well as its challenges and complexities are taken into account. We will then show how the literature on change differs in focus in terms of what key questions are asked and answered (the *how*, *what* and *why* of change). This way of structuring the field forms the pedagogical framework of the book, which more specifically differentiates between a tool-based, process and critical perspective on organizational change. Finally, we will further clarify the purpose of the book and give an outline of the different chapters.

BACKGROUND

In terms of what is often seen as being crucial for the success of contemporary organizations, there is hardly anything that is more important than the understanding and managing of organizational change. When we hear about organizational success it is often related to having productively completed some form of change, as was illustrated in the introductory cases. But successful change is complex and often calls for reflection and thoughtfulness rather than merely following fashionable trends and recipes and models for how to realize change. A central tenet in this book is that reflection and thoughtfulness about organizational change are enabled by having a broad repertoire of concepts and models of change, a repertoire that recognizes the variety within the field and facilitates a differentiated approach to the subject. Environmental forces and organizational challenges and problems are seldom clear-cut and unambiguous in terms of what needs to be changed, which is why any change agent will benefit from having appropriated a broad and nuanced understanding of what change is about and how it can be managed. Therefore, our basic premise is to go beyond sweeping views of change and to recognize that organizational change – in spite of all the success stories indicating otherwise – is challenging and often requires differentiated knowledge that facilitates an intimate understanding of the local and situational contingencies. The challenges that come with trying to critically understand and manage change thus forms the background of this book and its pedagogical framing of organizational change in three different perspectives: the how, what and why.

In order to provide an overview of the research on organizational change in terms of how, what and why, it is natural to acknowledge the historical background of writings on organizational change. The history of research on organizational change dates back several decades and even if many concepts have been around for years, some are still valid and significant in understanding as well as managing change. Furthermore, managerial ideals tend to reoccur, why the historical lessons learned about the effects of certain managerial practices, still can be highly relevant for contemporary organizations. We will devote a substantial amount of space to the history of organizational change by reviewing some of the classic traditions and the concepts that developed from these traditions, especially in Chapter 4 where we discuss concepts of change from the early classics of the Human Relations tradition to the highly popular Organizational Development (OD) approach to change that established itself during the 1950s and 1960s. Approaches and concepts of change have become increasingly sophisticated and inclusive, especially in terms of recognizing people (as more than cogs in the machinery), relations, interactions, group dynamics, organizational culture as well as broader orientations such as strategy.

In acknowledging the increasing sophistication of the field and the various approaches to change that have emerged during the last decades, it is also important to recognize that managing organizational change often means a lot of additional coordination such as managing projects, motivating, allocating resources, controlling, influencing organizational culture, etc. Following this, it goes without saying that change is difficult and messy, as there are plenty of traps and pitfalls that may lead to failure. There can be many reasons for the lack of success. Sometimes there is a lack of realism – the need for time, knowledge and insights quite simply is underestimated when change programmes are formulated and implemented. Sometimes it is due to a lack of understanding of the importance of existing organizational arrangements, such as the routines, organizational culture and structure. Often the importance of history and traditions are underestimated when attempting to make changes. Sometimes it is due to a lack of commitment, will or knowledge among those who are set to actively implement the transformation, which can ultimately be connected with too narrow a view of what it really entails to implement more extensive changes. As most people who have been involved in change attempts surely know, there is much that can go wrong.

Nevertheless, change management is still characterized by great optimism, and new radical and comprehensive change programmes are launched in organizations on a daily basis. Maybe over-optimism is inevitable when one talks about the need for change. Many authors on the subject – both in popular management books and in more research-oriented writings – are arguing their own case, so to speak, when they introduce new models of transformation. Of course, this is also true of this book, even though we also highlight the need for a differentiated view of change and a dose of scepticism about much of what is said about the need for change. To what extent organizational change is really needed often calls for considerable reflection and thoughtfulness. One seldom hears any author writing about the importance of being careful with change and to thoroughly consider the value of embarking on change programmes which are hard to control and which have uncertain outcomes. Given the rather frequent occurrence of change attempts in organizations, there doesn't seem to be much widespread scepticism of the view of the significance of change among practitioners. Many see it as more or less inevitable. To engage in organizational change can also be seen as an expression of drive and leadership, and can therefore enhance the status of those involved in it. Change attempts make it possible to profile oneself as a leader and to create an image of how you want to be perceived by others both within and outside the organization. Change is also a part of our times, and hardly anyone wants to be seen as an ordinary supervisor or administrator of an existing organization compared to being seen as a change actor (which, by definition, is often related to leadership) full of initiative. Some talk of organizational change is, in other words, about image and identity. It is also generally hard for organizations to ignore something that many people – practitioners, consultants and academia – agree is vital for the survival of organizations. Organizational change can thus be about promoting a certain image of the organization in order to gain recognition from internal and external actors who value and stress the importance of change.

That changes can be about identity, image and recognition doesn't, of course, exclude the possibility that transformation of an organization can be needed for highly rational reasons. As stated earlier, increasingly faster technological development is taking place, which, together with financial turbulence, political instability in many parts of the world and often unpredictable socioeconomic conditions, normally gives rise to increased demands for change. Added to this, today there are increasingly higher institutional and ethical demands in business, which means that many organizations have to show that they are good citizens, that they need to demonstrate not only economic efficiency but also societal legitimacy, i.e. that they care about ethics and corporate social responsibility (CSR) questions in general. For example, PwC conducted a study in 2018 on how companies globally prioritize and report on the sustainable development goals (SDGs)[1] for their businesses. The study showed that 72% of companies mentioned sustainable development goals in their annual report or their sustainability report, and that 54% of those that prioritized the goals also included them in their business strategy (PwC, 2018). Furthermore, in many public organizations, partly governed by fashions, trends and the opinion pressure of the media, it can be seen as equally important to work with how you are perceived in moral terms, such as through value issues, for example, as it is important to show results. The outside world is

---

[1]SDGs are a collection of commitments made by the 193 members of the United Nations in 2015. They set 17 goals and 169 targets to achieve sustainable development by 2030.

thus becoming increasingly multifaceted and this shift in character contributes in many cases to improved business intelligence and greater attention to readiness for and the possibilities to formulate and implement organizational transformation. This has led to a huge increase in interest for the field of change in the last decade.

REVIEW QUESTIONS 1.1

| Explain | Discuss reasons for managers to be (overly) positive and optimistic towards initiating organizational change. |
| Reflect | Do you think there could be groups of people who are less positive and optimistic towards change initiatives? If so, why? |

Understanding organizational change

How should one approach an area like organizational change, and what can one actually gain from theories and models? The diversity within the subject is substantial, and there is no scarcity of terms and models which facilitate and explain change. In the literature, knowledge that facilitates change tends to be at the forefront, that is knowledge that enables actors of change – consultants, leaders, bosses or co-workers in general – to perform better in change processes. Many people that have the ambition to change something normally look for writings about change in order to enhance their competence about it to be able to realize change more successfully. People are thus often looking for the recipes and tools for success. This is also the ambition in much of the mainstream literature covering change, where several more or less technical models of change have been developed that explain how it is done. Consequently, much of the literature within the field strives to be relatively clear in terms of how to formulate and implement change successfully. Within this genre you find practitioners, consultants and scholars who jointly try to emphasize guidelines and the principles for successful organizational change.

In much of this literature it is supposed that change will be implemented in fairly distinct steps and at specific periods in an organization's development. Sometimes this view of change is described as episodic – i.e. that change takes place in specific episodes – in a specific time or episode of the organization's history, and between these episodes organizations are assumed to be relatively stable. Episodic change is often characterized as radical and long-term, i.e. having significant organizational impact such as strategic or organizational cultural change. In this line of thinking, the organization is thought of as a rather static entity which typically changes when an internal or external force exerts pressure specifically for change, e.g. a planned initiative from management or radical change in the environment of the organization. It can, however, be questioned whether it is possible to formulate an abstract recipe that is generally applicable when the local and concrete realities in which the changes are supposed to be implemented in consists of more than thousands of situational contingencies. For example, many n-step models – viewed as the implementation of a number of sequential steps – are challenging to draw upon in real-life organizations as local and situational conditions seldom align well with the assumptions upon which the model rests. Sometimes people might not understand the meaning or the purpose behind abstract and general formulations of change directives and are therefore forced to spend a lot of time and energy trying to interpret and understand what is supposed to change more concretely in local situations. Plans and intentions are always interpreted on the basis of the background of specific local and situational conditions and the experiences and interests of the people involved in the process. Occasionally people don't agree on a decided course of change and may actively try to resist change and thereby complicate a well-formulated plan of change.

But even if recipes – such as n-step models – are problematic to interpret and translate to local conditions, they still provide us with a general toolbox of ideas and considerations of how to work with change management. In addition to the simple recipes of *how*, it is also central to develop an understanding of and feeling for *what* is happening in specific change processes in real-life organizations. This means that it is important to acknowledge that change includes questions that deal with diversity in interpretations, imitation, legitimacy, power, politics, conflicts and other challenges that one might not want to embrace in change situations that are supposed to express optimism and drive. To this, one can add other aspects that deal with norms, values, meaning and identity, the latter of which is related to what individuals or groups see as being distinctive about themselves. These themes are partly discussed in the literature that is more descriptive and interpretative compared to the more technically normative, i.e. prescriptive (in terms of advising how to accomplish change) literature. The aim of the descriptive is to portray organizational change processes in practice, i.e. the initiatives behind change and the processes and results. This also includes understanding how those targeted by change initiatives relate to them. Here the significance is placed on what happens to initiatives of change as people interpret and relate to them based on their position, interest, background, etc. For example, how do people who are targeted for change look at the initiatives and what is done with ideas of change in an organizational context? Are they accepted and embraced or contested and resisted? Are they ignored by people who either don't understand their meaning or just don't care about them very much? What are the unforeseen consequences of embarking on change projects and how can these consequences be explained and perhaps avoided? These are central questions in an interpretative and descriptive view of change, where understanding and meaning are central aspects. Of course, there are opportunities to find practical knowledge also, but opposed to the more anecdotally-based prescriptive literature, the descriptive literature is based on empirically comprehensive narratives of organizational change in practice. The ambition is to gain a deep and thorough understanding of the processes of organizational change and, from this, to formulate qualified learnings and insights rather than the seemingly handy tips in a simple instruction book. The process orientation can also be prescriptive, but then the importance of understanding the organizational context in which the changes are taking place and how the people within the organization look upon and relate to the changes are often highlighted. Interpretation is a central theme in the process orientation.

Besides the prescriptive (how) and descriptive (what) orientations, there is also a substantial and contemporary critical literature that takes a more sceptical approach to organizational change as a phenomenon by asking 'why change?'. Within this orientation, organizational change is often critically viewed as an expression of different groups' ambitions to secure their own interests. Power and politics are central aspects within a critical orientation, where the main aim is often to expose the motives and ambitions behind (managerial) organizational changes and to highlight the conflicts of interest between different parties. From the critical orientation, the need for and the possibility of management-driven change is scrutinized and questioned on a more fundamental level. These are questions that are often taken for granted in the technically normative orientation.

EXERCISE 1.1

Make a list of three highly renowned texts on organizational change and examine them in terms of what key orientations to organizational change they seem to express. Are they mainly focused on the question of how, what or why?

A prescriptive orientation – answering the question of 'what' – seem to dominate within the field of organizational change. Why do you think that is?

Three perspectives on organizational change

Based on the discussion above about the *how*, *what* and *why* of change, we can formulate three perspectives on organizational change: a tool-based perspective, a process perspective and a critical perspective (Table 1.1).

TABLE 1.1   Three perspectives on organizational change

Perspective	Tool-based	Process	Critical
Key question	*How* are we supposed to make change happen?	*What* is happening in change processes?	*Why* work with change?
Key focus	Technical-focusing on the toolbox	Interpretative-based on understandings and meanings	Critical-focusing upon interests, power and ideologies
Means	Normative (prescriptive)	Mainly descriptive	Critical: Scruitinizing and questioning

To apply a tool perspective to change means to ask questions about how you implement change in the best way possible. What tools and models does one have at one's disposal? What models are most useful for the situation one finds oneself in? How does one proceed to implement change in an efficient way with as little friction and resistance as possible? Within the frame of this perspective, the idea is to be pragmatic and look for '*how*' to accomplish change in a practical manner. This is a most common perspective among practitioners and students of change, and consequently the most common approach in much of the change literature. We will cover this perspective but also provide two additional perspectives that facilitate a more differentiated reflection upon the topic.

A process perspective means applying an interpretative approach to change, where the main idea is to understand what happens in the process of change, especially from the perspective of those involved. We learn about how change unfolds in an organization, for example, from its design to its implementation and reception among those targeted by the change. This means focusing upon the dynamics of change in order to gain insights about '*what*' is going on as people work on change in practice.

Applying a critical perspective means examining the intentions of change and processes based upon what motivated them and who might benefit from them in terms of interests and privileges. The focus is on the question '*why?*' and on deconstructing the process of change with the purpose of laying bare motives of power, ideologies and interests.

Within each of these orientations there are varying amounts of perceptions, models, theories and terms about the how, the why, the what, the who and the when of organizational change. Why is organizational change needed? What is supposed to be changed? How is the process of change being implemented? Who influences it? When is one supposed to engage in organizational change? There are many questions and many possible answers. There is no universal organizational change theory that gives unilateral answers to all these questions.

Behind the three different perspectives there are different assumptions about organizational change and its nature, which we discuss in more depth in Chapter 2. In this introductory chapter the emphasis is on how we pedagogically frame the large field of writings about change. Arguably, the variety within the field is an advantage as the diversity provides us with a wide range of concepts, models and tools that will help us to better make organizational change understandable and also show us how to deal with and lead organizational change. In this book, therefore, we take the field's diversity seriously.

REVIEW QUESTIONS 1.2

Recall	What are the three perspectives of organizational change presented in this book?
Explain	Discuss the key focus of these three perspectives on organizational change and what it would imply to adopt each perspective.
Reflect	What might be the value of adopting a multidimensional approach to the topic of organizational change?

EXERCISE 1.2

Examine a recent and a presumed successful case of organizational change in a contemporary organization by drawing on information from secondary sources such as the internet, newspapers, business press, etc. How is the success explained? What variables are drawn upon in describing the success and what variables have been left out of the equation? Is it possible to say that a particular perspective of change – a tool-based, process or critical perspective – is more salient or has been expressed more clearly in the article?

EXERCISE 1.3

Read the case of Technocom below and reflect on:

- What approach to organizational change do you think dominated among the top managers at Technocom?
- How do you think they could have benefited from reflecting on alternative perspectives on change throughout the process?

CASE

Cultural change at Technocom

The management team in a high-tech organization wanted to radically change its direction and organizational culture and structure by instilling new values, such as creating outstanding customer relations, more inspirational leadership and strong teamwork. Top management was highly involved and the programme was designed according to a technically very sophisticated version of a classic n-step model by consultants from a global consultancy firm (with quality checks by other local consultants). A lot of resources went into the programme, including a kick-off general meeting, formal communications and talks between the management team and the workforce, a management club for questions and answers, managerially led workshops, documents, videos, and a toolkit with exercises, etc.

(Continued)

In spite of all these resources and initiatives many employees never felt part of the change process. The employees felt that the kick-off meeting failed to engage and inspire people to be part of the change. Top managers also had problems in pedagogically explaining the ideas behind launching a large change project: their input was uncertain and vague, and the new culture was seen by many as fluffy and without concrete substance. In many of the workshops where middle managers explained the new culture and its vision and mission – such as where they wanted the organization to go in the future – the managers failed to reach the sceptical professional employees, most of whom were engineers. The exercises that were supposed to be performed at the workshops – such as conducting analysis of the organization in terms of its leadership, commitment, empowerment, etc. – failed to produce any result that could be taken back to the top managers or HR. As many of the middle managers also had problems in identifying with the change ideas, they failed to communicate the ideas in a convincing and persuasive manner.

All in all, many of the middle managers and employees said that nothing happened, nothing changed and the change project was looked upon more as 'paper and talk' and 'bread and spectacle for the people'. Why?

Part of the experience among junior managers and employees was that there was a fundamental confusion around the basic image and expectations of the change project. Among the junior managers there were expectations that top management would push for the change and act as key drivers all the way through. Junior managers also expected that top management would specify and more or less command – as change agents – the new practices and new behaviour in a concrete way; they said: 'We do as we are told.' In contrast, top management expected that the formulation of a new direction and organization – culture and structure – would function as an eye-opener and that once people's eyes were open, they would spontaneously act differently, without the need for more guidance. Top management also talked about the change as a wave (like in sporting events) and that the insights about the importance of change would spread from person to person naturally: 'We initiate as the architects, and the middle managers will implement and act as culture carriers and change agents.' This suggests that it was unclear who were meant to be the change agents and the central drivers of the change process. As a result, there was confusion and resistance. This partly relates to the issue of identities and meanings in managing change. There were misalignments around:

- the overall meaning of the project;
- their own situated identities, e.g. how they defined themselves in this context;
- the ascription of positions to others (roles); and
- their own models of how the organizational world looked and their own (limited) place in it.

The result was that the implicit culture already in place in the organization took over. What was to be changed became reproduced. The non-visible leadership and distrust in management, limited teamwork, and the focus on technology all continued and became even more entrenched. This is how the existing culture and structure can become traps in change work.

Source: Alvesson & Sveningsson (2015)

This case illustrates why recognizing the complexities of change might be a good idea. Top management primarily seemed to have a tool-based view on change: they were highly involved in the design of the change and focused on how to implement the change plans. Tools and models were the top priority, and consultants were engaged to provide expertise in this area. What happened along the way in the change process, that is, how the employees interpreted and responded to the change attempt, seemed to be of less importance. The managers seemed to expect the change to spread down the organization like a wave. Adopting a process perspective, and focusing on what the change programme meant to the employees further down in the organizational hierarchy, could have revealed that the suggested change did not fit with the employees' view of what the company needed to change. In addition, it represented a misfit between what the junior managers and the senior management expected their respective roles to be. A critical perspective, in turn, could have encouraged managers to question the suitability of the change in the first place and encourage a more reflective and realistic approach when deciding upon action. Furthermore, it could also have created an awareness of the potential consequences of not considering employees' voices. Embarking upon a change program like this might look like a quick fix but could in the long run lead to mistrust towards management and cynicism towards this kind of change attempt.

THE PURPOSE OF THE BOOK

The main purpose of the book is to provide an overview of where we stand today when it comes to knowledge about organizational change. We do this by considering how organizational change is understood from the three different perspectives. This gives us a breadth that enables us to examine and discuss the concepts and models created by academics, practitioners and consultants. As many authors in the field of organizational change often position themselves between these different roles as well as contribute to more than one of the three orientations, it is difficult and not very meaningful to make strong demarcations between them. We will therefore mainly connect different theories, rather than authors, to the three perspectives. Furthermore, in our account, we focus on a few and especially critical and dominant concepts and models. The idea is not to include everything, but instead to have a more limited and in-depth discussion about the central models, partly by putting them in a historical knowledge context.

Three areas of significance in change processes

Besides the three perspectives of change discussed above, we pay specific attention to three areas that are often said to be particularly important in the context of change (Table 1.2).

TABLE 1.2   Three areas of recognition in change processes

Area of significance	Organizational culture	Identity	Leadership
Key focus	Shared understandings	Understandings of who 'I am' and who 'we are'	Processes of influence
Key question	What is the relevance and significance of shared understandings, norms and values in change processes?	What is the significance of how people look upon themselves in change processes?	What role(s) do leaders play in organizational change?

The *organizational culture* is often said to be a key element in change since it can be considered a fundamental dimension of organizational life. To concern oneself with the organizational culture can mean that one places a more anthropological perspective on organizations with the aim of understanding the creation of meaning in a more qualified way and, above all, how meaning is expressed and how it affects other common organizational phenomena, such as strategy, systems, control, motivation and leadership.

Closely related, but with a larger focus on how individuals and groups understand and talk about themselves, is *identity*. Identity involves questions about what makes an individual or a group distinct – especially in comparison to other individuals or groups – and is often realized in the context of organizational change, especially when more radical change is taking place, where one's own understanding can be problematized and challenged.

Leadership is viewed as central in how one leads and drives processes of change, and therefore more attention has been paid to leadership than to many other organizational conditions. We will discuss how leadership is looked upon, but we will also problematize the phenomenon and show how an inflated belief in leadership might even undermine the possibilities of implementing change successfully.

REVIEW QUESTIONS 1.3

Explain	In what ways can the concept of organizational culture facilitate understanding and managing organizational change? Refer to the Technocom case in your answer.
Reflect	Does leadership matter in understanding and facilitating organizational change? Why?

THE STRUCTURE OF THE BOOK

The book is divided into ten chapters. In this initial chapter we have formulated the book's pedagogical idea and purpose.

In Chapter 2 we further develop the three perspectives on change and examine these in more depth by also reviewing the assumptions – labelled knowledge-interest – on which they are based. The aim of the chapter is to provide the reader with a conceptual platform. Within the organizational change literature there are established concepts that the reader should to be familiar with in order to better understand the reviews in later chapters. Among others, these are concepts that describe differences in the size and control of change.

In Chapter 3 we discuss what causes and motivates change. Initially we examine what triggers organizational change. Sometimes it is a question of external forces, for example, technological, political, demographical, economical and socio-cultural forces, and occasionally it is a question of internal forces, such as the growth or consolidation of businesses. With the help of a few illustrations, we show how trends can govern the occurrence of and the quality of organizational change. We will also discuss different theories explaining the dynamics of change: evolutionary, life-cycle, teleological and dialectic theory of change. By doing this, both the focus of change and its origin are considered and change in single as well as in multiple organizations are recognized.

Chapters 4 and 5 will be dedicated to the tool-based perspective on change. Here we will describe typical models and concepts that have dominated in academia, but that have also been very popular with many consultants in the field.

Chapter 4 will include a historical review of the topic of organizational change. We start at the beginning of the 20th century and then move along through the Human Relations approach to view change as a question of Organization Development (OD). OD might have had its heyday in the 1960s and 1970s, but many of its humanistic ideals, and the importance it places on the view that the organizational change must be seen as a process over time, are also expressed in many contemporary works about managing change, especially change based on more integrated organization models.

Integrated organization models are then followed up in Chapter 5. These models, which express a typical systemic view of organizations, today represent a dominant way of relating to organizational change. Here we look at organizations as more or less living organisms in constant interaction – and therefore in need of adaptation and adjustment – in relation to the environment. Alignment and long-term survival/health are key terms within the systemic approach. Chapter 5 reviews a number of the analytical models of organizations in general and examines different ways of achieving organizational change effectively.

Chapters 6 and 7 are devoted to the process perspective on change. We review much of the modern empirical research on organizational change in practice. Many authors who describe organizational change as an emerging process not only pay attention to interpreting and understanding the change process in practice, but also include suggestions on how to work with change, which is why some overlap of perspectives occurs. The ideal is, of course, to try to keep the principles for working with change solely within the tool-based perspective, and to let the process perspective be specifically about what the change is about in practice (i.e. the descriptive aspect). Counter to this, we can argue that we risk losing some of the context and the consistency with which some (prominent) authors have developed norms for organizational change. These norms are based on a rather specific understanding of the change phenomenon, for example understanding change through the help of languages and narratives.

In Chapter 6 we discuss the emergence of the process perspective, which can be partly seen as a counter-reaction and criticism of the view that change is controllable, or can at least be influenced, with the right kind of change design. We then explore the key characteristics of the process perspective and end the chapter with an account of a number of process-oriented studies, discussing their results and findings. There are several normative studies that focus on how change should come about but they often fail to describe what happens in practice when the plans are set in motion, which is the key topic of this chapter.

In Chapter 7 we discuss the conditions for interpretation and understanding by focusing on the circumstances that affect and shape people's meaning creation. Next, we examine the importance of language and narrative in the implementation of continuous organizational change. Terms such as discourse and narrative will be elaborated upon. Research in organizational change has in recent years focused specifically on the significance and role of language, especially how change takes place in everyday life through daily interaction and how language and communication can be central in planned change attempts. We also explore how identity connects to meaning creation and discuss how people's views about themselves and others impacts change processes.

The critical perspective on organizational change is discussed in Chapter 8. Characteristic of this perspective is that it problematizes many established theories on organizational change. The perspective examines and treats much conventional change management theory as a way to look at, talk about and describe change – as a discourse – rather than as an absolute truth. In the chapter we will discuss how critical theory problematizes change management theory and change management. The focus will not be on how change should be led, but whether change can or even should be led at all. The chapter is divided into two parts: the first problematizes a number of traditional beliefs and the second gives room for voices that tend to be marginalized in the context of change. The chapter aims to stimulate thoughtfulness and reflection.

In Chapter 9 we engage with a central and well-documented area in organizational change theory: resistance. Besides providing an in-depth understanding of this specific topic, the chapter also works as an illustration of the diversity of understandings within the field of organizational change. This chapter shows how a single dimension – resistance – can be viewed very differently depending on which of the three perspectives of change is applied. For example, we discuss resistance as a troublesome element, a valuable contribution, identity work and the terminology of resistance as an instrument of power.

In Chapter 10 we summarize the key points from the different chapters. We discuss what can be learnt from the different key points and what practitioners can learn from the claims and insights of the different perspectives. The chapter takes a relatively pragmatic approach to organizational change. We especially discuss what managers, based on the different perspectives, should pay attention to when working with and within change. The chapter aims to inspire reflection on some important themes in typical organizational change work.

| 1 Introduction |
| 2 Perspectives on change |
| 3 Why organizational change? |

| 4 The Tool-based Perspective: Planned Change and Organizational Development | 6 The Process Perspective: Focus on Interpretations and Understandings | 8 The Critical Perspective of Change |
| 5 The Tool-based Perspective: Integrated Organizational Models | 7 The Process Perspective: The Importance of Language | |

| 9 The Complexity of Resistance |
| 10 Managing Organizational Change: Practical Lessons and Key Insight |

FIGURE 1.1   Structure of the book

 KEY PRACTICAL INSIGHTS

What we can say about organizational change following this chapter:

- There are a number of simplified recipes on the market about how to drive change, but it is important to realize that there are seldom any quick fixes. To solely rely upon general, decontextualized advice when driving organizational change is not recommended.

- Much of the literature on change tends to be overly positive and optimistic about the need for and possibility of implementing large-scale organizational change. It might be a reasonable way forward, but it is not the only solution to organizational difficulties. Strive to base decisions on a realistic view of the possibilities to achieve the planned change.

- Accomplishing change in an organization can be a complex endeavour that calls for a broad and in-depth understanding. Gaining and applying a model and concepts that recognize the multifaceted and complex nature of understanding organizational change is advisable.

- The three perspectives on organizational change presented in this book are complementary and facilitate a broad and comprehensible understanding of change. In particular, they encourage the reader not only to look for *tools* for change, but also to strive to *understand* organizational processes on a more thorough level and to *critically* reflect upon the actual need for change as well as the potential conflicts of interests embedded in such an endeavour.

 # FURTHER READING

Go online to access free and downloadable SAGE Journal articles related to this chapter at **https://study.sagepub.com/sveningsson**

Collins, D. (1998). *Organizational change: Sociological perspectives*. London: Routledge.

Dawson, P. (2003). *Understanding organizational change*. London: Sage.

Helms-Mills, J., Dye, K., & Mills, A. (2009). *Understanding organizational change*. London: Routledge.

Pettigrew, A., Woodman, R., & Cameron, K. (2001). Studying organizational change and development: Challenges for future research. *Academy of Management Journal*, 44(4), 697–713.

Sturdy, A., & Grey, C. (2003). Beneath and beyond organizational change management: Exploring alternatives. *Organization*, 10(4), 651–662.

 # VIDEO

Go online to view video clips related to the key themes discussed in this chapter at
https://study.sagepub.com/sveningsson

PERSPECTIVES ON CHANGE

LEARNING OBJECTIVES

When you have completed your study of this chapter, you should be able to:

- Analyze and understand the substance of change in terms of its scale, scope and defining characteristics (strategic, structural, cultural, etc.).

- Understand the relevance of how the substance and defining characteristics of a change process is partly contingent upon who is doing the analysis.

- Recognize the benefit of using metaphors when analyzing organizational change work.

- Explain the difference between change as planned and as emergent.

- Identify the distinction between a prescriptive and a descriptive approach to understanding change processes and their manageability.

- Understand the concept of 'knowledge-interest' and the key characteristics of the technical, interpretative and emancipatory knowledge-interest.

- Analytically describe and contrast the three different perspectives on change (the tool-based, process and critical perspective).

In this chapter we explain and develop the perspectives on organizational change that we introduced in Chapter 1: a tool-based perspective, a process perspective and a critical perspective. The aim of the chapter is to discuss and explain the key terms, beliefs and models that are associated with these perspectives. Some of the concepts and ideas that we review in the chapter are used in all three perspectives, but our ambition is to go beyond their common ground and to point at typical concepts and dominant ideas that make the perspectives distinct from each other, in order to identify their central features. Besides the typical concepts, we also discuss how use of different perspectives implicitly suggests various assumptions about the functions of organizations more generally. The ambition is to provide a short and concise overview that can serve as a basis for the more in-depth analysis that will take place in subsequent chapters.

We begin by discussing what organizational change is normally about in terms of tempo and scope. Then there is a description of how one can understand change metaphorically and how that can be used in the context of organizational change. We then move onto the question of the significance of who is involved and who has influence over a course of change. Based on this, we move back to the three different perspectives and the chapter ends with Table 2.2, which outlines the terms and assumptions about how organizations typically function using these perspectives.

DIFFERENT TYPES OF ORGANIZATIONAL CHANGE

Change varies in terms of content and scope, from small and perhaps trivial change to radical and revolutionary change. To purchase a new copying machine or to change the office furniture is probably not as radical or as fundamental as starting a programme to change the organizational culture, to initiate mergers with organizations or to dismantle large parts of organizations. The first example is normally not seen as a huge challenge and seldom leads to severe conflict or opposition that creates political power struggles or locked situations, and in the cases when it does, it is often an indication that aspects such as status, power or privileges are significantly threatened. Minor change seldom threatens people's sense of belonging and identity. Some might call these changes trivial and inconsequential, even if they do in some cases influence the work and can lead to long-term and maybe even decisive consequences.

Radical changes are more challenging and complex and one can expect that employees will react to them with greater force and engagement. Some may feel that the change not only threatens current ways of working and working methods, but also undermines their feeling of belonging and identity, i.e. how they look upon themselves at work. Radical changes often give rise to worry and anxiety about what it means for the individual. Questions that deal with how individuals look upon themselves and what competencies and capacities they have are accentuated to a greater degree, and one can therefore speak about changes that are more identity-intensive (in contrast to being identity-neutral). Radical changes normally mean that there is a higher risk of conflict and opposition, where power and politics become central ingredients.

MINI CASE 2.1

Radical change at IKEA

A fundamental business idea at the global furniture retailer IKEA, known as the flat-pack furniture pioneer, has been that the customers are actively involved in the distribution process. Customers drive to a shop where they pick up the goods from stacking shelves, and transport and assemble them at home. In line with this idea, IKEA has for decades been building stores on the edges of cities in order to make it easier for customers to drive there.

IKEA is currently radically transforming this concept. The new business model is built upon online shopping, home delivery and assembly services. Some of the stores on the outskirts of towns have therefore been turned into distribution centres. The company is instead experimenting with considerably smaller store formats located in city centres, such as a kitchen showroom in Stockholm and a showroom for bedrooms in Madrid.

This is a radical shift for the global organization as it fundamentally transforms the original business model. The new ideas have been up and running for a while in different parts of the world. On the Spanish island of Mallorca, customers do not select the goods themselves; rather, this is done automatically by robots. In London and other large cities, around half of all goods are already home delivered. In Hong Kong, IKEA has established a smaller store where home delivery represents about 80% of the orders.

Furthermore, the company is working with interactive technologies, such as augmented reality (AR) and virtual reality (VR), to make it possible for customers to project a piece of furniture into a room in their own home before buying it online. This technology is supposed to supersede visits to a physical store. A key ambition behind these changes is to take sales into the digital era and thus also reach new generations.

Sources: Milne (2018); Marr (2018)

In between these extremes we find many of the ongoing organizational changes that take place in organizations and that are a part of the typical organizational life for the employees, such as changes in ways of working through the standardization of administrative routines, the implementation of educational programmes for competence development or the use of new reporting systems or new performance evaluation systems. Change sometimes involves only a smaller organizational unit, a work group or a department, or larger units such as divisions, areas of business or sometimes the whole organization. Organizational change can thus mean many different things, with the only commonality being that it involves some form of change in the way employees work or how they organize the work. It can be about everything from a radical change to a less significant, operative change, and it can involve the whole organization or only a local, limited part of it.

Within the organizational change literature, it is common to distinguish two types of change – revolutionary change and evolutionary change. This categorization is based on both scope and the rate at which the changes take place.

Revolutionary change

Revolutionary changes are extensive and profound changes that affect the whole organization. Sometimes these are labelled as large-scale changes. Organizations are changed in a revolutionary way when their fundamental orientation – in terms of culture, structure and strategy – is changed. For example, *organizational culture* changes typically involve changing the broader understanding and interpretation – or meaning creation – of an organization. Some organizations are, for example, characterized by formal and rigid organizational cultures in which a strong emphasis is placed on titles, rank and hierarchal conditions such as position and formal status. In some organizations, especially governmental organizations, where there is a high demand for legal certainty in the handling of cases, this can be justified, but an inflated importance placed on formula and procedure risks jeopardizing flexibility and an ability to think creatively and innovatively. It is therefore not unusual, especially if one finds oneself in a changing environment, that one tries to change overly rigid structures in order to facilitate change and renewal.

MINI CASE 2.2

Cultural change at Netflix

At Netflix, cultural change was driven by reinventions in the management of HR. During the time Patty McCord was the chief talent officer (1998–2012), radical changes were made to the HR practices in the company. The CEO, Reed Hastings, said that: 'Many of the ideas in it seem like common sense, but they go against traditional HR practices', and asked why others are not more innovative regarding talent management.

A key idea was to abolish formal policies and instead ask employees to think for themselves. According to McCord, this led to better results and lowered costs. Among other things, instead of relying on formal vacation policies, employees were allowed to take as much vacation time as they felt was appropriate, and to work it out with their boss. Formal travel and expense policies were also abolished in favour of a brief expense policy to 'Act in Netflix's best interests' – as if the company money where your own. According to McCord, this reduced costs and delegated responsibility to the frontline managers. Formal performance reviews were also eliminated. They were too ritualistic and infrequent, according to McCord, who claimed that bureaucracy and 'elaborate rituals around measuring performance usually doesn't improve it'. Instead managers and employees were asked to have conversations about their performance on a regular basis and reviews were also given by peers in informal 360-degree reviews. 'If you talk simply and honestly about performance on a regular basis, you can get good results', McCord claims.

Sources: McCord (2014); Taylor (2015)

Revolutionary change can also involve changes to the horizontal and the vertical division of work and the level of formalization and centralization, so-called *structural* changes. This can involve creating more divisions or unbundling earlier product- or marketing units, making them more independent in relation to corporate or organization management. These types of changes often tend to affects the power balance, accountability and relations with the environment, for example with the market and with clients.

Revolutionary changes at a *strategic* level typically involve an organization's external relations and connections, where competitive strategies, markets and associations with other organizations are in focus. Among the strategic changes we find, for example, the development of new products, launching existing products in new markets, or mergers and acquisitions.

Cultural, structural and strategic changes seldom occur in isolation but rather often influence each other in different ways. Cultural changes are often implemented with the objective to develop new products and to achieve new competitive advantages, i.e. a change in the organization's strategies. Strategic changes such as mergers and acquisitions often trigger people to clarify who they are (their identity), which can reinforce conflicts and culture shocks and, in extension, lead to cultural (or identity) change (whether spontaneously evolving or driven by management) (Kleppestø, 1993). In all these cases, it is appropriate to speak of revolutionary change, i.e. complex and far-reaching organizational change.

Revolutionary changes often occur over a limited period. If a radical change takes place during a short time period it can be perceived as being too revolutionary, and therefore threatening. However, radical changes do not have to be revolutionary. They can also be the result of long-term smaller and successional processes of change – evolutionary changes – and therefore not be perceived as revolutionary or threatening.

Evolutionary change

Evolutionary changes are smaller changes that occur continuously. Small-scale changes could for instance imply changing the office furniture, deciding to have a planning day, recruiting new co-workers, implementing a new course for marketers and the implementation of new routines for meetings or procedures to deal with employee matters. It is common to characterize small-scale changes as changes that don't challenge existing strategies, norms or structures. It may be that an organization has expanded in a growing market and therefore needs to recruit more employees to sustain levels of production and maintain the strategic course for the organization. It may also be a question of acquiring new production equipment to safeguard the quality of products or to train staff in customer relations in order for them to better meet client demands and wishes.

MINI CASE 2.3

Meituan Dianping

The Chinese company Meituan Dianping is primarily known for its food delivery business, where lunch boxes are brought to office workers. It is currently China's largest on-demand food delivery firm, and in 2017 it had 531,000 active delivery staff members and 310 million transacting users. The combination of high urban population density, relatively low labour cost and an underdeveloped offline service sector in China have made it possible for the company to prosper. Besides delivering food, the company also provides services such as travel and hotel bookings and restaurant reviews, all in a lifestyle services app. It is now possible to arrange haircuts, yoga classes, babysitting and home repairs through their single app. The ambition is to expand horizontally, by moving into other areas of services related to O2O (online to offline) business, i.e. connecting traditional businesses to an online platform. The latest initiative is the launch of a ride-hailing service. What characterizes this type of expansion is that the company does not challenge the existing business strategy. It is therefore an example of the evolutionary model of organizational change.

Sources: Borak (2018); Guo (2018); Horwitz (2018)

The vast majority of changes in organizations are small-scale and evolutionary. Some systems for organizations, such as *kaizen* and other quality systems, deal with continuous, ongoing improvements. Sometimes evolutionary or incremental changes are described as continuous changes that have no tangible repercussions on the organization's core orientation. Yet the consequences of evolutionary changes can sometimes be quite radical (Weick & Quinn, 1999). A new recruit might not be perceived as being especially radical, but if the new recruit shows a talent for product development, and contributes with new ideas that lead to a number of subsequent changes, it could result in strategic change (such as the establishment of new products in new markets).

Based on an extensive and largely qualitative examination of what makes some companies successful in the long term, Collins (2001) highlights evolutionary dynamics as a central part of processes of change. From an external perspective, such as is often seen in the media and more popular management texts, it may seem as if organizations' development is the result of specific change programmes, decisive leadership action or occasions when someone has said or done something miraculously that will turn the whole organization upside down in a revolutionary style. However, a critical review of the development within these organizations suggests that such developments took place cumulatively and progressively – there were step-by-step, single actions and decisions that added together and after a while constituted the prerequisites for a breakthrough. The latter could, in other words, be seen as the results of lengthy evolutionary processes that happened over time, occasionally governed by a consistent organizational culture and sustained leadership (Collins, 2001).

MINI CASE 2.4

Evolutionary development with radical results

Developments within the global health and medical company Abbott illustrate an evolutionary change model that had long-term radical results. Starting out as a rather mediocre company in the lower division in the medical industry, Abbott developed into one of the most innovative and profitable companies in the pharmaceutical business when one of their managing directors, Cain, took over in the 1950s. Many circumstances contributed to this success, but some are seen as being especially important, particularly Cain himself. Although he lacked the charismatic personality that is normally accredited to CEOs when their organizations show success, he is said to have strongly disliked mediocre results.

The central element in the organizational work that he started was to eliminate an earlier all-encompassing family nepotism by changing the members of the management team and the board. The ambition was to recruit the best leadership resources in the industry, without considering specific family ties, and to let them develop the company. The interesting part is that Cain himself was a family member, with all that that usually means in terms of loyalty and obligations.

Some years later, the company started to experiment with the development of healthcare products in a broader sense, with the aim of achieving more cost-effective care, rather than working on finding medical blockbusters, which the big players, such as Merck, were occupied with. The company, Abbott, started to develop nutritional products for hospital patients that enabled quicker releases as well as new diagnostic instruments (one of the key ways to reduce healthcare costs is supposedly to get the diagnostics right). Gradually they developed market-leading products. They also developed management control systems that meant that all costs, revenues and investments were divided down to the level of the individual manager. All managers were given personal responsibility for results that needed to be accounted for.

(Continued)

Thereby financial discipline and possibilities for creativity and development had been created. The company recruited people who were regarded as entrepreneurial and gave them the freedom to decide for themselves how they would reach their goals. They also followed up on each manager's results. Within Abbott a disciplined culture evolved in which cost-effectiveness could be combined with entrepreneurial spirit.

Source: Collins (2001)

Interpretations of organizational change

Normally, revolutionary change can be more controversial, and these changes can therefore demand more politics and negotiations than evolutionary change. However, this is not always the case. As a change leader, it is a good idea to consider how a proposition for change is received. Is the change accepted or even welcomed? Or is it met with scepticism and doubts or even fierce resistance? It is not always possible to know how a suggestion for change will be interpreted. Sometimes the same change proposal can be interpreted in vastly differentiated ways by different people within an organization. For instance, a reorganization that senior management do not see as being very far-reaching can be interpreted by others in the organization as an extraordinary and radical change. For some employees these adjustments in the organizational structure can have profound consequences for how they work, and the organizational ideology behind the new ideas may seem very unfamiliar and unwanted.

This is something that the process perspective of organizational change emphasizes above all: it is not necessarily the change itself, but rather how the change is *interpreted* that is the key issue. Depending on perspective, a change can come to be interpreted and defined very differently. This classification problem is however not always clear if one views change or work with change exclusively from the perspective of a particular group. If change is primarily looked at from the viewpoint of management (as in the tool-based perspective), for example, it can very well be perceived as unanimous and agreed upon.

EXERCISE 2.1

Consider a large complex organization that you are familiar with (it could be a university, a large hospital, a bank, a construction or automobile company or a high-tech company). Imagine that the senior management of this organization wants to achieve a large-scale cultural change. The aim of this change is to turn the employees' key focus towards the customers (or towards the clients or students, depending on the organization you have selected), with the ambition to create and become recognized externally as an organization with extraordinarily strong customer relations.

What types of incidents, problems and particular challenges do you think might arise in such an endeavour?

A change initiative can be interpreted in very different ways by different people (employees, professionals, professors, HR staff, middle managers, or any other group of employees). Who do you think would react strongly and consider this to be a radical change, and why? And who do you think would hardly react and consider this to be a small-scale change, and why?

REVIEW QUESTIONS 2.1

Recall	What are the commonly used terms for (a) sudden, radical changes and (b) incremental, small-scale changes?
Explain	Discuss various reasons why radical changes are much more likely to cause conflict and resistance within the organization than small-scale changes.
Explain	What is the advantage of analyzing the scope and scale of change?
Reflect	Why could it be problematic to classify the scale of change?

We have so far discussed the possibility that one and the same change process can be interpreted in different ways. This can lead different organizational members and other stakeholders to talk about the same change in quite disparate terms. Another reason for discrepancies in wording can be that a deliberately planned change is depicted in a certain way by change advocators (or change opponents) in order to influence others. Through the creative use of language, change can be rewritten in beautifying terms, and the real intentions and ambitions can be cloaked. Presenting change in a certain way, accompanied by certain types of arguments, may make it more likely to be accepted (or rejected). It can also make the change advocators appear as both sensible and thoughtful, and therefore accepted as legitimate actors of change. This is a dimension that is key to the critical perspective of organizational change.

CHANGE METAPHORS

Metaphors are a common way to organize different fields of knowledge within organizational research. A classic example is of course Morgan's (2006) more theoretically anchored organizational metaphors – organizations as machines, as organisms, as brains, and so forth – but the idea has also been used within leadership, where it is suggested, based on studies of leadership in practice, that leaders can be seen as saints, gardeners, friends, commanders, bullies, and so on (Alvesson & Spicer, 2010).

A metaphor is a linguistic expression that can be used to explain a concept or a phenomenon – for example, an organization or leadership – in such a way that can be understood intuitively. This operation is based on analogy, where the starting point is the similarities and differences between two concepts or phenomena. The difference between the phenomena helps us to understand the similarities between them and therefore increases our understanding of what is being explained. When we want to explain how hyped up and focused a boxer is before a match, we don't say he is 'like a man', but we might say he is 'like a tiger'. The former expression is flat and pointless, while the latter one, by comparing a man with a tiger, immediately makes us understand how hyped up the boxer is.

Metaphors can also be used to describe organizational change, and just as in the case of organization and leadership, the use of different metaphors for change express different values and approaches to change. Marshak (2009) therefore suggests paying attention to what metaphors of change are adopted within an organization. The use of different metaphors has various moral and ideological consequences, but especially practical consequences. Since metaphors govern our way of thinking, they will influence how we understand and interpret the world and, in turn, how we act.

Marshak (2009) identifies four different ways of looking at change through the use of four metaphors for change (the last of which is the most radical):

- Fix and maintain
- Build and develop
- Move and relocate
- Liberate and re-create

The metaphor *fix and maintain* suggests that organizations are seen as machines that need maintenance and repairs – some operative and simplified changes that enable their current orientations. Change from this perspective is undertaken to ensure the organization is continually kept in good working order and is not aimed to challenge current strategies, systems or structures. The problems that the change addresses are seen as unambiguous, and it is not necessary to spend a lot of time in advanced problem identification or analysis. The leader of change can be likened to a mechanic who repairs and executes preventative maintenance. This metaphor could for instance be applied to mechanical repairs in a production facility and the maintenance of IT systems in communication networks, but it can also be applied to social issues, such as the management of a conflict between two departments in order to maintain a collaborative spirit among the people in the groups.

The metaphor *build and develop* likens the organization to a building under construction or a person who is developing and learning new things. Change here means a development and expansion of the organization that in no serious way challenges existing organizational conditions and is often seen as something positive (getting bigger and better, and so on). Development and expansion here allude to a more organic view of organizations, where the change leader can be seen as a coach or a mentor who enables employees' learning and development. The problems that these changes are trying to solve are less clear or self-evident. They cannot be solved with the help of tricks and maintenance, but are rather more uncertain and demand an openness to what the outcome of the change might be. The metaphor could be applied to recruitment, further training of a group of employees or expansion of market share by advertising. Both 'build and develop' as well as 'fix and maintain' changes are primarily about single-loop learning in the sense that they improve established practices rather than challenge and revise the organization in any fundamental way.

The metaphor *move and relocate* portrays change as a journey – an organization is supposed to move from point A to point B. It is about a more radical change than the two previous metaphors and is occasionally described as a transition or move between two stages. As it is about transitioning between systems, for example between different organizational forms, move and relocate often comprises much analysis and planning. The leader of change is someone who plans and guides people in the transitioning between different systems. Change is not about repairs or expansion of current organizational systems but about changing systems. It can, for example, involve the outsourcing of some function, the creation of a new organizational structure, for example divisionalization, or the consolidation of organizations in conjunction with acquisitions and mergers (Child, 2005).

The metaphor *to liberate and re-create* portrays change as encompassing and profound. This is the most advanced form of change and it not only applies to transitions or relocations forward but is also about changing the core orientation and status of the organization. The change not only encompasses what one does, but also who one is, which comprises a change of fundamental values and mindset. The change actor is here seen as a visionary or a creator who contributes to more profound organizational cultural change. This refers to changes that embraces the whole organization and its reinvention, involving several different organizational contingencies in parallel and challenging current norms and assumptions. In terms of learning, this change is referred to as 'double-loop' learning.

These metaphors can be used in a few different ways. For example, they can be used by change leaders to contemplate how they put forward suggestions for change and, by extension, avoid communicating in one way and acting in another. Furthermore, the metaphors enable analysis of how the people in an organization talk about change, which in turn can be related to how they view change. We can therefore, with the help of the four metaphors (and related concepts), form an opinion about which assumptions and beliefs about change seem to be dominant in an organization. Initiatives for change can be perceived in different ways. It is therefore important to make sure that most people who are involved in a process of change have the same image of what type of change is about to be implemented. If someone primarily is talking about 'fixing the friction between units' or about 'tools to repair systems' it signals a 'repair and maintain' approach to change. If people instead talk about 'growing to keep up with development' or 'building on the company's strengths', they seem to give voice to a 'build and develop' approach. If anyone says 'we must move to a new location' or that the change is about 'fitting the costume to the current market', it is more a question of a 'move and relocate' approach. Talking about 'visions, reinvention and innovations' or that it is important to 'think outside of the box' points to a thinking that indicates a 'liberate and re-create' approach to change (Beech & McIntosh, 2012).

Furthermore, if one wants to change the culture of an organization with a dominant view of organizational change as primarily a question of fixing and maintaining, a lot of work is normally needed to uncover the existing view on change, otherwise one risks ruling out a change of the organizational culture. Metaphors and related language contain the potential for identifying this kind of problem.

At the same time, it is important to be aware that the language used – concepts, expressions and vocabulary – cannot always be seen as expressions of what people think or their intentions. The correlation to action is not always there either. The language can provide some indications of how someone thinks about change, but care needs to be taken in order to avoid overinterpreting expressions and concepts as they often mean different things to different people. There is occasionally a strong variation in terms of what people mean by different concepts and expressions, and sometimes they might not mean much at all. People might use terms and expressions that are typical in an organization or use ones that they think have a high approval rating with other members of the organization, but the use of language might be relatively disconnected from the type of change they want to embark upon. Someone might want to liberate and re-create – for example, changing the organizational culture – but formulate the ambitions for change in a more technical way – 'fix' or 'relocate' – maybe because they are heavily influenced by that specific vocabulary or believe that the ambitions for change will have a bigger impact if they use that vocabulary. In the latter case, they might want to pre-empt opposition and resistance to change.

It's also common for people to use expressions because they sound good or are popular – they might occur in media and popular science magazines or in other organizations. Furthermore, actions and practices are not always in line with how people talk about change. People often say one thing but do another and, as has been mentioned before, change is often about politics. This is why the ability to implement change is, among other things, dependent on the ability to seem convincing, to persuade or generally to use symbols and rhetorical tricks with the aim of appealing to people's interests and wishes. In other words, it can be difficult to draw any simple conclusions from language alone when considering how people think about change in an organization (Beech & McIntosh, 2012).

EXERCISE 2.2

Consider the case below and answer the following questions:

- What change metaphors can you identify in the case? Pay close attention to the language used by the managers and employees. Use Marshak's (2009) metaphors or suggest alternative ones.
- It seems as though different people use different metaphors when describing the upcoming change. Furthermore, the change is described differently in different situations. In what ways could this be problematic for the possibility of implementing the change successfully?
- Why do you think the managers played down the scope of the change when they first communicated and presented it to the employees? Do you think that the downplaying of the scope of change is common when senior managers communicate and suggest changes? Would you have done the same thing? Why or why not?

CASE

No 'musical chairs' – or...?

AlphaTec (a pseudonym), a small Scandinavian IT company founded during the dot-com boom in the late 1990s, had been growing rapidly, from four people to 170 in less than five years. By that time, the senior managers realized that there were fundamental deficiencies in the financial control system. The managing director of the company, Lennart, thought that in the long run a complete overhaul of the company was needed. The production manager, Ove, who had experience of working in a large multinational company, thought that the business did not work at all, that it was unstructured and chaotic. Ove believed that the main problems were that there were no means to overview company policy and there was no financial control whatsoever; he said the company 'did not even have functioning support systems', so it was impossible to make follow-ups.

The managerial plan was to change the organizational structure first and in parallel to introduce financial control. Their next aim was to continue to improve project management.

(Continued)

The basic idea was to divide the production department into smaller units and appoint experienced unit managers. The intention was to focus and clarify the areas of responsibility in the organization in general and to introduce an accounting system in order to allow follow-ups. According to Ove and Lennart, the business needed to be fundamentally restructured. To them, the changes that were needed were obvious and inevitable.

The tone at the explanatory meeting with all employees was different, though. The managing director started to talk about the company being a leader in its field. Then he emphasized the importance of financial awareness and hinted that there would be certain changes in the company activities. He supported his presentation with PowerPoint slides showing a road leading straight ahead, all the way to the horizon. Among other things, he declared that the production department would be divided into smaller units in order to increase efficiency and improve the financial follow-up. It will be more fun to work then, he explained, since it will be easier to get your voice heard. He assured the audience that there was no plan for radical change or some kind of 'musical chairs'.

Right after the meeting a project leader commented: 'Finally things start happening!' But a developer said: 'Mmm, we'll see if there will be any changes, or if things just continue as usual.'

A few weeks later, when more specific organizational plans were presented to the developers, many of them expressed a striking incomprehension and disapproval of the upcoming reorganization. For instance, they said that they did not understand why they needed to change the organization, and claimed that there were no arguments for it at all. They thought the plan to divide the department into units was 'a very stupid idea'. It would limit the opportunities for them to work on exciting projects and to exchange ideas and knowledge with people outside the unit. The developers talked about the division into units as confining: 'If you happen to be placed in a certain unit you risk being stuck there forever.' Another developer expressed a fear that they would be 'locked into a little corner, each one for themselves, and not be able to talk to one another except within the unit'.

Source: Sörgärde (2006)

REVIEW QUESTIONS 2.2

Recall	List at least three different change metaphors that indicate different scopes and scales of change.	
Explain	How can the application of metaphors in analyzing change help us to manage change in a more insightful way?	
Reflect	Why can it be insufficient solely to consider language usage (how people talk about change) when attempting to understand change processes?	

PLANNED AND EMERGENT APPROACHES TO CHANGE

Sometimes a distinction is made between planned and emergent changes. Within strategy research, it has been something of a rift for nearly 40 years. Some advocate planned changes in which careful analyses and well formulated plans precede implementation, while others propose emergent changes that are the results of local and more *ad hoc* adaptations due to changes in the organization's environment.

Planned change has received the most attention in literature about change, and the core logic is simple: action is thought to follow objectives and intentions. The norm is that action always follows what one wants to achieve, so that implementation of change follows its formulation. This often involves large-scale changes, such as changes related to either the 'move and relocate' or the 'liberate and re-create' metaphors, discussed above. The literature on planned organizational change are primarily prescriptive (Figure 2.1) and contains several n-step models for deliberate and sequentially planned organizational change. These suggest that planning and implementation follow several more or less preordained steps that are ticked off as the work of organizational change progresses. The idea here is to look upon changes as a rational pattern of separate and sequentially organized activities. Many classical change models, such as the integrated models described in Chapter 5, emphasize as their starting point a clear identification of the problem, followed by an analysis of different approaches and consequences from following different approaches. Finally, one assesses whether one has reached the objective with the change in question.

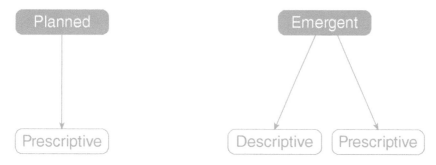

FIGURE 2.1   Planned vs emergent change and descriptive vs prescriptive aim

In contrast to planned change, there is what is labelled as *emergent change*, i.e. change that grows – in an evolutionary manner – over a longer space of time, through small and often local initiatives and engagements. Within the literature on emergent change, two broad theoretical orientations can be traced: one that is more descriptive and interpretative (focusing on meanings and understandings) and another that is more prescriptive and tool-oriented (focusing on how to influence and control). These orientations occasionally overlap, but in order to differentiate between the two we highlight their typical characteristics below.

Emergent and descriptive approach

For many years there has been an empirical research tradition that involves the close observation and examination of how strategic and organizational changes emerge in practice. These studies are often process-oriented and the ambition is to generate deeper knowledge and insights into the complexity, logic and dynamics that characterize different processes of change. Here, it is not assumed that all processes of change are similar. The idea is instead to achieve more credible descriptions and narratives of the unique and complex reality of how those involved in the processes commonly meet and experience change. What is emphasized, among other things, are people's interpretation of ambitions and initiatives of change – how suggestions and ideas are understood – and the challenges (uncertainty, anxiety, etc.) that organizational change sometimes mean for those involved in them. These studies also acknowledge and recognize time and knowledge limitations, identity and culture. These are questions about resources and the motivation of those involved as well as questions related to power and the political gambit for resources that is an almost unavoidable part of managing change.

To look at organizational change as emergent is not a new idea. Already in the 1970s, Henry Mintzberg and Andrew Pettigrew, among others, launched a variety of concepts and ideas on processes of change that radically parted with and challenged the then dominant planning ideal. Both strategic and organizational changes were here portrayed as the result of local, temporary, historical, knowledge-based and political circumstances. Since then there have been countless studies on the emerging and complex processes of change where the importance of complexity, culture, politics, identity and interpretation for the development of these processes have been considered (Dawson, 2003). Many smaller local changes are not necessarily a direct consequence of management initiatives, and sometimes many unexpected outcomes develop even from very well formulated change attempts. Sometimes processes of change almost seem to take on a life of their own and do not follow the pre-formulated plans at all; the results of attempts at change can even be the opposite of what was originally intended (Alvesson & Sveningsson, 2015).

Following this, it is common to suggest that organizational change should be viewed as rather unpredictable and challenging to manage. A proposed alternative is to consider organizational change as a constant emergent process, where the employees who are involved are also considered as active actors who interpret and reinterpret managerial plans and suggestions as well drive their own initiatives. The classical distinction between formulation and implementation is here seen as a misleading description of what actually happens in practice. In this book, we will discuss this descriptive view of change as a part of the process approach to change.

Studies of change in practice have given rise to a lot of critique towards the planning ideal and its inherent idealistic assumptions about the functioning of organizations, leadership and control. The complexity of organizational change and a generally more turbulent and unpredictable contemporary world is viewed by many authors as contributing to the fact that many planning models are inadequate as tools for managing organizational change. Taking this into account, is it at all possible to control or influence processes of change, or are they completely beyond control or influence? This is discussed in the following section, about change as an emerging process in more prescriptive (normative) and tool-based terms.

Emergent and prescriptive approach

Following studies of organizational change as emergent, many alternative managerial tools for influencing change have been developed. The view of the manager as the one in charge, managing the organization top-down – with the help of elaborate plans, commands, hierarchical arrangements or information technologies – is then questioned. Many of the advocates for emerging change instead talk about the importance of acting as a *leader* or a *coach*. Here, change is viewed as something best governed and formed by more indirect organizational means rather than lengthy plans and centrally controlled information technologies. Today it is common among change researchers to talk about shaping change with the help of the appropriate leadership, education, competence improvement, recruitment, award systems and organizational culture, but also structural arrangements are often mentioned. Some, such as Burnes (2004), argue that managers of change need to reconsider their role and approach towards their employees:

> Instead of controlling employees, they have to promote employee empowerment and engage people. Instead of directing and controlling change, they have to ensure that the organization's members are receptive to the change process, and have the necessary skills, motivation and power to take charge of it. (Burnes, 2004, p. 296)

This view of organizational change gained popularity in the 1980s, partly through the bestseller *In Search of Excellence* (Peters & Waterman, 1982). Themes such as organizational culture, visions and leadership received a considerable boost as being central for change. The trend was amplified during the 1990s by Kotter's ([1996] 2012a) ideas of leadership as something distinct (and important) in relation to management. Also, work by Collins (2001) about what creates sustainable organizations gave an injection to themes such as leadership, culture, recruitment principles, passion and longevity.

A lot of the literature is about encouraging organizational change where the co-workers feel motivated to take the initiative and act. An ideal is engaged, motivated and knowledgeable co-workers who feel that they have the mandate to act based on what they regard the organization needs. The initiative can be local adaptations based on interpretations of, for example, co-workers' or clients' needs or wishes. An example of this would be adapting an agreement or delivery terms against the background that a client is at that moment buying large quantities of a product. It can also be a question of adapting the handling of a service (e.g. the handling of a complaint) in a way that deviates from established routines and standards. It can involve small and maybe inconsequential changes, but if they prove successful, they might in the longer run contribute to more extensive and permanent changes in operations. The idea is that management should form organizational conditions that support learning and development. A central element in theories around emergent change is the importance of organizational culture in order to make long-lasting and evolutionary changes possible. Rather than single and large revolutionary changes (as a result of comprehensive plans), the importance of governing and managing change in accordance with organizational conditions such as structure, culture, award systems, recruitment and other personnel tools are put forward.

Based on this, one can say that even if organizational change in this emergent form is seen as more complex and harder to manage compared to the planning ideal, the message is not that it is impossible to influence the outcome of change. If the planning idealists are overly optimistic in their view of how much one can manage and control change, then one can say that the advocates for emergent change are moderately optimistic when it comes to effecting change through purposeful organizational architecture. Taken together, it is primarily the content of the organizational change toolbox that differs between the two viewpoints. The commonality for both is the view that organizational change is something that top management can affect in different ways and, in some cases, control. Therefore, in the following chapters of the book, we will include both planned and emergent change as different varieties within the tool-based perspective on change.

EXERCISE 2.3

Describe a situation where planned change seemed to be inevitable in order to avoid serious problems. The plan could, for example, have been triggered by falling profitability, complaints of the quality of products/services from customers/clients, negative feedback from employees about work conditions, a changing institutional situation (such as political or regulatory changes), or any other complaints from an important stakeholder that needed to be recognized.

Base your description upon personal experience or by drawing on media accounts (from newspaper or business magazine articles) of a contemporary organization. Can you identify any unintended consequences that occurred when the plan was implemented? Discuss critically whether the change could have been avoided and how. Finally, reflect upon why you consider the change to be inevitable.

EXERCISE 2.4

Read the case below and answer the following questions.

- How would you characterize the organizational change in terms of scale and scope?
- Would you consider this to be a case of a planned or emergent change? Discuss.

CASE

Changes at the Brazilian company, Semco Partners

Semco is a supplier of marine pumps for the shipping industry, founded by Antonio Semler in the 1950s. It was taken over by Antonio's son Ricardo in the 1980s. During the 1980s Ricardo implemented a variety of traditional control systems and tight authoritarian management in order to enhance efficiency and productivity at Semco. But rather than increasing efficiency, these moves led to a counterproductive control culture and highly demotivated and distressed employees. On top of this, Ricardo himself collapsed and ended up in hospital. From then on, everything changed.

Returning to the company, Ricardo decided to start changing himself by abandoning his philosophy of control. This included abandoning beginning-and-end-shift surveillance of employees, ditching the formal dress code so that employees could dress however they wanted, eliminating expense reports (so people could monitor their own spending), installing open-plan office spaces, abolishing reserved spaces in the company parking lot, starting to share power and information, installing democratic decision-making and encouraging dissent.

As the company developed, it also restructured to introduce teamwork, a worker-led recruitment system (almost eliminating HR) and flexible working hours. Later on, the company moved towards a transparent culture whereby any employees could attend any meeting, and read any report or memo that they wanted to. Everyone was allowed to attend budget meetings, where among other things production quotas were decided. The company also installed systems for evaluating managers that were posted for the entire company to see and created routines for letting employees set their own salaries. By the end of the 1980s, Semco had one the highest growth rates in Brazil and had won awards for labour relations. Sales had risen significantly and the company had become a market leader in many industries. In 2018, Semco's development is considered highly successful and Ricardo is seen as something of a legend of leadership and organization.

Looking back at the history of Semco, Ricardo said that there was no grand plan behind its development. The thing that triggered it all was his feeling that the company lacked enthusiasm and motivation and that the employees weren't happy about working there. In contrast, people seemed overly burdened by their work and the traditional management control systems just amplified the lack of motivation and enthusiasm. By radically removing the traditional and managerially oriented hierarchical control systems Ricardo aimed at liberating the inner motivation and passion among employees, thereby creating an organization full of life and joy.

Source: Maddux (2014) http://www.semco.com.br/en/

At first glance, the Semco case study can be seen as an example of revolutionary strategic and organizational change that may appear planned according to a classic rational logic. Upon closer examination, however, Semco's development is much more emerging and processual than it seems. Expressed differently, on the one hand, Ricardo implemented planned radical changes top-down in the sense that he abandoned a number of rules, changed the office design, and started to share information and decision-making. On the other hand, the development following the abandonment of tight behavioural control emerged organically. At least Ricardo stated that he had no grand plan. The theoretical distinction between planned and emergent change is seldom clear-cut in practice.

REVIEW QUESTIONS 2.3

Recall	What is the distinction between a descriptive and a prescriptive approach to change?
Explain	Explain the difference between planned and emergent change.
Explain	(a) Describe the assumptions on which linear n-step models typically are based. (b) Discuss an alternative approach for managers to drive change, an approach that does not follow planned, sequential steps, but is still driven from the top down.
Reflect	Would you say that managers give up control and power if they abandon formal, centrally decided plans on how to develop the organization? For example, were the employees in Semco freer and less controlled after the changes made by Ricardo? Try to find arguments for both a 'yes' and 'no' answer.

THE TOOL-BASED, PROCESS AND CRITICAL PERSPECTIVES

As demonstrated above, there are several classifications and terms that are crucial to understand in order to know what organizational change is about. We have so far suggested that changes can be classified by focusing on the character of the change in terms of its scope and how controversial the change may be considered (i.e. how radical the change is for the employees). We have also contrasted changes depending upon tempo (revolutionary vs evolutionary changes) and origin (planned vs emergent change). These are basic dimensions that can be used to specify a situation at hand, and subsequently what theoretical input could be useful. Based on this, we turn to the three perspectives on change introduced in Chapter 1 – the tool-based, process and critical perspectives – and discuss what kind of knowledge of change they provide us with.

A way to grasp what these perspectives are all about is to consider how they differ in terms of the knowledge produced about organizational change, i.e. what knowledge-interest they are based upon (Habermas, 1972).

Different knowledge-interests

A key division between the perspectives on organizational change relates to their approaches to the subject, including their primary motivations. The three different approaches suggest that it is important to study and understand change in order to:

- provide recipes, techniques and tools to control change processes, or
- provide insights and a better understanding of change processes, or
- critically scrutinize organizational practices and conventional theoretical ideas.

The sociologist Jürgen Habermas (1972) launched the concept of 'knowledge-interest' with the purpose of emphasizing the diverse motivations behind different types of knowledge creation about a social phenomenon. The concept of knowledge-interest describes the reasoning behind knowledge production, and distinguishes between a technical, an interpretative and an emancipatory motivation. The three perspectives, the tool-based, process and critical, can be related to these motivations.

A *technical knowledge-interest* generally focuses on creating and providing resources for human survival. It is a question of trying to control nature and social contexts so they can be exploited economically for human gain through rational problem-solving. The technical knowledge-interest warrants the creation of knowledge of how to manage and regulate social processes, such as human interactions and organizational change, in order to gain control and predictability. This means isolating objects (such as change) and processes into dependent and independent variables to ascertain regularities and causations. It is well articulated in the empirical–analytical sciences. The general aim is to produce knowledge that enables applications or provides technologies within different areas, such as production and distribution. In the context of change, knowledge from a technological knowledge-interest aims to explain and improve organizational practices such as productivity, efficiency and growth. This is in line with the tool-based perspective on change.

An *interpretative knowledge-interest* is generally about understanding and interpretation, and therefore language, meaning and culture are the key ingredients. This knowledge-interest is sometimes referred to as 'hermeneutics', from the Greek word *hermeneuo* meaning 'to interpret'. General insightfulness is the ideal here. One assumes that context and patterns are typically complex and that the role of knowledge isn't primarily to give techniques or a recipe, but rather to make the complex and uncertain – such as an organizational change process – a bit clearer and to develop ideas to better understand the world around us. Ideally, and traditionally, this is seen in the cultural sciences, which therefore are also sometimes called hermeneutic sciences.

In the context of change, the ambition is to interpret organizations and processes of change in order to get a more in-depth understanding. This is in line with the process perspective on change.

An *emancipatory knowledge-interest* aims not only to interpret and understand but also to critically review organizational practices and theories. It is about critical reflection and the primary goal is to enable liberation (emancipation) from a variety of cognitive blockages, limitations and assumptions that constitute people's thinking as well as in established knowledge. This is a perspective that looks at the darker side of organizations and that doesn't assume that organizations are systems in harmony. Instead, it highlights the presence of conflicts of interest – such as that an organizational change process is not necessarily in everybody's interest – and marginalization and suppression of alternative voices. An emancipatory knowledge-interest is thus all about reviewing and scrutinising different forms of knowledge and revealing the power interests behind actions and behind different representations of the current conditions. This is particularly prominent in critical management theory. The point of adopting a knowledge-critical approach in terms of organizational change is to promote liberation from conventional mindsets and ideas and to call for a reflective approach to knowledge, especially in relation to the more technically and pragmatically oriented knowledge about organizational change. For instance, is it reasonable to assume that 'the rate of change becoming faster and faster' (Burke, 2002, p. 9), as many authors claim, or could it be that the environment was far more turbulent at the beginning of the 1900s (Grey, 2003)? This approach emphasizes independent thought and critical reflection. Increased organizational efficiency is not a main ambition, even though a critical mindset can of course also contribute to it.

These knowledge-interests all fill their respective functions, and the relationship between them and the three perspectives explored of the book is summarized in Table 2.1.

TABLE 2.1   Three perspectives on change: the tool-based perspective, process perspective and critical perspective

	Tool-based perspective	Process perspective	Critical perspective
Knowledge-interest	Technical	Interpretative	Emancipatory
Aim	Explain and improve	Understand	Liberate

The starting point for this book is that all three dimensions are needed – that technical and instrumental knowledge is important from a pragmatic perspective, but so is critical knowledge stimulating reflection and liberation. The aim to understand what is going on in change processes might be even more basic. Depending on what perspective is adopted, different aspects of change and change management will be highlighted and different questions will be answered: *How* can change be managed? *What* does the change mean for those engaged in it and what social dynamics are in play? *Why* work with change in the first place?

The tool-based perspective

Applying the tool-based perspective suggests following a prescriptive orientation, with the aim of providing ideas on how to successfully implement intended change, whether it contains grand plans or whether it is about creating the organizational requirements for emergent change. A key focus is placed on the tools – often models of change – that can be used to formulate, plan and execute organizational changes. The changes are initiated by managers, usually as an answer to altered circumstances in the business environment, handled in either an offensive or defensive way in order to secure long-term survival.

From this perspective, organizations are often understood as living organisms, consisting of a variety of subparts that must be aligned with each other and adapted to the environment in order to survive in the long run. This expresses an open systems view of organizations, viewing the organization as a system which is part of a larger whole (the environment) that consists of a number of different subsystems (or subparts) between which there must be harmony and alignment in order to have a working whole. Subsystems can refer to strategy, culture, structure, reward systems, HR, management control systems, recruitment systems, management, leadership and any other significant part of an organization. According to this view, it is suggested that achieving alignment between the subparts means that the whole becomes more than the sum of its parts, which then promises the organization's long-term survival. Survival is, however, not only about alignment between the different subparts of the organization, but also about harmony and alignment between the organization and the larger system – the environment in which it exists, with its separate stakeholders, or other systems such as clients, suppliers, banks, the state, lobbyists.

As the world is constantly changing, it becomes important to find the appropriate tools to manage change successfully. These can be techniques about how to accomplish strategic change and implement explicit programmes of change with well-formulated intentions and goals. These can also be prescriptions about modifying organizational conditions – structure, reward systems, recruitment organizational culture, etc. – with the purpose of achieving emergent change.

Taken together, the major focus of the tool perspective is on how managers can control and shape the process of change so that its intentions are realized. Key questions are: How can change be accomplished and what are the appropriate tools to use?

The process perspective

The process perspective on change is in line with an interpretative knowledge-interest and implies a descriptive focus on how one can understand and gain a deeper insight for the complexity of the change processes. Unlike managing and controlling the process of change, the primary focus here is on understanding what happens in actual change processes, in particular from the viewpoints of the people involved. An important focus in much of the literature is on how meaning is created by the different actors in the change processes; how they make sense of and interpret what is going on as they are involved in the change. Above all, it aims at facilitating an understanding of the complexity, dynamics and logic of different types of change in order to gain deeper insights into the phenomenon. It is about understanding diverse interpretations and focusing on sensemaking and its relation to identities, values, symbols and organizational culture in general.

From a process perspective, culture is not seen solely as something an organization *has*, as a subsystem among others. Culture is also considered as something the organization *is* (Smircich, 1983). Even though many theories emphasize the importance of organizational culture, it is not always certain that organizational culture is approached from an interpretative knowledge-interest. Often the question of whether one can govern and control the culture (in line with a technical interest) dominates rather than the ambition to interpret and understand the culture and people's constructions of meaning. Furthermore, this perspective opens up the possibility of several cultures, rather than a single, stable and homogeneous organizational culture. Within the same organization, several cultures can be at play, originating from different departments, professions or even nationalities. The process perspective takes the cultural dimension into account whether it is reasonable to talk about cultural consistency (a single corporate culture), cultural differences (subcultures) or cultural fragmentation. The idea is to develop knowledge to gain more wisdom in order to improve the understanding of change processes in all their complexity and imperfections: Why do people interpret a suggested change process in different ways? What importance does the question of identity have for how people make sense of change ideas, or in what way does it influence the dynamics of change? Structural conditions are also focused upon, but still from the perception of those involved in the organizational change.

The critical perspective

When we talk about different perspectives of change, it might come across as if change is something self-evidently positive or at least something that organizations have to launch in order to survive in a changeable world. That is not always the case of course. In some cases, attempts to change are initiated because other organizations are seen to be engaged in change or because a new CEO wants to show drive and make his or her mark on the organization. Maybe a manager has picked up an idea at a management training session or has learnt something about how to make an organization more effective by personal networking, or someone may just be bored and want to do something exciting. It is not always certain that there are clear and rational reasons behind attempts to change. The critical perspective on change, in line with an emancipatory knowledge-interest, suggests a focus on power and politics in order to be able to shed light on the underlying interests and motives related to change processes. A key focus is placed on the divergent interests, disagreements and conflicts that often are expressed during attempts at change. It is not uncommon for mainstream organizational change literature (implicitly) to assume an absence of conflict of interests in organizations, with the result that organizational changes tend to be regarded as clear-cut and beneficial to all the members of the organization. If anyone opposes the change or asks questions of the propositions of change, it is often viewed as opposition against a more or less given development. Opponents always risk being described as resisters who are against progress or as blockers of natural development. From a critical perspective, however, it is stressed that organizational change is never a given or inevitable; it always emanates from some individuals' interests for change, especially interests coinciding with position and power. Here organizations are looked upon as political systems, consisting of (groups of) actors with different interests and agendas, who are involved in various power struggles. This approach highlights that organizational changes always have political consequences for the people affected by them, and that organizational changes thus should not be looked upon as neutral, unpolitical answers to changes in the environment. A key ambition of the emancipatory knowledge-interest and the critically-oriented literature on change is to question what tends to be otherwise taken for granted in order to look beyond the obvious. It could, for instance, be to encourage reflection on why change is necessary or to unveil diverse interests: whose interests are being served and whose interests are being ignored, and what could be the power-political consequences of a certain change? A focus on these types of issues can create possibilities for emancipation from ideological or mindset blockages that are not uncommon in processes of change.

TABLE 2.2   Terms and assumptions of the three perspectives on change: the tool-based, process and critical perspectives

	Tool-based perspective	Process perspective	Critical perspective
Knowledge interest	Technical	Interpretative	Emancipatory
Aim	Explain and improve	Understand	Liberate
Means	Normative: Provide advice and guidelines	Descriptive: Describe and interpret the course of action	Critical: Scruitinise and question the given
Empirical focus	Managerial programmes for change, tools for change	Sensemaking of the involved actors	The hidden, marginalized, not spoken about
Dominant view on the organization	Organism	Culture	Political system
Dominant view on change	Controllable and desirable	Dynamic, complex and ambiguous	Conflict-filled (conflicts of interest)
Central terms	Systems, planning and control	Interpretation, dialogue and context	Power, politics and interests
Treated in this book in	Chapters 4–5	Chapters 6–7	Chapter 8

EXERCISE 2.5

Identify the key problems associated with solely adopting a process approach to organizational change. Write a list of what can cause those problems and another list of how you can solve them by adding insights and concepts from the tool-based and critical perspectives, respectively.

EXERCISE 2.6

Think of an organization that you are familiar with or have some experience of. Imagine that you were given the task of exploring possibilities of implementing an organizational change in line with a new strategic direction within that specific organization. You need to make a multidimensional analysis, drawing upon the three perspectives on change – the tool-based, process and critical perspectives of change. How would you set up this task?

Suggestion: For each of these perspectives, list the following: Who would you primarily talk to? What aspects would you focus on? What types of questions would you like to be able to answer?

EXERCISE 2.7

Consider the case below and answer the following questions.

- How would you characterize Electronic Engineering Ltd? What kind of organization is it?
- What kind of change in terms of scope and scale does Weston suggest? What are the defining characteristics of the change?
- What key aspects do you think Weston has failed to consider in this seemingly rather large change project?
- Provide five recommendations for Weston in order to improve the chances of success.

CASE

Electronic Engineering Ltd

When Stanley Weston was appointed as new CEO for the renowned company Electronic Engineering Ltd, many people in the company, the business community and the business press applauded. Weston was seen as a young company leader and represented a modern management philosophy. He had also been trained in many of the most celebrated international engineering companies.

Upon arriving at the new company, Stanley Weston took some time to familiarize himself with the history of the company, its current strategic direction and its future prospects. After a few weeks, he organized an important meeting with the management team and union representatives in order to discuss the long-term strategy of the company. Early in the meeting Weston stated that:

> After performing an analysis of the company, I have reached the conclusion that we need to develop the electronic engineering department by introducing more sophisticated flexible manufacturing systems. I think it is important to make this change in order to facilitate the use of computer-controlled machines such as robots in the production process. This will also help in enhancing the valued added in our products and move us towards selling whole systems rather than just being a supplier of simple electronic components.

Even though people in Electronic Engineering Ltd were concerned when thinking about flexible manufacturing systems and robotization, many said that they felt good about that the new CEO assumed responsibility for the technological development of the company.

However, during the year following the strategy formulations of robotization by Weston not much of a substantial change happened. In connection to the annual planning meeting a year later, the question about the company's objective, strategy and long-term orientation was once more raised and emphasized. Again, the need for change towards robotization and systems solutions was formulated, but subsequent to the meeting nothing happened. The procedure was simply repeated over the next two years. The whole organization seemed to support the ambition to change to a new direction, but even so no concrete changes seemed to materialize. Three years after Weston had assumed his position and despite the ambitions for strategic change being formulated every year in the strategic plan, the company was still strongly oriented towards simple electronical engineering.

During a conversation with his friend from college, Anna Stevens, Weston described the situation as follows:

> The situation is troubling. On every occasion I have talked about the necessity to change technology and turn to robotics and systems solutions. I think we have made a decision to do that on at least four occasions. And although everyone agrees, nothing happens. Everyone just continues in the traditional wheel tracks. How am I going to get change to happen?

REVIEW QUESTIONS 2.4

Recall	List at least three key characteristics of the tool-based perspective, process perspective and critical perspective on change.
Explain	Explain how and why a certain basic understanding of the organization (as an organism, culture or political system) can be related to a certain perspective on change (tool-based, process, critical).
Reflect	In what ways can a critical approach to change facilitate organizational change work in practice?

SUMMARY

Change varies in terms of tempo, scope and managerial intervention. It is common to contrast revolutionary and evolutionary changes. The difference can be important for the way one relates to change in terms of management. Revolutionary changes often mean greater political intensity, which can have consequences when it comes to considerations regarding power, time, control and decision-making. Evolutionary changes are often less politically charged and therefore tend to invoke another type of organizational dynamics when it comes to power and influence. In this chapter we have raised the political aspect as a central element in order to understand what organizational change is about – it is not just a question of resistance in the traditional meaning of the word; it also involves questions dealing with interests, engagement and participation.

Organizational change can also be characterized with the help of metaphors. Metaphors can contribute to an increased understanding of the progression of change and its dynamics as well as how to influence and manage change processes. Metaphors can help with the understanding of how to relate to and look at organizational changes in specific organizations, how to talk about them, motivate them and look at the possibilities of successfully implementing them. Another common way to describe organizational change is to speak of planned and emergent change, respectively. Planned change is the most classical way of looking at change. The planning ideal is dominated by a distinct pragmatism and there is a vast array of n-step models available, suggesting that organizational change should be implemented along a series of different steps. Within the genre of emergent change, two comprehensive orientations can be found: a descriptive approach based on understanding and a prescriptive and tool-based approach. The first orientation puts the focus on how processes of change develop in practice, and is often based on how those involved look upon what happens in processes of change, and the second focuses on factors that promote organizational change and launches recipes for how to work more successfully with change.

We concluded the chapter by further specifying and contrasting the three perspectives on change: the tool-based perspective, the process perspective and the critical perspective, with the starting point being the three different knowledge-interests. The tool-based perspective implies a distinctly tool-based view on change, i.e. *how* one makes change happen. Here the view on change is pragmatic. It expresses a will to try to control the change process, irrespective of whether the plans are big or whether it is a matter of managing incremental, emergent change with slightly more subtle forms of control. The process perspective comprises *what* organizational change work means in practice. When does change occur and what dynamics can be traced in the process of change? Finally, a critical perspective means that the importance and need for organizational change should not be taken for granted. Rather, this perspective encourages critical reflection and asks *why* change is needed and *why* it evolves in a certain way. It tries to identify the interests that lie behind the change process and examines the power-political effects that organizational change can entail.

 # KEY PRACTICAL INSIGHTS

What we can say about organizational change following this chapter:

- The scope, scale and content of change is a matter of interpretation and thus concerns the perspective of the interpreter. Therefore, it is important to follow up on how employees view a suggested change, rather than assuming that they experience and understand the change in a similar way as those change agents who have designed and formulated it.

- A way to understand how people interpret change is to acknowledge and recognize how they talk about it. What metaphors of change seem to be in use?

- It is often sensible to strive to create and uphold a shared understanding of what the organizational change implies. Contrasting and conflicting images can be confusing and undermine commitment.

- Recognize that portraying organizational change in a certain way always privileges some interests while downplaying interest of others.

- Planned or emergent organizational change offers two distinctive but also complementary ways of understanding and managing change. It is important to acknowledge that organizational changes can and will take place even though they are not centrally planned.

- Most successful organizational changes are evolutionary. Incremental and evolutionary changes tend to be less threatening to people's identities, while revolutionary changes can trigger anxiety and worries and imply more politics and negotiations. Therefore, it is often advisable to work with long-term goals and implement changes incrementally. Evolutionary changes, too, can achieve radical results in the long run.

- Radical changes can at times mobilize huge efforts and commitment among employees, in particular if the organization is in a crisis and people are receptive to ideas of change.

- Social engineering models of change often underestimate the importance of considering that organizational change primarily involves people rather than systems, structures and strategies, which tend to cause more problems than necessary.

- Organizational change involves people and therefore often requires an intimate understanding of meanings, identities, emotions, symbols, politics, etc.

 # FURTHER READING

Go online to access free and downloadable SAGE Journal articles related to this chapter at https://study.sagepub.com/sveningsson

Burke, W. W. (2017). *Organization change: Theory and practice*. Thousand Oaks, CA: Sage.

Marshak, R. J. (2002). Changing the language of change: How new contexts and concepts are challenging the ways we think and talk about organizational change. *Strategic Change*, 11(5), 279–286.

Palmer, I., & Dunford, R. (2008). Organizational change and the importance of embedded assumptions. *British Journal of Management*, 19, 20–32.

Pettigrew, A., Woodman, R., & Cameron, K. (2001). Studying organizational change and development: Challenges for future research. *Academy of Management Journal*, 44(4), 697–713.

Tsoukas, H. (2005). Afterword: Why language matters in the analysis of organizational change. *Journal of Organizational Change Management*, 18(1), 96–104.

Weick, K. E., & Quinn, R. E. (1999). Organizational change and development. *Annual Review of Psychology*, 50, 361–386.

WHY ORGANIZATIONAL CHANGE?

LEARNING OBJECTIVES

When you have completed your study of this chapter, you should be able to:

- Identify and describe the external and internal factors that can trigger organizational change.

- Classify change based on the unit of analysis and the nature of its emergence.

- Compare and critically discuss what is referred to as the evolutionary, dialectical, teleological and life-cycle models of change.

- Explain and discuss the significance of interpretation and perspective in relation to the drivers of change.

- Identify and illustrate the role and relevance of imitation and fashion-following in change processes.

- Critically discuss the significance of identity in change processes.

In this chapter we devote our attention to the question of why changes occur. What is it that makes organizations embark on changes? What is so tempting about change, especially as most people know that it is very complex and that many organizations fail? We have already touched upon these questions in the previous chapter, but here we examine these issues in more depth with the help of some popular models and classic concepts.

We begin the chapter with a discussion about what is often referred to as the triggers – or driving forces – of change, which refers to the various external and internal conditions that are often seen as giving rise to change. Next, we discuss different ways of managing the triggers. Should triggers be regarded as more or less unavoidable, as forces that will uncon-ditionally change an organization in a particular way (a regulating and determining view), or can change rather be explained as the outcome of a more thoughtful and intentional plan? Also, should change primarily be understood in evolutionary terms (that might be following a certain pattern), or something that occurs in specific and limited episodes, driven by corporate management? Should we try to understand change from a single organizational unit, or should we rather focus on trying to understand change from a broader view by shifting the focus to organizations' employees?

We then more explicitly turn to the process and critical perspective and emphasize the significance of viewing organizational change as a result of how individuals interpret and understand the organization and its relation to the environment. Based on that view, it is com-mon to depart from the idea that there is an objective environment consisting of external or internal forces that somehow compel or drive an organization to change. Rather, change can productively be seen as a matter of people's interpretations of the organization and its context, interpretations based on people's interest, commitments, wishes, background and identity. It is not uncommon, for example, to examine how managers rhetorically motivate a change by referring to so-called unescapable forces in the environment, in spite of the fact that it may perhaps be better understood as the manager's wish to express decisiveness and mark his or her distinctiveness and power.

DRIVING FORCES OF ORGANIZATIONAL CHANGE

There are different reasons for organizational change. Based on a view that changes occur epi-sodically, it is very common to talk about organizational change as a result of the presence of external and internal driving forces or triggers. Some significant external triggers commonly include (Child, 2005):

- Technological developments
- Political forces

- Demographic factors
- Economic factors
- Sociocultural forces
- The emergence of new knowledge
- Changing competitive and industrial conditions (often as a result of the driving forces mentioned above).

It probably goes without saying that technological development influences organizations in many ways. What springs to mind in contemporary society is perhaps the development of new forms of technology of information and communication, which trigger and enable new ways of working (distance work, for example), and which subsequently also drive increased globalization. Also highly significant are technological developments such as mobile commerce, online transaction processing, electronic funds transfer, internet marketing and electronic data interchange (EDI), which have all facilitated a massive development in what many are familiar with as e-commerce. There is an increasingly large number of companies and services – Amazon, iTunes, Alibaba Group, eBay, and Etsy – that draw upon this technological development and have subsequently changed the traditional retailing landscape on a global basis. The internet also facilitates public organizations (e.g. the police force or social services), such as when people interact and accomplish a variety of tasks online that traditionally needed physical meetings. New information technologies can also form the basis for the proliferation of economic control systems, such as scorecards and other methods that target increased measuring and the quantification of ways of working and productivity, that contributes to greater standardization, formalization and centralization in many contemporary organizations (Kärreman et al., 2002).

Political driving forces refers to changes in broader national and international regulations and trade agreements. For example, a reduction of international trade restrictions – within consumer products or services – may expedite the development of new international markets. Changing regulations may enable organizations to enter alliances or establish themselves internationally through acquisitions or close collaboration. Trade agreements, for example by the World Trade Organization (WTO), may have significant consequences in terms of possibilities for expansion and development. Most companies in the UK face new and complex challenges in terms of trade with many countries following Brexit. At the time of writing (October 2019), limited access to the single market of the European Union may force many companies to reconsider their global strategies and organization, especially if it becomes difficult to reach a deal on some sort of partial integration.

Demographic factors influence the ability to recruit and the composition of the workforce, and other internal conditions that relate to career, education, promotion, motivation and rewards. An increased level of education can boost expectations on ways and forms of working in terms of influence and participation, something that can impact decision processes and the distribution of power in organizations. An important factor that has been widely discussed is that millennials are an increasingly important demographic group which have an impact on workplaces, recruitment, leadership and consumption more generally. In terms of the latter, it is sometimes suggested that millennials often look for convenience and flexibility, encouraged and facilitated by mobile technology. Having grown up with mobile technology, millennials expect to use it – to consume and pay, chat, engage in social media, do online searches and many other things – in a convenient and flexible manner. Arguably, this puts pressure on companies to develop user-friendly apps and systems in order to reach and keep millennials (McGee, 2017). In terms of consumption, millennials are also often said to expect a more customized experience, making them feel valued and wanted.

MINI CASE 3.1

Nordstrom

The American retailer Nordstrom has invested substantially in personalized shopping experiences. The company examines which items are popular via the social network site Pinterest – Nordstrom's Pinterest community – and then displays the 'top-pinned-items' in its stores. The items are also displayed with a Pinterest logo. In this way, Nordstrom is able to draw upon popular things and interests in social media and thus better personalize their offers to align with what they perceive the shopper wants. As stated by the social media manager at Nordstrom, Bryan Galipeau: 'Pinterest is in many ways the world's biggest wish list – and so it also fits well with our goal of having our merchandise show up in our customers' wish list'.

Sources: Lutz (2013); McGee (2017)

Economic factors, such as growth, interest rates and unemployment levels, can impact organizations in a multitude of ways. For example, in a recession with a high level of unemployment, it can be easier for organizations to recruit personnel and they do not have to compete with other employers by offering high wages or other benefits. Economic downturns can also increase the demand for studying at university. In contrast, in periods of economic prosperity, organizations may need to pay greater attention to employer branding in order to attract new employees. Interest and exchange rates can also affect the demands from markets.

It is also important to emphasize how changing cultural conditions can drive changes in organizations in an increasingly significant way. There are a variety of demands on organizations to be not only economically efficient but also socially legitimate and acceptable. This normally means that organizations need to consider and relate to broader societal trends and norms with respect to, for example, environmental or gender issues, or ethics.

MINI CASE 3.2

#MeToo

In October 2017, an investigation revealing recurring sexual harassment and rape allegations against a Hollywood executive was published in *The New York Times*. The story brought new energy to the #MeToo movement, which was originally founded by Tarana Burke in 2006 to support women of colour from low-income neighbourhoods who had been sexually abused. The #MeToo movement – fighting against the oppression of women – quickly spread across the United States through tweets, headlines and demonstrations, and continued to spread internationally throughout the following year. By 2018, the #MeToo movement had led to more than 250 men being removed from their positions in the entertainment industry, in business and in politics in the US alone.

The movement also got a strong hold in the tech industry. For instance, more than 20,000 employees at Google (including senior management and staff from around the world) participated in the 'Google Walkout for Real Change' demonstration, which was demanding changes to the oppressive workplace culture. The protests specifically focused on how Google had handled sexual harassment allegations, following a report that a former executive had received a $90 million exit package after being accused of sexual coercion. Signs stated 'I reported, and he got promoted' as well as 'Happy to quit for $90M—no sexual harassment required'. The following week, Google, followed by Facebook, announced a number of changes to harassment and discrimination policies, including an end to forced arbitrations; it should now be possible for employees to bring their claims to court.

The events related to the #MeToo movement show how previously silenced voices were finally heard due to a large-scale movement that put the oppression of women on the global agenda. The societal trend more or less forced companies to act on issues that had previously been marginalized and covered up.

Sources: Klich (2018), Marwan (2018)

Many of these broader societal questions are sometimes framed under the common label of societal responsibility or *corporate social responsibility* (CSR). In order to deal with these questions – and also to avoid negative exposure and damage to reputations – contemporary organizations to an increasing extent engage in social issues. However, the extent to which this has any substantial effect on the core business is more uncertain. Some would argue that organizations create administrative routines and ways of working that have little substantial effect on the core business, but rather work at legitimating the organization, based on current societal norms and views about what is right, good, ethical, etc. (Meyer & Rowan, 1977). Organizational change may occasionally also be the result of that organization's appropriate new knowledge about, for example, management and control of organizations such as quality systems (TQM) and control systems such as the previously mentioned scorecards, or organizations subject themselves to different accreditation systems, such as the International Standards Organization (ISO). Appropriation of new knowledge might give rise to substantial changes in the core business of an organization, but they are also difficult to apply and can often lead to more superficial changes.

Sometimes, however, efforts at improving the image of an organization might also have a rather substantial and long-term impact on an organization and its products and services. For example, a significant global trend among business schools is the increased demand for accreditation, something that is seen as serving mainly business schools' quality assurance for themselves and their stakeholders, providing marketing benefits, and that also facilitates benchmarking and networks with peer business schools. Although most countries have some form of basic quality assurance agency that supervises higher education, voluntary management education accreditation by non-governmental, international accrediting bodies – such as European Quality Improvement System (EQUIS), Association of MBAs (AMBA), Association to Advance Collegiate Schools of Business (AACSB) – has grown increasingly popular in business schools all over the world. This is partly as a result of an increasing number of educational agencies – such as educational agents or consultants that provide students with advice about which school to choose – all over the world that keep track of how different business schools are performing in terms of the view of the accreditation bodies. Occasionally these accreditation bodies can have a substantial impact on the operations of business schools and give rise to organizational changes.

MINI CASE 3.3

University accreditation

In a large national business school, preparations for upcoming accreditation contributed to a variety of changes. Some of these were the result of increased formalization procedures, such as requiring much more detailed annual reports of staff and faculty at the school. This was more or less expected by the employees. More surprisingly in this case, however, the preparations also led management to facilitate more fundamental and long-lasting organizational changes such as designing a variety of new courses within different disciplines. The aim was to enhance the global image of the school and, in turn, its international attractiveness to students all over the world.

Some of the triggers discussed above often also lead to changes in competition dynamics, as when organizations establish radically new competitive strategies. In Sweden, for example, a large number of international consumer electronics companies – often with a chain of stores – have recently established themselves, with radical consequences for many national corporations in the form of increased competitiveness and subsequently higher demands on efficiency and aggressive marketing. Another example, related to the development of e-commerce, as discussed above, is digitalization, providing possibilities for radically new business models, which in turn have transformed the media, music and film industries. To this we can also add the significance of more or less radical entrepreneurs who constantly look for new business opportunities and who often challenge traditional business dynamics with new business models and ideas. We can note, for example, how the UK entrepreneur Richard Branson, and his creation, Virgin, has challenged existing organizations for more than 30 years, in both traditional and highly regulated industries, such as music, airlines, railways, and soft drinks. These are businesses that new organizations would normally avoid due to their established and regulated nature. But the case of Virgin has shown that it is possible to redefine industries in terms of barriers to entry and competitive advantages, something that in many cases has also contributed to changes among the established organizations within those industries. Redefining business is also something that Amazon and Netflix have been particularly successful in doing, as well as Airbnb and Uber.

EXERCISE 3.1

Consider the case below and discuss in what way(s) you think:

- The entry of Airbnb has affected traditional companies in the hotel business.
- The entry of Uber has affected traditional companies in the taxi service business.

CASE

Airbnb and Uber

Airbnb and Uber are two companies that have challenged the traditional logic and economics of the hotel industry and taxi services, and they experienced remarkable growth while doing it. Both of these business models are built upon an online platform that connects customers with service providers. Airbnb connects home owners willing to rent a room/house with customers, while Uber connects taxi-drivers with customers. Both businesses have transformed and opened up new competitive landscapes.

In contrast to traditional hotels, Airbnb does not own or manage any physical accommodation. Instead, Airbnb manages a platform that connects customers and house owners and

(Continued)

takes a percentage of the rent. Likewise, Uber does not own any cars. The drivers use their own cars and Uber facilitates connecting the customer with a driver.

Airbnb was founded in 2008 but already has more rooms than InterContinental Hotels or Hilton Worldwide. Airbnb, like Uber, does not involve owning or managing physical assets, so the risks for these businesses are low and expansion is easily facilitated since no large investments are needed in order to scale-up.

Source: Kavadias et al. (2016)

There are also what are labelled internal driving forces. These involve situations where an organization has experienced rapid growth and needs to realign its structure to accommodate the larger size or where an organization has differentiated its products or services and consequently needs to increase integration in order to reach economies of scale and secure efficiency. Internal triggers may also have their origin in individuals' interests and wishes for specific changes. It is difficult to imagine much of the product development taking place at Apple during the last 20 years without acknowledging and recognizing the interests and wishes of Steve Jobs. Much of the spectacular product development that Apple embarked upon after Jobs returned in 1997 – the iMac, iPod, iPhone and iPad – is often directly attributed to his personality and management style (Isaacson, 2011).

External and internal triggers naturally interact and influence each other in complex ways. This is why it is often important to examine the relations between them in order to understand the broader logic and dynamics of systems and to see how different triggers interact. For example, the globalization of markets (driven by technological and/or political factors) often lead to intensified competition that subsequently increases demands on effectiveness and renewal (which can be possible by utilizing technological development). Increased demands on effectiveness might trigger increased standardization and ambitions to remotely control organizations with the help of a variety of modern control systems (new knowledge). An illustration of this can be seen in the pharmaceutical industry, which, following globalization and increased organizational consolidation, increasingly strives to standardize and control knowledge-sharing and knowledge development by coding (facilitated by modern information) and communication systems (i.e. people's competencies and skills).

MINI CASE 3.4

Mitsufuji Corporation

The Tokyo-based fabric company Mitsufuji has combined changes in demographics (an ageing population) and technology and used it to transform its main business. Founded in 1979, Mitsufuji was originally a conventional textile manufacturer. In the 1990s the company started to develop, manufacture and sell the silver-metalized fibre (AGposs®) for antibacterial products. When it became known that these fibres had high conductivity, the company got into the business of the Internet of Things (IoT). Now they are developing, manufacturing and selling smartwear, that is wearable IoT products (hamon®). These clothes can be used to monitor breathing and hearth rate, body temperature and humidity. From a transmitter attached to the fabric, data can then be sent to mobile devices.

Smartware can be used in various sports as well as in uniforms for factory workers, but Mitsufuji has paid attention to the growing interest in these types of clothes from Japan's ageing population and collaborated with university researchers to develop smartwear that can detect when heat stroke may occur. The majority of the 105 people who died of heatstroke in Tokyo in midsummer 2018 were over 70 years old. In this way, the company has turned external changes in demographics as well as new technology to their advantage.

Sources: Forbes (2018); www.mitsufuji.co.jp/en/ (accessed 6 December 2018)

Furthermore, it is also important to remember that it is not always easy to classify whether a trigger is external or internal, or identify what the initiating trigger was, as organizations relate in different ways to their environment. Some organizations choose to be more innovative and agents of their own fate, while others choose to be more cautious and benchmark the development of other organizations. The latter is more defensive and conformist in terms of pioneering. To what extent different triggers are seen as unavoidable and determining for how organizations develop or if organizations can manage and relate more actively to them, is something of a classic divide in the literature of organizational change. From an empirical perspective, it might be wise not to be too rigid in tackling this question, and rather regard the different explanations as a rich source for understanding change. The discussion so far has been oriented towards how single organizations can relate to various triggers, but there are also some theories about changes regarding employees of organizations, and we turn to this in the next section.

EXERCISE 3.2

Consider the case entitled 'No "musical chairs" – or…?' in Chapter 2 (pp. 31–32) and answer the following questions:

- List as many triggers to change you can identify in the case.
- Are the triggers related to each other in any way?
- Could the need to change the organization, as expressed by the managers, have been foreseen?

REVIEW QUESTIONS 3.1

Recall	List at least five external and two internal potential triggers of change.
Explain	Describe, by providing vivid illustrations, how triggers can interact and enhance the need to change.
Reflect	The theoretical division between external and internal triggers to change might look clear-cut, but it is seldom so in practice. Reflect upon potential reasons why the distinction can be blurred.
Reflect	Why is it important to understand the triggers of change? Try to come up with at least three distinctive 'lessons learned' on the topic.

AN EXTENDED UNDERSTANDING
OF WHAT DRIVES CHANGE

As indicated in the last section, understanding the variety of organizational change normally requires more than one perspective or approach. In an effort to categorize and classify theories of change and encourage a more multidimensional analysis, Van de Ven and Poole (1995) introduced a framework consisting of two dimensions – unit of study and mode of change – that intersect with each other in the form of a matrix.

The first dimension, *unit of change*, concerns the focus of the study. In some cases, the change relates to a specific entity, for example, a single organization or the development of a particular product or service. The focus here is on the particular organization or product and its progression, for example, how an organization develops as it grows and matures through the phases in a life-cycle. In other cases, the unit of change concerns a broader perspective with multiple entities, such as a change process for a larger group of organizations (within an industry or a market) or the development of a group of products within an organization over time.

The second dimension, *mode of change*, concerns the source or origin of change, and how the change is governed. Within this dimension, a distinction is made between theories that regard changes as predetermined, and in some sense unavoidable because the changes are driven by uncontrollable forces (the prescribed view), and theories that, in contrast, emphasize the actions of those initiating and involved in the change process (the constructive view) (see Table 3.1).

Combining these two dimensions in a matrix consisting of four different approaches to change:

- An evolutionary theory of change
- A life-cycle theory of change
- A teleological theory of change
- A dialectical theory of change

TABLE 3.1   A typology of change process theories (Van de Ven and Poole, 1995)

Theory of change	Unit of change	Mode of change
Evolutionary	Multiple entities	Prescribed
Life cycle	Single entity	Prescribed
Teleological	Single entity	Constructive
Dialectical	Multiple entities	Constructive

Evolutionary theory of change

According to the evolutionary theory of change, organizational change is governed by conditions and demands in the environment, for example competitive forces and demands on efficiency, profitability and development. The focus of attention here is not on single units – organizations or products – but on how groups of organizations, labelled populations, emerge, develop and eventually fade. Inspired by biology, this theory is characterized as an ecology of a population, suggesting that only those organizations that are best adapted to their environment will survive. Adaption to the environment becomes a natural necessity, as living organisms have to adapt to their environment in order to survive. This is a kind of 'survival of the fittest' or Darwinian approach (Hannan & Freeman, 1977). The founder of the Boston Consulting Group, Bruce Henderson (1989, p. 143), once suggested that: 'Human beings may be at the top of the ecological chain, but we are still members of the ecological community. That is why Darwin is probably a better guide to business competition than economists are.'

According to evolutionists, organizations can always develop different competitive strategies through product innovation or more efficient means of production and more competitive prices, but in the end, it is always the environment that dictates the terms of competition. The environment (e.g. the industry or market) determines which organizations are best adapted to survive – a kind of natural selection. Within population ecology, there is a rather pessimistic and gloomy view on the ability of organizations to control and manage any change direction. It is the market and other regulating forces – institutional, political, economic, etc. – in the environment that dictate the existence and life of organizations, and thus form the conditions that enable only the fittest, often most economically efficient, to survive. It is about adapt or die. It is commonly understood that managers (and others), in spite of comprehensive analysis and efforts to characterize their situations, have difficulty in understanding an increasingly ambiguous and complex environment, and that successful adaption is often more the result of luck and coincidence.

A more optimistic take on the population ecology theory is that it helps us to understand the significance of analyzing and mapping the environment (such as existing competitive conditions and the development dynamics within an industry) in order to improve adaption and alignment to environmental conditions. In addition, if survival is contingent upon adaption, it is important to create structural flexibility and organizational cultures that encourage change and reduce resistance and friction. Organizational symbols and histories that emphasize swift organizational change and adaption to environmental circumstances become highly significant tools for managing change. It is not uncommon for change actors to create stories about heroic efforts of change that function as encouraging illustrations of how an organization has previously managed to adapt to difficult circumstances and avoided failure and possible closure. Indeed, many change actors often talk in terms of change or die.

Life-cycle theory

According to the life-cycle approach, organizations follow a specific life-cycle trajectory from birth, development and maturity to decline and death. As in the evolutionary approach, organizations in the life-cycle approach are viewed as living organisms and change is given a biological explanation (Greiner, 1972). In the life-cycle theory, however, it is the specific and single organization or product that is in focus. Change is, as in the evolutionary approach, viewed as unavoidable and the orientation of change is determined by the pressure that is contingent upon the phase or stage in the life cycle in which the organization is located.

Applying this view to product development, it is crucial to accomplish a broad variety of development activities that enable a continuous stream of new products that can renew, for example, maturing organizations. The alternative is an organization finding itself in a situation where its product portfolio consists of only maturing and declining products. A life-cycle approach can also help organizations to recognize and understand typical problems that occur in different life-cycle phases. In the growth and expansion phases, it is usually important to encourage creativity and to experiment in order to preserve the organization's ability to develop and renew. As an organization matures, the emphasis shifts towards increased formalization and the installation of reliable systems of control to secure continuity and sustained efficiency. In parallel, it is vital to prepare for the downturn in the life cycle that follows the maturity phase. This normally means trying to maintain an element of creativity and a climate of innovation in order to develop new products and services and thus new life cycles that prolong the life of an organization.

Viewing organizations as organisms progressing through different life-cycle stages has also received some criticism. A particular criticism suggests that living organisms are too different from organizations in order to explain the life and development of organizations. For example, many start-ups and small entrepreneurial organizations never survive to grow beyond the initial phase and many organizations are liquidated after having been around for a short or relatively short period of time. How should such common developments be explained assuming the life-cycle theory of living organisms? Should we label these common developments among organizations as instances of 'sudden infant death syndrome' and 'cardiac arrest' or is this to stretch the metaphor beyond what makes sense? It is also said that the life-cycle theory is limited in explaining change among organization as it assumes that change takes place in relatively short periods of time while in reality change is often more continuous and evolving, such as in the process approach.

A third form of criticism limiting the value of the life-cycle model suggests that the assumption that organizations face relatively similar kinds of challenges and possibilities independent of contextual contingencies such as institutional, social, cultural and industry conditions is too sweeping. This kind of sweeping determinism means that it may be less helpful in understanding and managing change than is often assumed.

EXERCISE 3.3

The life-cycle model suggests that organizations follow a life trajectory that ultimately leads to an unavoidable demise. But most of us can probably think of some organizations that don't follow that logic. Why is that? Why do some organizations manage the mature stages and prolong their lives in ways that seemingly contradict the model? And what does that tell us about change in organizations?

Teleological theory of change

Within the teleological theory of change there is a focus on the specific and single organization or product. In contrast to life-cycle theory, changes are here seen as a result of an internally driven change process rather than a result of an unavoidable pressure. Teleology originates from the Greek word *telos*, meaning an objective or goal. Changes are thus a result of intended and premeditated plans and actions by change agents and other individuals with the ambition to change. This involves looking at change through purposeful and goal-driven strategic activities (which are commonly driven by management). Organizational change is initiated deliberately to achieve improvements or develop the organization, based on some broad visions or ideas of a future state. Changes are thus the outcome of formulated goals and intentions – a constructive mode of change – rather than the consequence of external, prescribed or regulated influences. In the teleological approach it is common to talk about strategic changes that are planned and actively driven by management in a repetitive sequence of goal setting, formulation of plans, implementation and evaluation. Thereafter goals are remodified and the process is repeated.

Teleological theory assumes that changes can be managed as a rationally-driven process. Shared interests and consensus about the goals and the appropriate means for accomplishing those goals among those involved in the process are assumed (or are seen as being possible to accomplish). Power and politics are seen as unnecessary disturbances of an otherwise rational and neutral process. Interpretations and understandings of the process that deviate from or interrupt the goal are regarded as resistance, which needs to be managed with the help of different strategies, such as improved communication, the provision of information and negotiations with employees (see more about resistance in Chapter 9). From a managerial point of view, this often means making an effort to stay focused on the goal of the change process and assuring that results in line with the original plans and ambitions are accomplished.

The teleological perspective dominates in most of the popular and academic management literature on organizational change, and consequently also receives a lot of coverage in this book. We discuss this approach under the tool-based perspective in Chapters 4 and 5 in particular. Planned change is a very common way of looking at change that is initiated by management for the purpose of correcting some internal or external problem.

Dialectical theory of change

The fourth and final approach is the dialectical theory of change. In contrast to the teleological approach to change, the dialectical theory has its origin in conflicts and antagonism, which is often viewed as being an unavoidable, and sometimes advantageous, dynamic of organizational change. The assumption is that conflicts between different views of how the organization should be governed and developed are natural and expected. Individuals and groups of individuals typically hold and express contrasting views of how to run and develop an organization in terms of strategies, structures, cultures, recruitment, policies, etc. The dialectical view is based on a classic reasoning about how an idea, a *thesis*, meets with and confronts a radically different idea, *antithesis*, and thereby creates a conflict. The antithesis struggles to replace the thesis, and if that occurs, the conflict ends. The conflict can also end if a completely new idea, a *synthesis*, which contains elements of both the thesis and antithesis, emerges in the process and establishes itself as a result of the confrontation.

These kinds of conflicts and struggles typically occur in organizations when a dominant business idea – embodied in strategies and organizational culture – is replaced by an alternative view of how to run and develop the organization. A classic case is when a production-oriented logic of an organization is replaced with a more market- or customer-orientated logic. But rather than totally replacing the former orientation, it is often more common that a synthesis emerges that contains elements of both orientations, even if a particular view usually emerges as the more dominant one. Organizations are often targeted by various ideas, such as control, development, change and leadership. These ideas compete for attention among managers and other opinion leaders within organizations. Sometimes these ideas may help to reframe organizations in a new light by challenging old habits and entrenched ways of thinking and enhance learning. Sometimes these ideas may not be very helpful at all. For example, many of the theories of leadership that focus on change management – such as transformational and charismatic leadership – are less helpful in actual managerial work and primarily function as managerial identity support (by enhancing a positive and influential view of oneself) (Sveningsson & Alvesson, 2016).

According to the dialectical view, therefore, it is conflicts and challenges that drive change. This is not primarily about conflicts between people, even though that also can be a productive part of organizational life (as in sports), but more about conflicts between ideas (Beech & McIntosh, 2012). If conflicts are seen as primarily about ideas rather than individuals, it is normally less difficult for employees to back the winning ideas and change suggestions.

The dialectical approach is based on a pluralistic view of the world in general, which means assuming that (groups of) people have different and contrasting views and values and typically strive in different directions in order to realize these. According to this, the world consists of colliding events and forces that result in change or stability (see for example, Bartunek, 1984; Bartunek & Reid, 1992). Thus, conflicts are seen as unavoidable, rather than as a result of a badly managed change process, as these emerge when different ideas and interests are confronted.

The dialectical view has been criticized for its one-sided emphasis on conflicts and confrontations. As a result, an alternative view has emerged, labelled 'trialectic', which stresses that change involves not only pressure, force and opposition, but also attraction, enticement, appeal and temptation, something clearly noted, for example, in the lure of all management fads and fashions (Ford & Ford, 1994).

The theories outlined above provide us with rich language that enables a broad and nuanced understanding of the various dynamics of change and provide insights into how organizational change can be managed. Depending on how we understand a specific change situation, certain challenges and alternative ways of managing organizational challenges will surface. This theoretical pluralism is arguably advantageous considering the increasingly complex and ambiguous challenges facing contemporary organizations.

EXERCISE 3.4

Consider the case below and discuss the changes in light of the four approaches to change. In particular, consider:

- How can developments in the print industry be understood from the evolutionary and life-cycle approaches to change?

CASE

The global decline of the print newspaper industry

An industry that has encountered severe difficulties – some would argue impossible challenges – for the last two decades or so is the traditional newspaper industry. For many years the environment has demanded significant rationalizations and an increased emphasis on efficiency measures if the industry is to survive. For example, technological developments – initially television (in the 1950s), but now of course especially the internet – have undermined the traditional markets of newspapers (markets for newspapers and advertisements) in ways that have led to a radical consolidation of the industry and also put many large newspaper corporations into difficulties.

With the advent of the internet, which is always available via mobile phones, iPads, computers, etc., people can instantly upload any news content, often for free. This has seriously undermined circulation figures and the number of subscribers of print media. The major revenue from advertising, especially for the morning newspapers, has been diminished due to digital ads. There are thousands of jobs sites, such as Monster, LinkedIn, Google for jobs, etc., that serve people on a global basis. Local classified ads, which are especially important for local newspapers, have been replaced by digital forums, often serving local markets. This development is expected to continue.

In the wake of these technological developments, there has been a significant consolidation in the newspaper industry, even if this has not always strengthened the financial positions of the surviving companies. For example, studies of the US market suggest that:

- Readers of digital news like to get their content for free. Only 11% of US readers paid for online news in 2014, according to a University of Oxford survey. The remaining readers said they'd never pay, or pay only a small amount – $8 a year on average.
- Each month, 8 in 10 Americans read newspapers' digital media.
- Millennials are 39% more likely to read newspapers on a mobile device than other age groups.
- Half of those who consume content in a digital form during a month do so on a mobile device, i.e. not using a desktop or laptop computer.
- A majority of US adults (62%) get their news on social media and 18% do so often.

We can note how various combined forces have created a very unfavourable situation for print media. In particular, there has been a steady decline in circulation and advertising revenues, which has been the lifeblood of print media. No wonder, then, that the circulation figures for all newspapers fell 24% between 2005 and 2015, and that newspaper advertising revenue fell by 60% during the same period.

Dealing with these developments within the confines of print media is highly challenging, and measures have not reversed the trend, with falling profitability as a result. Measures include cutting down publishing frequency or turning to a mainly digital-only publication with print editions once or twice a week. Others have turned to paywalls, charging readers for access to content, but this is an uncertain route, according to many studies. Only a select few, such as those that provide premium and exclusive content, have been able to sustain this model. Other measures include facilitating for advertisers to communicate to more focused customer segments by using videos but this has still not changed the prevailing economic dynamic very much. Besides such measures, there are also the traditional cost-cutting measures, targeting both back-office staff as well as journalists and editors. For example, in the US, employment within news companies has dropped by 23%.

Observers note, however, that all these managerial actions have not reversed the industry trend in general, only slowed the rate of decline: 'Overall, newspaper publishing operating income has not improved despite the implementing of paywalls and cost-cutting initiatives...' The news audience still exists, but it favours digital news media in a shorter news format. Digital media with ad-supported free content seem to be what most audiences would increasingly prefer in the future.

Sources: KPMG (2008); Mitchell et al. (2013); Pew Research Center (2018)

Taking an *evolutionary* perspective of the newspaper industry provides insights to the difficulties of remaining competitive within a declining industry. From this perspective, the print newspaper population is undergoing a natural process in the survival of the fittest. In this case, one would expect the most economically efficient companies to be the fittest, those that are large enough to still attract subscribers and that can afford to experiment with paywalls, for example. This evolution in the newspaper industry accelerated in the 1970s and has been in process ever since, increasingly so over the last couple of decades. The consolidation in terms of reducing the number of print newspapers towards the more economically profitable, and often larger and stronger, brands is common in most countries in the Western world. This suggests that only a few print newspapers will survive. However, looked at from a *life-cycle* perspective, the whole industry has reached a downturn, where there is no escape – death is inevitable. Trying to maintain the print newspaper from a life-cycle perspective is thus futile. It is just a way of providing artificial life support to something that faces unavoidable decline. From a *teleological* perspective, we can note how individual newspapers try to manage the decline by employing different measures, which also suggests that they look more optimistically at the situation. However, as the numbers above also suggest, the print newspaper business may soon be only a romantic memory. From a *dialectical* perspective, we can ponder upon whether alternative voices (from the younger generation or others) promoting digital solutions within newspaper organizations have been heeded, and whether these have been allowed to flourish, confronting the more traditional views of what the newspaper business is all about. The dialectical perspective makes us aware of the fact that opposition and conflict drive change.

REVIEW QUESTIONS 3.2

Recall	List the key characteristics of the following approaches to organizational change: evolutionary, life-cycle, teleological and dialectical. Emphasize specifically what differentiates them from each other.
Explain	In what ways can a dialectic understanding of change processes facilitate change management?
Explain	Both the evolutionary and life-cycle approaches relate to a prescribed and rather deterministic mode of change. Discuss in what ways these approaches can aid managers and other organizational members to make wise decisions about the future of the organization.
Reflect	All perspectives have blind spots. Reflect upon what aspects are underdeveloped in each of the four approaches – the evolutionary, life-cycle, teleological and dialectical theory of change.
Reflect	Discuss how the evolutionary and teleological perspectives on change can complement each other in providing a more comprehensible understanding of organizational change.

THE COMPLEXITY OF DRIVING FORCES: INTERPRETATIONS, IMITATIONS AND IDENTITY WORK

It is common for driving forces to be seen as objective and unambiguous, in particular, but not only, when it comes to the more prescriptive (regulating) views on organizational change. A process perspective on change, however, emphasizes how change actors and other individuals interpret and understand events in the environment and how they draw upon and use those interpretations in order to push for change (Pettigrew, 1985).

Interpretations and impression management

From a process perspective, it is not assumed that people behave in a predetermined way contingent upon objective stimuli such as triggers of change. Rather, people are viewed as acting based on how they interpret and understand events and occurrences. Accordingly, in these terms, people are viewed as interpretative and meaning-creating subjects – rather than pre-programmed objects – where elements such as understanding, intentions and feelings are central. External driving forces in the environment are understood and regarded differently by different people, something that also creates room for variation between organizations in terms of development and renewal. For example, how a particular manager interprets the environment, is contingent upon personal interests, education, organizational culture, history and how other organizations act in relation to events. Driving forces are thus not to be seen as determining how people act in organizations – there is always a certain room for individually and idiosyncratic manoeuvring and acting (Smircich & Morgan, 1982; Tsoukas, 2005).

How people interpret the need for change is therefore contingent on many circumstances. Broader cultural trends, such as current social atmosphere and popular notions about what is right and wrong on the basis of popular knowledge, are important to note here. Much of this explains why change actors and managers introduce and drive change programmes and what may lead to these attempts being accepted or rejected by those at the receiving end.

Change actors that drive a specific change often construct a change agenda, for example, such as 'going global', based on the idea that the expression 'going global' is something superior and good and thus worth striving for. Such popular expressions – sometimes labelled as discourses – are drawn upon by change actors as a way of formulating and framing a change agenda that supposedly sounds good in the ears of others and that may enhance the status of those formulating it and perhaps also the image of the organization. To the extent that the expression 'going global' is also used by other organizations, it may gain a broader impact, which potentially can accelerate its acceptance and proliferation among organizations and society at large. Being a rather general expression, one can also expect a variety of local interpretations regarding what it actually means to 'go global' in a specific organization.

Even though it is often emphasized in the business literature that originality and creativity are wise in order to facilitate innovation and renewal, it is also common, as suggested above, that organizations follow trends and implement changes in ways that they interpret that other organizations do (Sahlin-Andersson, 1996; Sevón, 1996). This may involve an imitation of the latest management fashion or the organizational models that everyone is talking about. This could be about 'agile leadership', 'core competencies', 'sustained competitive advantage' or broader expressions such 'the employees are our greatest asset' or some other good-sounding statement. Patterns of imitation are rather common and widespread in most industries, and organizations within a certain industry tend to change in similar ways and often in parallel (Czarniawska & Joerges, 1996). Management ideas might also spread across industries. For instance, several studies have described and discussed the transfer of business practices such as TQM (total quality management), re-engineering (Bigelow & Arndt, 2000) and mergers (Comtois et al., 2004) into the healthcare sector. In many cases, ideas have been imitated without consideration of local appropriateness, with the result that organizations end up with practices that are unsuitable for them, sometimes with devastating outcomes.

The ambition to benchmark what other organizations are presumed to be doing facilitates a fast proliferation of popular change models – often encouraged by academics and consultants – and sometimes without any close examination or critical review of their substance and potential impact. The problem is that these fashions are not always – or are rather seldom – grounded in more serious investigations or deeper analysis of organizational processes in real-life organizations (Collins, 1998).

There are countless recipes for change and success, but organizational complexities are difficult to capture with all too simple solutions or models that often fail to recognize the complications of the real world. It is also often the case that many organizational change efforts result in increased frustration, irritation and cynicism among those targeted by them, rather than achieving relevant and meaningful change. A former and legendary Swedish bank manager and later chairman, Jan Wallander (2002, p. 115), once wrote that:

> Examples of fashion trends within the corporate world are many. A constant driving force is the fear of ending up at the residual map. I used to say that corporate managers [...] are like a sheep herd standing and eating on a meadow. And then one sheep somehow hears that it is greener on the other side of the hill and rushes over, whereupon all the other sheep rush after.

An area that has traditionally been linked to possibilities to express originality and creativity in problem solving is strategy. Many classical writings on strategy, such as Ansoff (1965) and Andrews (1971), emphasize that strategy involves the ability to create a unique and original development, something that later on was also emphasized by many process-oriented writers, such as Mintzberg and McHugh (1985). But strategy concepts, similar to many other ideas, can also be drawn upon for the purposes of impression management, i.e. efforts to depict an organization and its development in a brighter and more rational light. Drawing on the concept of strategy may allow an organization to exhibit a façade of rationality that makes them more legitimate in the eyes of important constituencies such as finance markets, customers, the state and others that emphasize the significance of profit maximization and cost efficiency.

This is not to say that the introduction of concepts such as strategy may give rise to real and substantial change. Changes that some may see as important may be seen as less favourable and productive for an organization by others who take a more critical perspective. Some argue that a classic knowledge of strategy, which still often dominates in management and leadership education, shapes the identities of managers in an analytically distanced and financially limited manner, making them less inclined to understand the deeper value of how to create a meaningful organization in the service of a multitude of constituencies (Mintzberg, 2005).

CASE

Strategy as a driving force for diversification and organizational change

An illustration of how organizations view each other and how certain ideas gain broad impact in an industry can be seen from the development of the Swedish newspaper industry in the 1970s and 1980s. Before the 1970s, Swedish newspaper organizations were mainly occupied with publishing one or two newspapers and were understood as pursuing single-business strategies. Over a relatively short time in the 1970s the single-business orientation of the newspapers changed radically as many newspapers transformed into what are commonly understood as multi-business organizations. These organizations started to acquire businesses besides newspaper(s) and developed their existing businesses in ways that contributed to the emergence of a multi-business model and larger groups of organizations. This development was highly unexpected as Swedish newspaper organizations had exclusively been occupied with just print newspapers, basically to avoid risk and to maintain what at the time was called editorial integrity. The editorial integrity was based on the idea of being economically independent, something that was historically seen as impossible if they were to be part of a larger business group consisting of a variety of different businesses.

In the 1970s, however, editorial integrity was challenged by the emergence and growing popularity of the idea of strategy. The reproduction of strategy knowledge challenged the single-business model as many newspaper companies embarked on a diversification trend by acquiring businesses outside the core newspaper business. Even if the development was highly controversial and attracted strong resistance and conflicts in the newspaper organizations, it also contributed to radical development and company growth. The largest Swedish newspaper, *Dagens Nyheter* (today in the so-called Bonnier group), was leading the development, but other newspaper organizations soon followed and tried to imitate their competitors.

The development had far-reaching organizational consequences as it also facilitated structural divisionalization into business units and increased the commercialization of the different business units. Subsequently, the organizations also installed new forms of profitability control and an increased focus on the economic status of the organizations. The proliferation of the strategy knowledge within the newspaper business gave rise to strategic and organizational changes in many newspaper companies as they imitated each other. However, it is also important to emphasize that the newspaper organizations did not just imitate a given version of strategy knowledge, but rather interpreted a general view of strategy to suit their own local and specific organizational situation. Based on an individual understanding of the organizational context, the impact of strategy varied between the newspaper organizations.

In sum, the strategy knowledge approach resulted in an increased attention to the economic environment and an expanded view of the organization – its economic and strategic status – as well as diversification as a strategic option. It was reproduced in many newspapers although it impacted them somewhat differently, depending on company traditions and history as well as different economic and structural organizational situations. Varied interpretations of the significance of the strategy knowledge among leading managers in the companies also resulted in different organizational impacts. Recognizing the

(Continued)

differences in responses in the organizations, it can be argued that external or internal driving forces do not just reproduce a given and predetermined behaviour. It is necessary to include people's understanding in the change equation as well as the historical context and the specific conditions of the organization.

Source: Sveningsson (1999)

Based on this case, we can note how the attractiveness and popularity of a specific field of knowledge can trigger a substantial change in a specific direction, and subsequently change the character of a whole industry. This is, of course, not always the case. In contrast to this development, we can note how ideas of modern leadership – such as strategic and visionary leadership – seem to be highly significant for how managers look upon themselves but also how that seems to have only marginal relevance for what managers actually do in modern organizations. In a large and international pharmaceutical company, most managers claimed to exercise strategic leadership in spite of being distanced from the market, having relatively limited business responsibility and little input in product development (Alvesson & Sveningsson, 2003). But leadership as well as strategy are very attractive concepts for managers to relate to when describing themselves (their managerial identity), even when they may not exercise very much of it in practice (Sveningsson & Alvesson, 2016).

EXERCISE 3.5

Read the case below and answer the following questions.

- These cases primarily concern imitations of business ideas, products and features. What other types of imitation tend to occur among organizations within the same industry?
- Can you identify any examples of imitation in other industries?
- What is the basis for imitations like these? Discuss.

CASE

Business imitations...?!

Instagram introduced stories, which was the same feature that *Snapchat* had introduced before them. It was considered highly successful for Instagram and added 250 million users in the year it was launched, 2016. It also dwarfed Snapchat in terms of revenues.

In contrast to what many people would think, the large crowdfunding company *Kickstarter*, which started business in 2009, is not the inventor of online crowdfunding sites. The rival *Indiegogo* began online crowdfunding a year before, in 2008. Both companies have been highly successful in their businesses.

Since the 1990s, the gaming company *Sega* has been trying to dethrone *Nintendo* as the largest gaming company in the US. Back in the 1990s, Nintendo, with Super Mario, had a market share of 90% of the video game industry. Sega created Sonic the Hedgehog and at one point mobilized around 55% of the market. In 2017, Nintendo introduced Nintendo Switch, the fastest-selling console in US history, and ended 2018 with $9.6 billion in revenue. It is still the market leader.

The Chinese technology company *Xiaomi* is often accused of copying *Apple* when it comes to smartphones. In 2014, the chief design officer at Apple at the time, Jony Ive, even talked of 'theft' in describing what Xiaomi was good at. Xiaomi, on the other hand, says there are differences, despite the smartphones looking strikingly similar.

In 2015, *Amazon* Inc. released a personal home assistant called Echo. It is a multifunctional and interactive system providing updates on a number of issues, including the weather. A year later *Google* released a similar home assistant system that includes a Google response to whether it is raining outside. A year later, at the end 2017, *Apple* released a similar system (although reportedly with fewer functions) called Homepod in order to target the industry for home assistants.

Sources: Nyberg (2018); Perez (2018); Zaleski (2017)

Organizational change as following popular trends

We have previously stated that what triggers and motivates a specific change orientation is commonly associated with change actors' ability to mobilize driving forces in a way that makes the change appear rational for those targeted by the change efforts. As highlighted by the process perspective, driving forces do not speak for themselves. It is rather a case of people – often managers – interpreting these and their significance for the need to embark on organizational changes. Sometimes managerial interpretations of external or internal triggers face contrasting and opposing interpretations of subordinates, suggesting that there may be less motivation for change. People might not agree with or understand the motives behind managerial change initiatives. And sometimes even well-motivated and seemingly rational efforts at organizational change may occasionally also be seen as resting on rather shaky ground, as is shown below in the case on 'Change as a result of trends'.

Several studies of contemporary organizations point at organizational changes that increase standardization and control, leading to more regimented bureaucracies (Kärreman et al., 2002). This represents a trend with the aim of enhancing top management control by reinforced centralization and the introduction of more elaborated and refined management control systems, such as scorecards and more explicit accountability measures. In some cases, greater centralization has resulted in a transformation of many formerly legally independent subsidiaries in large organizations to mere sites of production, with local site managers, rather than, as previously, more independent CEOs. Increased control and the accompanying bureaucratization have also contributed to a standardization of production and development processes, with augmented demands on formal documentation (Alvesson & Thompson, 2005).

CASE

Change as a result of trends

Senior management in a global pharmaceutical organization initiated a radical organizational change project with the ambition of strengthening the management of the research and development processes by increasing structural control and emphasizing a market focus. The change amounted to an increased formalization and standardization of working roles and ways of working, while the strengthened business focus aimed at changing the organizational culture. In general, the changes aimed at bolstering the role of managers and managerial influence over R&D.

By enforcing more explicit structural control and market orientation, management hoped to be able to remedy several years of weak product development and what they regarded as an indolent organizational culture. The poor product development track record and relaxed organizational culture were seen as a result of weak control and a lack of understanding of the role of a strong market-oriented culture. By mobilizing both internal and external triggers – internal control systems, the economy, market development and competition – managers wanted to rationalize and make the change legitimate in the eyes of employees.

However, in interviews with the managers involved, a much more nuanced picture about what motivated the organizational change emerged. In contrast to ideas of weak control and an unproductive (indolent) organizational culture, a variety of alternative, and partly contradictory, explanations were advanced as reasons behind the low productivity in product development (few new drugs had been developed over a lengthy period of time). Some suggested that the weak productivity in product development was a result of recruiting the wrong kind of managers, in this case people who did not understand how to manage and lead R&D operations, because managers were not acquainted with the peculiarities of the pharmaceutical industry. Others suggested that the company had too many junior employees with limited research experience, while still others said that, in sharp contrast, they had too many senior employees who lacked motivation – being professionally saturated and looking forward to retirement – to renew and revitalize the company. Some managers said that the absence of product development was a strategically intentional decision – the company wanted to prolong the patents of existing products rather than develop new ones – rather than an organizational failure.

Managers also suggested that the company was very divided in terms of a cultural fragmentation, while others suggested that the overall organizational focus on comfort or well-being took precedence over a work ethic – with staff taking many coffee breaks and a lot of employees spending a substantial amount of time in the company fitness centre. A few talked about how the organization had a more academic orientation than was inappropriate for a business organization and some said they just lacked any strategic or structural control. All in all, there existed a variety of different explanations for the absence of product development. However, in spite of this rather ambiguous picture, management interpreted things very simple; the problem was weak control and a lack of business culture, both of which needed to be remedied.

The organizational change focused on the formalization of working roles, routines and reporting relationships, and promoted efforts at creating transparency, centralizing decision-making and implementing new management control systems.

Looking at the more multifaceted and ambiguous picture of the company history, one could argue that the suggested change – formalization and centralization – appears less well grounded, because it was not based on a more thorough analysis of internal organizational structures and external market conditions. What really did trigger the radical change in this organization? It does not seem too far-fetched to suggest that this change was motivated by current trends and fashionable management ideas.

Source: Alvesson & Sveningsson (2011a)

The development described above is often regarded as highly problematic in many organizations, especially among those framed as knowledge-intensive. Knowledge-intensive organizations normally rely on the professional commitment and intellectual competencies and skills of the employees. These people have a professional background and are often seen as the core competence of the organization, with a decisive significance for strategic development, motivation and culture. Leadership in knowledge-intensive organizations is often exercised with the aim of facilitating autonomy, learning, flexibility and knowledge-sharing. Enhancing the control of managers and explicitly emphasizing the significance of bureaucracy – as was the case within the R&D function in the pharmaceutical organization above – may be an exaggeration of the role of managers and structural control in such operations. Such managerial control would be more appropriate in a manufacturing company (such as one producing toothpaste, soft drinks or jeans) or within the production function – manufacturing standardized pills – of a pharmaceutical company. By following management trends, organizations may thus end up in a situation where they embark on changes that are not appropriate when examined with a more nuanced and thorough understanding of the specific and local context. But it is also important to emphasize that organizations cannot ignore the relevance of occasionally following ideas and trends that also make them more legitimate in the eyes of important stakeholders, such as markets, suppliers, financial institutions, employees, unions and governmental authorities. Even so, it would seem that in the case of the pharmaceutical company, the solution (i.e. strengthening the management orientation) preceded the problem (i.e. a weak market orientation). Indeed, the problem seems almost to be constructed to fit a particularly favoured and popular trend within management thinking, something which occurs if managers conform too easily to management fashions in order not to appear old-fashioned or outdated.

In addition, we can also note that many contemporary ideas about learning, flexibility and leadership, which aim to support development in organizations, are often difficult to implement and therefore remain at the level of ideas. Many organizations make strong claims about their organizational identity in terms of learning and flexibility, but remain bureaucratic as formal control, regulations, structure and systems take precedence over ideas that may be difficult to practise in a meaningful way (McSweeney, 2006; Tengblad, 2003). Also, for the purpose of increasing tempo and efficiency, many organizations also work with quite strict rules for resource allocation such as time and elaborate reports, etc. (Kärreman et al., 2002).

EXERCISE 3.6

Identify a recent and highly debated (in mass media, internet and other secondary sources) change process in a contemporary organization. Examine and discuss critically how different people in the change process – those within the organizations as well as observers outside such as journalists or others – explained what actually triggered the change process. What triggers are used by different actors and what conclusions can be drawn by the analysis?

REVIEW QUESTIONS 3.3

Recall	What is the key difference between how a tool-based and a process perspective consider (and in turn approach) triggers for change?
Explain	Explain why it is important to appreciate that the triggers of change are dependent on who is talking about them and their presumed relevance.
Explain	Explain in what way(s) managers' identities can play a role in decisions made about organizational change.
Reflect	Why is it important to understand that organizations have a tendency to imitate each other in terms of organizational change processes?

SUMMARY

There are many reasons why organizational changes occur. In this chapter we have provided a broad view of factors that trigger and provide energy to organizational change processes. A starting point in this chapter was that a productive way to try to understand why changes occur is to examine its triggers or driving forces. We find examples of external triggers in the environment of organizations; they often involve the economy, politics, demography, fashions, trends and technological development. Internal triggers include growth, strategies and political ambitions. These external and internal triggers can be intertwined in complex ways and it is not always easy to separate them.

By introducing a broader framework, distinguishing between evolutionary, life-cycle, teleological and dialectical change theories, we have shown a productive variety of approaches as to why organizations change: some orientations claim that it is possible to detect explicit intentions behind organizational changes, others claim that it is rather a matter of broader industry logics or life cycles that govern the development. While some state that it is possible to study and understand change based on a single organization, others mean that we need to consider broader populations of organizations in order to understand the dynamics of change.

In addition, we suggested that there are good reasons to be attentive to the fact that change often occurs as a result of change actors and managers who want to express decisiveness – that they are in charge – and demonstrate their legitimacy to important stakeholders. Organizational change can also be initiated due to managerial identity work in the sense that managers want to show themselves and others that they are leaders (transforming work practices) rather than just managers (maintaining the status quo), in order to avoid being regarded as old-fashioned or plain boring.

We ended the chapter by discussing management fashions as a background for radical change and illustrated this theme with cases. In the first case, we showed how the strategies of Swedish newspaper organizations developed during the 1970s and 1980s as a result of the establishment of and reproduction of forms of strategy knowledge. In the second case, we showed how a seemingly well-motivated change initiative in a pharmaceutical organization could be seen as an anxious adoption of a popular management ideal, rather than a genuine consequence of internal and external conditions.

 # KEY PRACTICAL INSIGHTS

What we can say about organizational change following this chapter:

- Examining external and internal triggers of change can be a fruitful way to understand organizational change and register new opportunities and threats. Particularly, the identification of change triggers might facilitate critical reflection on the pressure for change as well as its necessity.

- Change triggers are commonly quite complex and stand in interaction with each other, which needs to be taken into account when analyzing them.

- Change processes can be understood as evolutionary, dialectical, teleological or in life-cycle terms. These approaches differ in their unit of analysis (a single organization or a broader industry) and their origins (more voluntarist or more deterministic), and taken together they facilitate a broad and varied understanding of change processes and a person's role in it.

- Change triggers don't speak for themselves but are interpreted differently by different people depending on how they view themselves (their identities), their interest for change, company position, rank, etc. It is therefore advisable to go beyond viewing external and internal triggers as clear-cut, objective and neutral facts, and rather to consider them as social constructions with potential powerful effects.

- Imitation patterns, such as anxious fashion-following, are widespread among organizations. Popular fashions often include simple managerial or organizational recipes – such as agile organizations, Total Quality Management (TQM), Balanced Score Card (BSC) – for dealing with various problems. Therefore, when working with organizational change, critical reflection is crucial to avoid embarking upon change programmes that do not suit the organization.

 # FURTHER READING

Go online to access free and downloadable SAGE Journal articles related to this chapter at **https://study.sagepub.com/sveningsson**

Sahlin, K., & Wedlin, L. (2008). Circulating ideas: Imitation, translation and editing. In R. Greenwood, C. Oliver, R. Suddaby, & K. Sahlin (eds.), *The Sage handbook of organizational institutionalism*. London: Sage, pp. 218–242.

Sevón, G. (1996). Organizational imitation in identity transformation. In B. Czarniawska & G. Sevón (eds.), *Translating organizational change*. Berlin: de Gruyter.

Tsoukas, H., & Chia, R. (2002). On organizational becoming: Rethinking organizational change. *Organizational Science*, 13(5), 567–682.

Van de Ven, A. H., & Poole, M. P. (1995). Explaining development and change in organizations. *Academy of Management Review*, 20(3), 510–540.

Watson, T. (1994). Management 'flavours of the month': Their role in managers' lives. *The International Journal of Human Resource Management*, 5(4), 893–909.

 VIDEO

Go online to view video clips related to the key themes discussed in this chapter at

https://study.sagepub.com/sveningsson

THE TOOL-BASED PERSPECTIVE: PLANNED CHANGE AND ORGANIZATIONAL DEVELOPMENT

LEARNING OBJECTIVES

When you have completed your study of this chapter, you should be able to:

- Understand the historical context of the tool-based perspective and describe the fundamental ideas of Scientific Management and Human Relations.

- Explain Lewin's Field Theory, the 3-Step model of change as well as the significance of group norms for understanding change.

- Discuss the central concepts, models and values of contemporary Organizational Development.

- Discuss OD in relation to the development of organizational consultancy.

- Examine and evaluate diagnostic and dialogic OD in terms of similarities and differences.

- Discuss and evaluate the relevance and significance of OD from a critical perspective.

Viewing organizational change as a result of various analytically conceived formulations – such as planned activities or the design of an organizationally well-aligned architecture of various subsystems (structure, culture, HR, systems, leadership, management, etc.) – is highly common as well as popular. Many imagine that organizations exist in a relatively stable state of normality that now and again needs to be changed based on new internal conditions and/or developments in the external environment. Planning changes are therefore seen as periodical activities that occur in episodes between the stable periods of the normal state of affairs. This type of change work implies following certain procedures and models with a rationalistic mindset. Among some of the contemporary authors following the idea of conceiving change analytically, there are those that downplay the idea of long-term planning in favour of designing various subsystems, for example culture, HRM, structure, systems and leadership, in a way that enables change. According to this technical approach, change is seen as something that is possible to managerially control and implement – more or less – in line with plans and designs. This chapter is devoted to this approach – here labelled the tool-based perspective – to change.

Common ground for different models within the tool-based perspective is a belief in the possibility to control organizational change, even though it is often portrayed as being complex and messy. Consequently, several models have been developed with the focus on the change of social systems, where the people in the organization are taken into account. In this chapter we discuss the dominant models within the area and provide insights into and discuss their practical applicability.

The chapter starts with a historical background which includes a review of Scientific Management and its theoretical counterpart, Human Relations. Since many of the ideas developed in those historical streams of thought are still present in many contemporary ideas on organizational change (although not necessarily always in ways that are salient or obvious), the lessons learned remain of great relevance and significance. Next, we discuss Kurt Lewin's reasoning and models for change and development; these are ideas that have made a huge impact on the field. Based on this foundation, we look at alternative schools and views on organizational change that can be placed under the relatively broad heading of Organization Development (OD). We also discuss the critique that has been placed on concepts and perspectives within OD.

THE TOOL-BASED PERSPECTIVE – BACKGROUND

When discussing approaches to change in organizations (for example, changes in organizational design, working methods or forms of control), it is common to relate to two important historical streams of ideas: Scientific Management and Human Relations. Both of these have had a major impact on how organizations in general and change in particular are understood. In addition, with the establishing of these schools of thought, more systematic studies on change dynamics, efficiency, effectiveness and control in organizations were initiated.

SCIENTIFIC MANAGEMENT – THE FUNDAMENTAL IDEA

Although Scientific Management and other classical management theories were established over 100 years ago, their ideas and principles are still applied in many modern organizations and expressed in more contemporary management concepts (Boje & Winsor, 1993; Ritzer, 2018; Willmott, 1994). Knowledge of the effects of this managerial orientation and its practices are therefore still highly relevant.

Scientific Management (or Taylorism) introduced ideas and suggestions on how to solve many of the typical problems – control, motivation and efficiency – that followed from the growth of the classical production factory. The background was that managers in particular experienced huge difficulties to motivate and control employees, which, for example, expressed itself in rising labour costs (Thompson & McHugh, 2009). A particular problem was that many workers maintained traditional crafts-oriented ways of working. These methods were seen as inefficient and also made it difficult for the managers to control the execution of the work done. It was in this context that Frederick W. Taylor developed the ideas which later became known as Scientific Management. A key idea was to split the whole work processes into finite and narrowly detailed, standardized, uncomplicated and repetitive tasks. These tasks were distributed among the workers – the muscle power – under the control of managers. This horizontal division of work and standardization of work processes enabled increased managerial control, efficiency and predictability of performances and work results. Furthermore, methodical work studies were performed in order to identify and eliminate superfluous movements. Based on these observations and measurements, the work process was analyzed and improved in a scientific way by the managers. As a result, the traditional craftsmanship was split up not only horizontally but also vertically, in the sense that the design and planning of the work (performed by managers) was separated from the doing of the work (performed by the workers). Through an increased level of managerial influence and control over the work processes, efficiency was to be improved.

The four underlying principles of Scientific Management (Taylor, 1911):

1. The development of a true science.
2. The scientific selection of the workman.
3. His scientific education and development of the workman.
4. Intimate friendly cooperation between the management and the men.

Taylor's ideas were framed as a scientific approach to work organization and were assumed to reduce conflicts between managers and the workforce as well as stimulate cooperation and harmonious relations (as long as workers were given appropriate monetary compensation).

Workers were seen primarily to be extrinsically motivated (i.e. interested in pay rises), rather than being interested in the work and its results as such. Based on the assumption that people would seek maximal reward for minimal input, it was essential to instruct in detail what each worker should do, and closely follow up those instructions – in other words, to apply a kind of strict behavioural control. In sum, Scientific Management implied a centralization of knowledge about work and work processes and, consequently, a stricter managerial control over deskilled workers with low bargain power.

Scientific Management is said to have had its clearest expression in the classic Ford Company car factories. As the production of the T-Ford, the world's first mass-produced car, began in 1908, a doubling of its assembly necessitated a doubling of the workforce. The application of the principles of Scientific Management together with the progressive assembly line enabled the multiplication of the production of cars with a reduced workforce – a revolutionary organizational change that had repercussions in industries across the world.

A Scientific Management approach to humans and organizations

Within Scientific Management and other classical management theories with a focus on efficiency, rules, formalities, the strict division of work, hierarchy and monetary motivation, organizations are seen as machines and humans are looked upon as cogs in the machinery (Morgan, 2006). This management logic is still present in modern society. Boje and Winsor (1993) write about the resurrection of Taylorism in Total Quality Management (TQM) and Willmott (1994) shows that Business Process Re-engineering (BPR) – in a manner similar to Taylorism – basically neglect and trivialize the human dimension in organizations and change management. Furthermore, Ritzer (2018) suggests that rationalizations, as suggested by Taylor, are far from a relic of the past by showing how even extended rationalized techniques are adopted in modern society. He labels this undertaking as a 'McDonaldization', which is characterized by the principles of efficiency, calculability, predictability and control of work. It has been suggested that McDonaldization is occurring in many sectors, including higher education and health services, creating so-called McJobs with respect to the nature of work, routine and repetitiveness (see Mini Case 4.1).

MINI CASE 4.1

McDonaldization of higher education?

The McDonaldization of higher education and the proposed rise of the McUniversity is occasionally discussed with reference to causal (cheap and flexible) labour, increased bureaucracy and regulations, the standardization of educational programmes, increased behavioural control and managerialism (Parker, 2012). However, a close and critical examination of these claims suggests a more nuanced and complex picture (Nadolny & Ryan, 2015). Based on interviews and survey material from causal academics and managers in an Australian university, Nadolny and Ryan (2015) argue that the McDonaldization label of work in higher education is misplaced and misleading as the nature of work of academics is diametrically opposed to the standardized input (homogeneous food inputs), work processes (repetitive work) and output (standardized hamburgers) at McDonalds. In contrast, their findings suggest that the personal relationship between teachers and students and the exercise of academic judgements cannot be controlled by or follow standardized manuals. In addition, the findings also suggest that the teachers can exercise control in relation to their academic judgement, suggesting a large degree of autonomy in a work that is overwhelmingly complex. Also, a very large portion (78%) of the casual academics expressed satisfaction with the nature of the work in itself. Using relational and creative processes in order to educate individuals – students – with different aspirations and abilities (input) to a heterogeneous group of graduates (output) can, accordingly, hardly be meaningfully regarded as McDonaldization (Nadolny & Ryan, 2015).

From a Scientific Management perspective, organizations are viewed as rational phenomena created with the purpose of executing well-formulated goals. They are supposed to build upon universally neutral and scientific principles of the division of labour and decision-making based on the idea that managers and workers are driven by economical rewards. Humans are here portrayed as a 'greedy robots', more or less without fantasies, dreams, feelings, group loyalty, friendship and other deeply held human dimensions (Rose, 1988). Critique towards this instrumental and, according to many, cynical view of humanity stresses that work without an inner drive contributes to low morale, demotivated employees and alienation. The vertical and horizontal division of work that has been driven too far creates subgroups and subcultures that risk generating conflict and clashes. The rigid application of rules and standards risks creating inflexible rule cultures that may counter and make organizational change highly difficult. A specific challenge is the exaggeratingly rational view of humans as the prolonged arms of the organizational machinery. It is a dark and cynical view of humankind that is expressed, and one of its foremost critics, Elton Mayo (1933), pointed to the fact that instead of contributing to efficiency, Scientific Management leads to the alienation of people and constitutes a basis for contempt of work and the organization.

Mayo argued that Scientific Management obstructs and counteracts personal development and that it constitutes a dehumanization of people that contributes to frustration and conflicts. In contrast, he thought that organizations should offer the workers more freedom and acknowledge individual and group concerns, thus facilitating greater commitment and enhancing motivation. In the 1930s these ideas were developed within the Human Relations movement, discussed below.

REVIEW QUESTIONS 4.1

Recall	What are the key ideas of Scientific Management?
Explain	Explain why the ideas of Scientific Management could (a) lead to extensive efficiency gains, (b) result in conflicts and unmotivated employees, and (c) hinder organizational change.

HUMAN RELATIONS – THE FUNDAMENTAL IDEA

The emergence of Human Relations should be understood against the backdrop of the generally stronger social awareness of the 1930s and more communal view on organizations and change in the western world. In the US, for example, this was expressed through President Roosevelt's 'The New Deal' from 1933.

Within academia, the background to this socially oriented view on organizations was a widespread discontent with work conditions, alienation and unrest among workers, which was especially evident during organizational changes. Resistance to change and sabotage of change processes were common, particularly when new technology that changed working conditions was introduced. The importance of paying attention to the social aspects of organizations became evident in the famous studies conducted by Elton Mayo and his colleagues at the Western Electric Company's plants in Chicago, the so-called Hawthorne experiments. One of the most famous experiments sought to ascertain the role that levels of lighting played in productivity. The ambition was to identify which level of light was needed to reach optimum productivity. An experimental group was created in which the light levels were altered in order to measure any changes in productivity. The assumption was that productivity would increase with increasing levels of lighting, but to the surprise of the researchers, productivity increased at both increasing *and* decreasing levels of lighting. Indeed, the production levels did not drop even when the workers could barely see what they were doing. Even in the control group, where the level of lighting was constant, productivity increased. Based on this, it was suggested that paying attention to and acknowledging workers as social beings may be more important for productivity levels than optimizing mere physical work conditions as, for example, levels of lighting. The recognition of the workers heightened their work morale and contributed to increased productivity, and this is known as the Hawthorne effect. Instead of being able to determine the optimum correlation between the physical working environment and productivity in line with the ideas of Scientific Management, the results of the experiments rather undermined the scientific principles and contributed to the establishment of its opposite movement.

A Human Relations approach to humans and organizations

In contrast to the focus on the individual worker (as was the case in Scientific Management), the Hawthorne studies contributed to an intensified interest in group dynamics and the group's influence on its members. Research showed, among other things, how group-specific norms and logics could affect how members of a group act and think. A key idea here is that group pressure often influences individuals to act in a certain way – it can involve work-pace, work-morale or other work-related qualities that affect productivity. The Hawthorne experiments also contributed to key insights about the importance of the more or less universal human needs of attention, recognition and belonging. The Tayloristic assumption that performance is primarily related to monetary rewards was questioned and countered by the notion that individuals also are driven by desires to feel included and to be confirmed as belonging to a group. An important conclusion related to organizational change was the significance of establishing cooperation with informal groups in order to implement change more effectively. According to Burnes (2004, p. 60), the Hawthorne experiments contributed to the 'Economic Man' being challenged by the 'Social Man' and to an increased understanding of the significance of social relations – human relations – for motivation, work satisfaction and change. Following this, the interest in leadership and communication related to managing organizational change was amplified.

Alongside Mayo, Roethlisberger and Dickson (1950) also demonstrated that the social dimension of organizations and change received insufficient attention when trying to understand how to implement change without creating distrust and resistance. These authors underlined that any problems with the workers' approach and receptiveness to change had less to do with specific technical demands on the work as such and more to do with the social and personal aspects. They emphasized the importance of active listening and partaking in workers' experiences and knowledge of change. Roethlisberger and Dickson also highlighted the importance of a democratic and participative leadership.

Theories of leadership and communication for motivation and engagement in change were also developed by Chester Barnard (1938), who stressed the importance of viewing organizations as social and cooperative systems. Barnard developed a *contribution and reward model*, in which the organization's relationships to a variety of stakeholders were in focus. Accordingly, organizations should reward their stakeholders (such as their employees), not only materialistically but also socially and personally in order to encourage them to contribute to the long-term survival of the organization. Furthermore, formulating a clear purpose for the organization to promote cooperation and a shared engagement was emphasized as one of the most important functions of management. Also, during this time, Maslow (1954) launched his renowned model of the hierarchy of needs, which recognized and emphasized the importance of social and personal needs as driving forces.

The Human Relations movement emerged as an attractive alternative to Scientific Management. In terms of organizational change, Human Relations contributed to highlighting the relevance and significance of relationships, leadership, informal communication, organizational purpose and values as well as participation. These ideas where then developed further by Kurt Lewin, among others, and through the establishment of the school of planned change, referred to as Organizational Development (OD).

EXERCISE 4.1

Think of an organization you are familiar with, where work (at least in some part of the organization) is designed according to some of the typical ideas of Scientific Management. It could be an organization with an extensive horizontal division of work (where work is split in small and repetitive tasks) and/or a vertical division of work (where doing is separated from thinking or where a major portion of the actual work – the core work process – is separated from the thinking of how it should be designed).

- Do you consider the work design appropriate? Why or why not? Who does it benefit?
- Taking the Human Relations approach into account, discuss the potential downsides of this work design.

REVIEW QUESTIONS 4.2

Recall	Briefly describe the Hawthorne experiment, which was designed according to the principles of Scientific Management but initiated the opposite movement.
Explain	Explain the key ideas of the Human Relations movement. Make sure that you relate your reasoning to the name of the movement.
Reflect	Why do you think that Human Relations had such a large impact at the time of its appearance and why is it still talked about as significant for understanding organizational change?

LEWIN AND PLANNED CHANGE

Kurt Lewin's ideas of organizational change have for decades dominated the theory and practice of change management (Burnes, 2004). As a humanitarian, with a key focus on how social conflicts – religious, ethnic, marital or business oriented – could be solved, he emphasized and developed knowledge about Field Theory, Group Dynamics, Action Research and the 3-Step model of change. In later years, his ideas have been treated as separate models, in particular Field Theory and the 3-Step model. However, Lewin's original idea was that these dimensions are related (Burnes, 2004).

Field Theory, Group Dynamics and Action Research

Similar to the Human Relations movement, Lewin (1951) suggested that organizational change – changing ways of thinking, behaviour, routines, etc. – is most likely to be achieved by focusing on and influencing group dynamics and group norms. This is in contrast to classical behaviourism, where the focus is placed on trying to change and control a single individual's behaviour in a social vacuum with external stimuli, typically materialistic rewards. Lewin argued that human thinking and actions are primarily influenced by the work group's norms and dynamic, which is why changes of external stimuli, such as individual rewards, are less productive in changing people's behaviour at work. Accordingly, thinking and action should be seen as a function of the work group environment. The latter is seen as being regulated by various driving forces that make up the group dynamics, and it is central to understanding how these driving forces – norms, values, processes – reinforces or weakens people's behaviours in processes of change. An important driving force in groups that often counteracts change ambitions is people's need for confirmation and recognition. People conform to group norms even though it may decrease the productivity

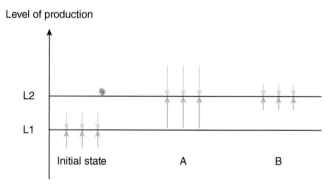

FIGURE 4.1   The force field

of their group or even threaten its survival. Numerous experiments have demonstrated that individuals tend to stick to the view of the group even if it is obviously wrong or against the individual's personal convictions.

According to Lewin (1947), an organization can be seen as a field where different forces – both driving and restraining forces – are at work, a so-called 'force field' (see Figure 4.1). Consider, for instance, work in a factory were the strain of hard work as well as group norms are forces that keep the production rate down while various incentive systems are forces that drive towards higher production levels. The production level can be understood as a 'quasi-stationary equilibrium' and in order to change it (from one level (L1) to another (L2) as illustrated in Figure 4.1), the key forces that uphold it need to be identified and altered. Change is made possible when the driving forces are stronger than those restraining change. This can be achieved either by strengthening the forces for change, such as introducing new incentives for working harder, which will make the production level rise to a new equilibrium (A). It can also be achieved by undermining the restraining forces, by changing group norms and established ways of working (B). Lewin primarily advocated the latter in order to make change legitimate and possibly avoid high levels of tension.

EXERCISE 4.2

Consider a change process that you have experienced. This can be personal and related to life circumstances in general (changing travel plans or weekend plans, or experiencing unexpected contingencies that force a reconsiderations of your ambitions) or related to more specific work experiences (moving between jobs, changing career prospects or work tasks, etc.).

- Try to identify the driving and restraining forces at that time.
- What do you think made the change possible? Was it primarily an increase in driving forces or a decrease in restraining forces?
- Could the change have been achieved using an alternative approach?
- Reflect upon your analysis: What conclusions can you draw from it? Consider both practical insights of the change processes and also reflect upon the relevance and usefulness of the model.

Central when working with change, according to Lewin, is therefore to identify the group dynamics – norms, roles, socialization processes, values and accompanying behaviours – and build the organizational change from there. This work encompasses a switch between reflection and action, which is often supported and facilitated by the participation of those affected by the change. Lewin worked with action research, which helped individuals to reflect and thereby better understand their situation which in turn could enable change (Burnes, 2004). Through a continuous movement between identifying problems and taking action, it becomes possible to continuously assess if there is any real change in the group dynamics, norms and behaviours.

The 3-step model of change

A common difficulty when implementing change is to make sure that new ideas are substantially embodied in thinking and acting. It is, for example, not unusual that new working practices return to their previous form when the formal change process is over. In order to make new ideas stick in thinking and acting, Lewin (1947) developed a model of change as a sequence in three steps. This is the most commonly cited of his ideas. It is often described in terms of an ice-cube metaphor.

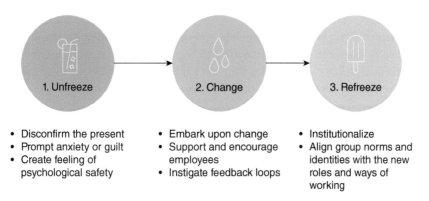

FIGURE 4.2   The ice-cube model

Schein (1987) has developed the model and describes the stages as follows (see Figure 4.2).

The first step, *unfreezing*, is the process of preparing for change through undermining the restraining forces. This entails making co-workers understand that change is necessary in order to survive in the longer term. Schein suggests three aspects of unfreezing as being particularly important:

a.   Clarifying the need for change, by convincingly identifying and demonstrating misalignments that may be less known to people in order to disconfirm the present and undermining current thinking. For example, this can be between how an organization views the quality of its products or services and how they are perceived by its clients, in particular if employees seem to take the relation to clients for granted. Clients may not be as happy as is commonly supposed, or the competitors may have products or services that are better than is generally assumed.

b. Prompting anxiety or guilt by clarifying the gap between results and ambitions. For example, identifying the gap between a desirable and the actual market position. Both (a) and (b) aim to open up to reflection and action, but they are not sufficient alone.

c. Creating a feeling of 'psychological safety' among the workers. This is important in order to avoid defence mechanisms, such as denial and projection, and to enable people to dare to internalize ideas for change and to start working with change. Fear of losing face or losing self-esteem often make people resist new ways of thinking and acting. It is one thing to promote the need for change by talking about it, but another to act on it without the fear of negative reprisals, which are usually uncertain and risky.

The second step, *changing*, involves the actual organizational change: the changing of thinking, acting, routines, procedures or other organizational conditions. If the unfreezing is successful in terms of mobilizing a will and urge for change, it is seen as highly important to embark rapidly on the actual change, for example with the help of workshops, meetings and seminars, even if the overall direction may be a bit unclear. This demands a lot of communication, managerial support and encouragement. Here it is important to begin testing and applying new methods and ways of working as well as experimenting with and implementing new systems and processes. It is a step that is occasionally likened to a trial-and-error process, in which it is necessary to adapt continuously to new ways of working and to reflect upon the results of the changes. An idea here is to implement change but in parallel to instigate feedback loops and learn about what works.

The third step, *refreezing*, involves those aspects that contribute to the long-term result of the change, i.e. to make sure that new ways of working, work methods and routines gain a foothold and are stabilized within the organization. This step is important as many ideas and designs of organizational change often never even leave the drawing board or remain as subjects of talk in endless workshops without any lasting organizational impact. Individuals might change their thinking about an organizational procedure in a workshop or a developmental activity in a remote conference facility. Returning to their ordinary work group, people easily return to their old way of thinking and acting. This is why it is necessary to work with changing the norms and behaviour of a group and to ensure that the new ways of working also harmonize with these. It is also important that the changes of working, roles and assignments align somewhat with the identities of the employees, i.e. how they see themselves and their capacities. Schein (1987) talks about alignment between new ways of working and self-image (identity). We will return to identity matters later in the book.

These three different steps overlap in several ways, and it is not always easy to clearly separate them in practice. Schein suggests, for example, that step 1 is partly about making the process of change (the implementation) possible by creating psychological safety, at the same time as step 2 (the change) is partly about getting people to identify with role models – managers or change leaders – who are supposed to facilitate understanding of what it is important to achieve. The former activity however seems to concern facilitating the change as such (step 2) and the latter seems to concern something that should have been accomplished already in the unfreezing phase (step 1). But even if there is some variation in how these steps are interpreted, and it may be difficult to separate them meaningfully in practice, they provide some valuable insights into how to manage change. A key message is that information, knowledge and employee involvement potentially reduce resistance and subsequently facilitate change, in line with the suggestion to focus on reducing the restraining forces rather than strengthening the driving ones (Dawson, 2003).

Even though the ice-cube metaphor may not be so explicit in contemporary literature about organizational change, many of its ideas and thoughts still form the basis for how many – academics and practitioners – view planned change, especially within the Organizational Development tradition.

EXERCISE 4.3

Unfreezing usually involves mobilizing an urge for change by creating some form of discomfort with the existing organizational conditions. What problems could you expect to encounter in such a process? Discuss. Bear in mind that the creation of discomfort means disconfirming people's belief of how something works and thus often entails considerable emotional stress and anxiety. What role could leadership play in that process (to the extent that it is relevant in the first place)?

EXERCISE 4.4

Read the case below and analyze it based on Lewin's ice-cube metaphor of change:

- What actions taken can you relate to the phases of unfreezing, changing and refreezing, respectively?
- Reflect upon your analysis: What conclusions can you draw from it? Consider both the practical insights of the change processes in the case and also reflect upon the relevance and usefulness of the model.

CASE

Unfreezing and refreezing the British Airway's way

At the beginning of the 1980s British Airways (BA) had financial problems and received considerable subsidies from the UK government. The deregulation of the international airline industry at the time had resulted in intensive price competition and further financial losses were expected. Faced with the risk of having to allocate further subsidies, the UK government decided to dispose of British Airways through privatization. In order to make such a disposal possible, BA had to become profitable.

So, a radical process of organizational cultural change took place, in which the organization – over a five-year period – went from being 'bureaucratic and militaristic' to 'service-oriented and market-driven', as described by the managers participating in the process. During this time, the airline grew both in terms of the numbers of passengers and in the volume of cargo flights, and in this way transformed a loss of US$900 million in 1982 to a profit of $435 million in 1987. In five years, the previously government-owned organization had changed into a private and highly competitive company.

The initial step in the change process was a considerable reduction of the workforce (from 59,000 to 37,000 employees). Although this was challenging for many, it was mainly implemented through early retirements with large financial compensations. The downsizing in particular reduced the number of hierarchical levels and a common understanding in the organization was that this provided the workers with more freedom and some autonomy to make their own decisions.

In addition, BA hired a new CEO and a new chairman of the board. The CEO had a marketing background that was quite different from his predecessors, who had been retired senior Royal Air Force officers. He explicitly stated the need to change the culture of the company and launched the strategy that BA should become 'the World's Favourite Airline'. To accomplish this change in mindset, among other things, a training programme 'Putting People First' was provided for the employees working directly with customers. The service orientation that was promoted was noticeably different from the established mindset and way of working.

Training programmes for senior and middle managers were also introduced, such as 'Managing People First' and 'Leading the Service Business', in which the managers received extensive feedback on their management practices. The programmes were designed to demonstrate how the prevalent management style was dysfunctional and thus inappropriate if the organization wanted to become market-driven and service-oriented. At the same time, these training sessions were supposed to lay a foundation for a new, more open and participative way of managing. A new bottom-up budgeting process was also introduced, in sharp contrast to the earlier centralized system.

The top managers were heavily involved in the change process, not least the new CEO, who visited most training programmes to answer questions and promote his view of a marketing-led organization. HR was trained to become internal change agents, with the role to support and help managers, and peer groups were established in which managers could support each other in the change process.

At the structural level, systems providing emotional support were developed, recognizing that airline service work could be tough and emotionally draining. A new bonus system was introduced too, in which employees shared the financial gains the company achieved.

Management worked continuously to encourage changes in thinking and acting. For instance, people who were seen as having the new 'British Airways values' were more likely to be promoted. A new performance appraisal system acknowledging how people embodied the new culture in practice was introduced. Customer service was emphasized all over the company and a performance-based reward system was established. The crew received new uniforms and the aircraft were renovated. Additional training programmes were also held, especially for managers. The company also developed feedback systems in order to trace changes in the organizational climate and foster learning.

Source: Goodstein & Burke (1993)

The transformation at British Airways (BA) was based on a 3-step model and has become somewhat of a classic illustration of Lewin's idea. It goes without saying that a lot has happened with BA since then. At the beginning of the 2000s, the German rival Lufthansa had more international passengers and the slogan 'the world's favourite airline' is no longer used internally. Subsequent to the events of 11 September 2001 and the succeeding aviation crisis, the company began a restructuring process which involved cutting jobs and suspending routes and which has been followed by additional cuts.

BA has since the turnaround in the 1980s been considered to be a top-league airline – inventing seats that turn into beds, offering a hot breakfast in arrivals lounges and the possibility to shower and have your suit pressed. But the industry has changed and BA has become much more cost-focused too. Lately, BA, driven by increased competition from low-cost carriers, has made a number of small cuts, in particular in the menu and meal offerings, and has started to charge for checked baggage and seat reservations. Alex Cruz, coming from a low-cost carrier, was appointed as new CEO of BA in 2016. When asked about future cost-cutting, he said: 'We're always going to be reducing costs, but there are no more programmes. It's now injected into the DNA. If one particular day we don't come up with an idea to reduce our costs, then we're not doing our job.'

Sources: Clark (2002); Gollan (2017)

REVIEW QUESTIONS 4.3

Recall	What are the three stages of Lewin's ice-cube metaphor of change? Briefly describe what they involve.
Explain	In what ways can the ice-cube model facilitate the process of implementing change? Discuss. In what ways can insights from Field Theory facilitate the process further?
Reflect	Why do you think it is often preferable to focus on diminishing the opposing forces rather than increasing the forces towards change?

ORGANIZATIONAL DEVELOPMENT – BACKGROUND AND TRADITIONS

Organizational Development (OD) is an umbrella term for various ideas and models about how to effect planned organizational change that have been launched since the 1940s and the 1950s. Even though the approach is quite fragmented, its intellectual roots are based very much in the Human Relations approach and Lewin's ideas of the significance of acknowledging the socio-psychological aspect in change processes. Often Maslow's (1954) research on motivation and McGregor's (1960) theories on how people's needs affect organizations' development are also mentioned as being important for the establishment of OD.

Humanism, democracy and broad participation are the cornerstones of OD. A key focus has been how to make people feel more included and involved in the planning of organizational change. The assumption was that as people participate in planning change, they learn more and develop themselves, and subsequently also perform better both in terms of engagement and creativity. Many efforts within OD can be seen as ways of trying to democratize working life and stimulate increased individual engagement and achievement. Based on that, much attention has been placed on training, reflection and feedback. The ambition has been to approach inter-personal and relational problems in groups by increasing openness and trust, the idea being to enhance group dynamics and problem-solving abilities. The focus within OD has not only been at the work group; concepts for approaching organizations at large, including developing organizational culture, have also been developed over many years.

However, the development of OD has not been without challenges. For example, Greiner and Cummings (2005) suggest that there still is a lack of a more thorough understanding of the results of the application of different OD concepts and models. Morrison (1981) reviewed a number of studies of OD interventions with a largely mixed result and suggested that more rigorous studies – including failures and possible long-term results – of specific work with OD is needed. Greiner and Cummings (2005) maintain that OD had already developed into a fashionable idea by the end of the 1960s, and that academics and practitioners embraced it with naïve idealism and without asking if the exercises (e.g. coaching and feedback exercises) were always suited to the purpose of development.

At the beginning of the 1970s, Greiner (1972) made a summary of what had been presented as the central problems with OD. First, it was emphasized that OD in practice was too centred on the individual and the group, rather than at the organizational level, and that elements such as strategy, structure and broader control systems were lacking. The narrow focus on the individual and group levels was said to contribute to a lack of understanding of the broader context for thinking and acting in work groups. Second, it was suggested that the rather strict focus in OD on informal relations resulted in a neglect of how formal structural arrangements (such as hierarchies) and demands for efficiency also affect relationships and group dynamics. Third, it was suggested that practitioners allowed the *principles* of OD to influence and govern decision-making rather than the local *situational* circumstances, the latter being advocated as a superior base for decisions. Organizational Development was seen by many as becoming a universal – and consequently less appropriate – approach. Fourth, some criticized that teamwork seemed to be taken for granted as the best solution to different problems, rather than proceeding from what the local organizational situation warranted. OD was seen by many as an abstract and ready-made development package that was not very well adapted to concrete local organizational challenges and problems (Greiner & Cummings, 2005). From this standpoint, organizations were seen as being forced to adapt to an abstract OD-world rather than adapting the OD-world to an actual organizational reality. In other words, reality as forced to conform to the map rather than the map conforming to reality.

Much of the critique was aimed at OD being developed into a universal doctrine, even a cult, that should be applied to all kinds of organizations regardless of local and specific characteristics and contingencies (Greiner & Cummings, 2005). This critique contributed to the loss of appeal of traditional OD for many years. The decline of interest can also be linked to the radical and strategic changes that took place in many organizations during the 1980s and 1990s, changes related to radical technological development, internationalization and an increasingly turbulent economy. Other factors included a growing heterogeneity among co-workers, greater social demands being placed on organizations and the emergence of new organizational models with a focus on competitive advantages, learning, innovation and strategic leadership, all of which prompted strategic changes and an enhanced focus on competitive advantage. Rather than personal development, fulfilment and creative expansion, concepts such as efficiency, consolidation, 'Business Process Re-engineering' (BPR), cost control and downsizing emerged as popular topics among academics and practitioners in the 1980s and 1990s.

REVIEW QUESTIONS 4.4

| Explain | In your own words, describe the key ideas behind the rise of Organizational Development. |
| Reflect | Why do you think OD became so very popular in the 1970s but by the end of the century lost its appeal? |

CONTEMPORARY OD – CONCEPTS, MODELS AND VALUES

During the two last decades, OD has developed by integrating many contemporary concepts and models about strategic development and competitive advantages, structures and systems, learning and emergent change.

From traditional to contemporary OD

In a study comparing traditional and contemporary OD, Greiner and Cummings (2005) suggests that the doctrine has developed in the following areas:

- From focusing on individuals and groups to also considering the overall company structure and strategy.
- From focusing on social processes to also including work processes and HR practices.
- From a managerial and co-worker focus to also considering clients, suppliers and other stakeholders in the organizational environment as being central to change.
- From a humanistic focus to including traditional efficiency criteria.
- From a typical focus on identifying problems and undertaking episodic change to a new focus on learning and continuous (emergent) development.
- From a focus on reducing resistance to a focus on building a positive vision at an organizational level.

Today, most people who adhere to this orientation express an explicit open-systems view of organizations. This implies viewing the organization as a subsystem within the larger system of the environment, which facilitates a stronger focus on strategy and how to formulate relationships with a range of stakeholders. Furthermore, contemporary OD emphasizes organizational learning as well as focusing on financial results and visions. The open-systems view is expressed in Burke and Bradford's (2005, p. 10) description of OD as a planned organizational change 'that focuses on all levels of an organization – individual, group, intergroup, total system and interorganizational'. In this version of OD, it is central to formulate and achieve change of an organization's mission, vision, strategy, leadership and culture, thus recognizing the significance of the organizational level in the change process. The change should be based on behavioural science; especially significant here are psychology, sociology and cultural anthropology, rather than industrial planning or social engineering project management.

Burke and Bradford (2005) also stress that OD is based on some joint values, among the most typical of which are:

- The aim for alignment between individual and organizational goals and ambitions. The idea is that what is good for the organization is good for the individual, and vice versa.

- Encouraging honesty and openness in relations.
- Creating options for learning and personal development, with the aim of personal fulfilment for co-workers.
- Reaching a balance between the individual's freedom of choice and organizational constrains. On the one hand, too much individual freedom can be harmful and contribute to undermining the operations of the organization, why additional constraints can be needed. On the other hand, organizational constraints can become too restrictive and undermine the freedom of the individual, why a decrease in constrains can be needed.
- Pushing collaborative changes. Those affected by the change should also participate in its formulation and implementation.
- Minimizing the power discrepancy between co-workers both horizontally and vertically.
- Making conflicts among individuals and between units visible in order to solve them, rather than trying to avoid them or ignore them.

Power and conflict are things to be solved in order to restore organizational coherence and harmony. OD is generally based on a harmonious view of organizations and a strong belief in democratic processes. It is assumed that it is possible to align individual and organizational goals and development; what is good for the individual is also good for the organization, and vice versa. Conflicts and distance of power can occur, but they should be made visible and dealt with.

Even today OD still focuses a lot on the status of the individual in organizations. However, the characteristic humanistic approach has been complemented with an emphasis on effectiveness and financial performance. Cummings and Worley (2009, p. 1) describe OD as:

> [a] process that applies a broad range of behavioral science knowledge and practices to help organizations build their capacity to change and to achieve greater effectiveness, including increased financial performance, customer satisfaction, and organization member engagement.

Within OD it is commonly assumed that organizational change initiatives come from top management. Following the managerial initiatives, increasingly more hierarchal levels and co-workers should be involved in terms of work groups and project groups in a long-term process of change, contrary to the 'quick fix' idea that is common in many mainstream management books.

Organizational change should also preferably be supported by an external change actor that continuously draws on findings from behavioural science throughout the process. OD is built on an explicit integration between theory and practice, a relationship that, among others, has contributed to the growth of professional organizational change consultants and clinical action research that constitutes a bridge between theory and practice.

The legacy from Lewin is still very strong in the academic field and among the practitioners and consultants of OD. This is well illustrated in the following list of the activities that are suggested to contribute to efficient change (Cummings & Worley, 2009):

1. Motivating change – creating readiness for change and overcoming resistance to change.

2. Creating a vision that describes the core ideology and the envisioned future.

3. Developing political support – assessing the power of the change agents and identifying the key stakeholders and other possible influencing stakeholders.

4. Managing the transition with the help of activity planning, commitment planning and management structures.

5. Sustaining momentum – supporting the change through resources, developing support systems to help the change agents, developing new competencies and skills, reinforcing new behaviours and maintaining the course.

This list of suggested activities aligns well with the ice-cube model. Initially, the management is encouraged to unfreeze the organization by creating the will for change and the motivation to move towards the future, which can be encouraged by visions and political support from the key actors. Next, the process of change itself should be implemented, in terms of the creation of the appropriate organizational contingencies in, for example, meetings, committees and planning. Finally, the organization should refreeze through, among others, competency development and the increased allocation of resources.

EXERCISE 4.5

Think of a change project that you have been involved in. It can be anything from a minor individual change attempt to a large-scale organizational change project.

Critically reflect on why you consider it to be a success or a failure. What factors lay behind the success or failure and to what extent can these be related to the ice-cube reasoning?

REVIEW QUESTIONS 4.5

Recall	Organizational Development is a broad field, but it is based on a number of shared values. List at least four of these.
Explain	Explain in what aspect(s) Organizational Development is based on a logic of harmony.
Reflect	Can you think of any organizational contingencies where OD would be a less suitable tool or inappropriate as a change manager?

OD and the consultancy development

Even if OD today has a broader organizational focus – considering organizations as systems and organisms – the development during the last two decades has contributed to the area becoming more and more fragmented, something that likely has resulted in its waning influence on the general view of the management of organizational change. In a certain sense, one can lament this in a time when alternative models of change are geared towards consolidation, cost efficiency, a focus on results, financial measurements and a common obsession with the measuring and subsequent quantification of organizational life – a trend that hardly encourages participative ambitions or more humanistic values, i.e. the core of traditional OD. Today, many OD consultants act as solution-oriented specialists rather than as supporters and facilitators of the development and learning of organizational members, encouraging them to act as problem solvers themselves (Burnes, 2004).

The widening of the OD orientation is partly associated with the development of new organizational change models in general. Since the 1970s, the area has developed into what could be likened to an industry of change management where consultants, academics and practitioners try to outdo each other with advice on how to best formulate and execute organizational changes. In the 1970s, several more or less extensive system models – organizations as open systems – were popular, which over time became more and more complex as they included an increasing amount of organizational aspects, from strategy and organizational culture to narratives and discourses (see for example, Grant & Marshak, 2011; Peters & Waterman, 1982). We will discuss these in the following chapters and here only mention a relatively recent development that contrasts to OD.

As in many other areas of organizational research, the area of change management is inhabited by a mix of people from academia, consultancy and practice, all of whom have a stake in the development. Arguably, organizational change has become an economically lucrative area why much of the development of ideas, concepts and models is quite naturally driven by consultants.

For the past few years organizational change has been very much about reductions, consolidations and the downsizing of operations that are no longer seen as financially viable. There are some variations in the terminology, but change management and business process re-engineering are two common ways among consultants and practitioners to describe consolidation and downsizing in many industries. Many of the more well-known consultancies – Accenture, Cap Gemini, Ernst & Young, IBM Business Consulting – have been part of this. They have all pushed their business agenda to include Change Management (and Business Process Re-engineering).

In a critical review of the development of OD, Marshak (2005) makes an illuminating comparison between OD and Change Management. For Marshak, OD and Change Management are two contrasting ways of approaching organizational change, both ideologically and in practice. Change Management presumes that it is possible to identify and implement organizational change with the help of strict planning and project management techniques. Management enforces the process together with change agents and consultants who plan and lead the work. Consultants are seen as active problem solvers who provide suggestions as to how effective change can be accomplished. Participatory methods can be applied, but primarily with the intention to reduce possible resistance. The primary objective of Change Management – understood as Re-engineering – is to develop competitive advantages and consequently the profitability of an organization. Marshak (2005, p. 22) describes Change Management ideologically as follows: 'To change organizations for economic gain'. The vocabulary, concepts and values emanate from an economic and business-like orientation with a focus on productivity.

This can be contrasted with OD, where successful organizational change always involves those who are affected by the changes. Not in order to reduce resistance, but to maximize the co-workers' commitment, creativity and knowledge. The change is not seen as a means to reach specific (economic) objectives, but as an important learning and development process in itself. The consultant functions as a kind of advocator and encourager of learning and development, rather than as a problem solver or manager of the actual change. The change actor should thus enable those targeted by the change to participate both in identifying and solving the problem, not only in the implementation of ready-packed solutions, which typically is the case of Change Management (and also of some later varieties of OD, where there is an overall organizational focus; see for example, Bullock & Batten, 1985). An important idea within OD is to view people as active and learning subjects rather than passive recipients of information and data about the correct way to effect organizational change. As suggested elsewhere in the chapter, OD aims to contribute to more humanistic organizations with focus on individual development, creativity and co-worker influence, which in turn should contribute to efficiency, development and profitability. The idea is to develop people in order to effect social and organizational development and profitability. OD draws upon and is often framed in a more social psychological and cultural anthropological language and expresses humanistic values. Here it is people's development and fulfilment that is assumed to contribute to the development of organizations.

Diagnostic and Dialogic OD

A relatively recent development within the field is the emergence of theories and practices that depart from the assumptions of traditional OD. Bushe and Marshak (2009), for example, contrasts between a Diagnostic and a Dialogic OD orientation, where the former corresponds to the traditional OD perspective. To avoid confusion, we will briefly describe the Dialogic orientation in this chapter, even though these studies also have several similarities to what we refer to in later chapters as the process perspective on change.

Dialogic OD, unlike Diagnostic OD, views organizations as systems of meaning, with the starting point that reality is socially constructed rather than being objective. Seen from this perspective, the importance of diagnosing the situation is toned down, as it is suggested that there is not necessarily one correct view of the organization and its problems and possible solutions, but rather many versions. Based on that, the focus is shifted from formulating and planning towards encouraging and creating solutions for self-organizing among organizational members. (We will return to this thought in Chapters 6 and 7.) Both orientations express the strong humanistic approach that is characteristic of OD. They are also based upon democratic values and view the consultant as someone who should support the process rather than control the content. They also share a focus on developing the organization through developing its members.

REVIEW QUESTIONS 4.6

Recall	What is the key difference between Diagnostic and Dialogic OD?
Explain	What are the key differences between OD and the so-called concept of Change Management?

Critique towards OD

As we already touched upon, OD has been targeted by quite a lot of critique. First, a particular critique towards OD is the assumption that change is primarily episodic (and not valid for all approaches of change within the OD tradition more broadly). Viewing change as episodic is particularly problematic in a turbulent world that is continuously changing and hence it becomes difficult to plan and execute changes episodically. Viewing change as episodic rests on the assumption that stability is the norm and change is something occurring only temporarily: a development or episode of change between periods where the organization is more or less frozen. Critics argue that complexity, uncertainty and turbulence is the norm of today, which is why planned, episodic change quickly becomes outdated and irrelevant.

A second critique is the lack of possibilities to utilize OD in more radical and comprehensive, organization-wide changes. Planned organizational development – which dominates classic OD – is seen as being primarily suitable for evolutionary development on an individual level and a group level rather than for more radical revolutionary changes, including the whole organization and its different subsystems – strategy, culture, control, systems and processes.

A third critique is the consensus orientation that is typical for planned change in its evolutionary form. It is assumed that it is possible to reach consensus through dialogue, communication and learning. This expresses a harmonic view that ignores deeper conflicts of interest or assumes that it is possible to reduce power conflicts and achieve politically stable conditions within a community of common interest and political accord. This expresses a political naivety which follows the profound belief in the ability to reach a common understanding and agreement through dialogue and wide-ranging participation that is expressed in many of the theories and models.

At the same time, seen against the background of re-engineering, outsourcing and a stricter focus on economic results as well as increasing demands for standardization, control and measuring, it is increasingly important to maintain the core values of OD, such as humanism and participative influence.

EXERCISE 4.6

Think of a contemporary organizational change process, either from your own experience or from secondary sources such as the internet. Critically analyze the case on the basis of some of the OD models reviewed in this chapter.

- To what extent did the change in question consider, implicitly or explicitly, some of the principles or ideas of OD? Relate to some of the common ground of many OD approaches, such as participation, dialogue, communication, recognizing the value of people's voices, plurality, etc.
- What implications do you think it had to the change process that OD principles or ideas were (or were not) involved?

REVIEW QUESTION 4.7

Reflect	Evaluate OD from a critical perspective: What dimensions of organizational life in general and organizational change in particular are not taken into account?

SUMMARY

The Human Relations approach constitutes a key intellectual platform for the overwhelming majority of theories and models about organizational change that were established up until the 1970s. That approach established the significance of relations, group logic and group dynamics as well as the importance of attention, appreciation, recognition and other aspects of the social and psychosocial work environment. These conditions had been trivialized by its precursor, Taylorism and Scientific Management, with its mechanical focus on designing work efficiently and implementing rational techniques in the working environment.

The Human Relations approach led the way for Lewin, McGregor, Maslow and many other organizational researchers, who focused on what counteracts and promotes change, including motivational and management questions as well as the importance of viewing change as a learning process.

In its wake, at the end of the 1950s, a specific approach within the broad field of organizational change was formed: Organizational Development. OD was a broad approach for a diverse variety of models and theories but with the common denominator that they have their base in a few core values: participant decision-making (equality), the reduction of too-visible hierarchal asymmetries between the decision levels in organizations (decision democracy), consensus orientation and humanism (Wooten & White, 1999). Many of the models and theories supported episodic evolutionary change at the individual and group level. In particular, the focus was on the group and emphasized how group norms can have a considerable impact on how individuals think and act in organizations.

In recent years, many OD models have taken a more organization-wide approach on change, based on an open-system views on organizations. Here organizations are looked upon as systems containing a number of subsystems; in other words, as a whole consisting of a number of mutually dependent parts. Through the open-system viewpoint, the focus is shifted from the individual and the group to the organization level when it comes to the context of organizational change. This is the topic for the next chapter.

 # KEY PRACTICAL INSIGHTS

What we can say about organizational change following this chapter:

- Insights from Scientific Management and its outcomes show that change processes that are driven strictly from the top down, mainly focusing on productivity and rationalizations and ignoring the human dimension, run a great risk of resulting in alienated workers who distance themselves from the work and the organization.

- The Human Relations studies have shown the importance of taking group dynamics into account. Informal groupings need to be considered and worked with in change processes. Group norms and values can have a significant impact on how group members think and choose to act. It has been shown that people tend to stick to the perception of the group even if those ideas are against their individual values.

- The Human Relations studies also provide insights into what motivates human beings. People are not only driven by extrinsic motivations (such as monetary rewards) but also by a desire to belong and to feel recognition, which is important to consider when implementing organizational change.

- Force field analysis encourages us to consider the driving forces for change as well as the restraining forces, and to pay specific attention to the latter. By diminishing opposing forces, change plans can be pursued with less risk of tension and conflict based on resistance to change.

- Lewin's 3-step model recognizes the value of problematizing – or unfreezing – the existing state of affairs of the change object. The basic idea is that dissatisfaction with the present situation stimulates reflection and action, in particular if the employees feel safe and not personally threatened. In line with the same logic, vision can be motivating, especially if it clarifies the gap between the present and desired state. It also emphasizes the importance of making sure that the changes gain a foothold in the organization – i.e. the value of refreezing.

- OD theories highlight several advantages in involving those targeted by the change initiative in the change process. A key message is that employee participation and opportunities for individuals to personally learn and develop fuel commitment and creativity.

- An over-reliance on OD models can be problematic because of their somewhat harmonious and idyllic (naïve) understanding of organizations, with their strong belief in democratic processes and the assumption that individual and organizational goals and interests can be aligned. Power and politics should not be forgotten when working with change.

CASE

Implementing transformational change through dialogue

A new national cancer strategy was developed by the government in a northern European country, which included an organization-wide structural change programme where six Regional Cancer Centres were to be established. This case concerns the change process that took place when one of these centres was formed, more specifically how the Oncology Centre (OC) became the new regional Cancer Centre West (RCC West).

According to the head of the OC, who together with other colleagues had the strategic responsibility to develop cancer care in their region, this was a major system-wide change. For him, there was a great need for a fundamental change, in particular in order to improve knowledge-sharing and increase patient satisfaction. A common critique raised against the national cancer care concerned the fragmented process that lacked continuity and involved long waiting times for the patients. At that time the organization was highly decentralized. As the head of OC saw it, national cooperation had become inevitable.

A key idea behind the change programme leading to shaping the new RCC West, was to create a patient-focused organization with specific and more efficient pathways for the patients with malignant diseases as well as forums in which new knowledge could be generated, shared and disseminated. Thirty-four senior physicians, all specialists with extensive experience, were appointed as Process (pathway) Owners. Each of the processes was focused on a specific type of disease, such as brain tumour, breast cancer, liver cancer, etc.

The head of the OC had a clear ambition to involve and engage the professionals in the process. He explained: 'They are the key. That's why we want to engage them as central actors – they know their processes best and how to develop them.' There was a history in health care of numerous change initiatives with poor results and he explained: 'Usually a fashionable idea comes along and an enthusiastic new manager tries to roll it out. As if a magic solution has finally been found.' This type of change driven from the top down was out of the question as he saw it: 'We are dealing with experienced professionals' who are 'rather tired of yet more change initiatives from the top'.

The head of the OC talked about the upcoming transformation as a cultural change, where the traditional territorial boundaries of different departments should be torn down. Instead of thinking in functional silos, a new, processual mindset was to be developed, where the patient perspective was in sharp focus. This meant, for instance, that the traditional gaps between practices of care and cure had to be bridged.

Together with his assistant, and in close cooperation with a team of action-oriented researchers, the head of the OC planned the overall process for the upcoming 12 months. Their key guiding principles were:

- Physician-led change process (empowering physicians)
- Ambition to create more value for the patient
- Organizational development and learning through individual development
- An appreciative approach (focusing on possibilities, not only on problems)
- An open-systems view (taking the complexity of healthcare systems into account)

A key practical component was the 'Learning Platform', which consisted of dialogue meetings every six weeks attended by the physicians who were process owners, OC/RCC West staff, the research team and an external consultant. In these sessions, the participants where taught process work and quality improvement techniques by the consultant. It also functioned as an arena for exchanging ideas and experiences. The physicians, in their role as process owners, received 20% paid leave to focus on development activities such as these.

A year and a half later the OC became the new RRC West, with strategic responsibility for a region with 20 hospitals serving 1.9 million inhabitants.

During the change process, the head of the OC drew heavily on the metaphor of an aqueduct, illustrating how the new organization was supposed to function. The key point highlighted

(*Continued*)

by this metaphor was that the top priority was to provide effective care to the patient, represented by the water flowing undisturbed along the top of the aqueduct. In order to make this flow possible, robust support structures needed to be in place underneath. These consisted of the care team, supported by the regional process group, which in turn was supported by the regional cancer centre. Furthermore, it was emphasized that no bricks should be wasted in the process of building the aqueduct; in other words, resources should not be wasted. Finally, it was of key importance that the vertical and horizontal levels were interconnected – that people in different parts of the organization cooperated – in order to achieve a smooth flow.

The message expressed through the metaphor was interpreted in three rather distinct ways by the healthcare professionals:

1. One group of professionals acknowledged the metaphor in a favourable way. In particular, they embraced the idea of turning the former organization upside down and to focus on the patients. They were open towards a cultural change which they considered to be necessary in order to add value to the patients and welcomed the redesign of the care processes.

2. The second group had a more ambivalent approach to the metaphor. For them patient-centred care primarily meant supporting the patients and their specific needs hands-on. They thought the metaphor was unclear and they had mixed feelings towards it. Their focus was more on their own professional role and they spoke about a need for acquiring better understandings of the work performed by others and talked less about the importance of switching perspective. In particular, they stressed that standardized solutions were inappropriate in the context of cancer care.

3. The third group was rather indifferent to and a bit sceptical of the metaphor. However, they were positive about the Learning Platform. For them it was less about a change process going on, and more about the fact that the dialogue meetings legitimized what they were already doing (supplying and drawing upon evidence-based knowledge).

Questions:

1. Would you characterize the change process as to be in line with diagnostic or dialogic OD? Why?

2. People in the organization did not seem to share the same understandings. Do you think the plurality of voices enhanced or reduced the possibilities for radical, innovative transformation to take place? In what ways?

3. There was a clear ambition to involve and engage the professionals in the process. What effects do you think this had on the process?

Sources: Huzzard (n.d.); Huzzard et al. (2014)

FURTHER READING

Bradford, D. L., & Burke, W. W. (eds.) (2005). *Reinventing organization development: New approaches to change in organizations*. San Francisco, CA: Pfeiffer/Wiley.

Burnes, B., & Cooke, B. (2013). Kurt Lewin's Field Theory: A review and re-evaluation. *International Journal of Management Reviews*, 15(4), 408–425.

Bushe, G. R., & Marshak, R. (2009). Revisioning organization development: Diagnostic and dialogic premises and patterns of practice. *Journal of Applied Behavioral Science*, 45(3), 348–368.

Cummings, T. G., & Worley, C. G. (2009). *Organization development and change* (9th ed.). Mason, OH: South-Western.

Grugulis, I., & Wilkinson, A. (2002). Managing culture at British Airways: Hype, hope and reality. *Long Range Planning*, 35(2), 179–194.

Hurley, R. F., Church, A. H., Burke, W. W., & Van Eynde, D. F. (1992). Tensions, change and values in OD. *OD Practitioner*, 29, 1–5.

Nadolny, A., & Ryan, S. (2015). McUniversities revisited: A comparison of university and McDonald's casual employee experiences in Australia. *Studies in Higher Education*, 40(1), 142–157.

Ritzer, G. (2002). An introduction to McDonaldization. *McDonaldization: The Reader*, 2, 4–25.

Wooten, K. C., & White, L. P. (1999). Linking OD's philosophy with justice theory: Postmodern implications. *Journal of Organizational Change Management*, 12(1), 7.

THE TOOL-BASED PERSPECTIVE: INTEGRATED ORGANIZATIONAL MODELS

LEARNING OBJECTIVES

When you have completed your study of this chapter, you should be able to:

- Explain and discuss the significance of the open-systems theory for understanding organizational change.

- Appraise the relevance of integrated organizational models for analyzing and managing organizational change.

- Recognize the significance of organizational culture in organizational change processes.

- Describe organizational change as a sequentially organized process consisting of a variety of steps.

- Critically evaluate typical n-step models in terms of their advantages and limitations as tools for managing change.

In the previous chapter we pointed out that the tool-based perspective originated in the planning approaches that were established during the 1940s and 1950s, where it was often assumed that organizational change took place in well-defined, episodic time periods. In some of the key approaches to change, such as Organization Development (OD), focus was traditionally mostly placed at the individual and work group level. However, during the 1980 and 1990s, OD developed an increasingly integrated view – a broader systems view – of organizational change that included a focus on, for example, organizational culture and strategy. In parallel with this, more integrated models of organizations and change were launched within organization theory, many of these with an emphasis on strategies and an organization's relations to its environment. Many of these models provide more or less practical tools to be used for analyzing organizations and as guidance for implementing rational and well-planned change work. According to these approaches, organizational change can and should be performed in a sequence of consecutive steps. Consequently, guidance often consists of a number of steps that should be executed in a certain order in order to succeed with change work, known as n-step models. In some approaches, the sequential idea is toned down and more advice is provided on organizational modelling generally, and in some cases a greater emphasis is given to change as an evolutionary process.

Most of the concepts, terms and models, discussed in this chapter, are founded in a systems perspective of organizations, both in terms of how organizations function internally and of their external relationships. We therefore begin this chapter with a brief description of organizations as open systems. This is followed by a longer account of some of the significant systems models that aim to allow for and enable situational analysis and subsequent change work. Thereafter, organizational culture is discussed, an area regarded by many as central to understanding organizations and change. We also highlight some typical n-step models for effective change work.

ORGANIZATIONS AS OPEN SYSTEMS

Many contemporary authors consider organizations as open systems (Kanter, 1999; Luthans et al., 2015). Considering organizations as open systems usually dates to the end of the 1950s and is most often linked to a view of organizations as living organisms. Biological systems have thus constituted an important source of inspiration for related terms and concepts. However, it is not only the world and vocabulary of biology that provides the starting point for systems-oriented social scientists and organizational researchers. Systems theory has established and combined terms from a range of disciplines (including physics, chemistry and technology), such as feedback, self-regulating systems, equilibrium, entropy, thermodynamics, cybernetics and homeostatic systems (Blegen, 1968). Even though the terms and theories from the systems world are highly theoretical and abstract, some of them have had a great impact on the view of organizations and organizational change among researchers, consultants and also practitioners.

There are many reasons for this. Primary is that the systems view emphasizes that entities that were previously seen as defined areas – departments, units, processes, cultures, organizations or entire societies – should rather be understood as subparts (or subsystems) of a wider context, with which these subparts (or subsystems) have different kinds of exchanges. Further, the theory can easily be scaled up or down; deciding where one wants to set the limits for the system one seeks to understand is simply a pragmatic question, and the systems view can, in practice, be applied at any level of any social phenomenon. However, it is most common to consider an organization as a system that interacts with the wider system – the environment – of which it is a subpart (or subsystem hereinafter). This kind of understanding of organizations poses several questions, of which two are discussed extensively in this chapter. First, how well are different subsystems aligned with each other and with the external environment? This is the key focus of situational analysis models, which aim to analyze the current situation to identify the need for change. According to a tool-based perspective of organizational change, analyzing is an important first step that precedes planning and implementation. Second, what kind of managerially-led changes are necessary in order to manage and correct mis-matches or misalignments between different subsystems (Katz & Kahn, 1966)? This is the key topic of integrated organizational change models. Later in the chapter we will also review some models for managing and implementing organizational changes, which often are expressed in terms of a prescribed sequential process.

THE ORGANIZATION AND ITS STAKEHOLDERS

Viewing organizations as living organisms puts the spotlight on themes such as what maintains organizational long-term survival, and thereby what provides their nutrition or input, as well as how organizations can manage the right conditions for long-term nutritional supply and organizational health (see Boulding, 1956). A focus on the entire organization and its environment thus becomes central. Following this, a range of approaches and models of the company's relationships with its environment has been established – characterized as consisting of a variety of stakeholders – known as *stakeholder theory* (Mainardes et al., 2011). Figure 5.1 shows the original stakeholder model devised by Freeman (1984) and Figure 5.2 is a refined model developed by Fassin (2009). In the later model, stakewatchers such as pressure groups that influence the firm (which are outside the large central oval representing the firm in Figure 5.2) and stakekeepers, such as regulators that control and impose regulations on the firm (the dotted lines in the figure) are treated as separate categories, differentiated from the real stakeholders who have a concrete stake in the firm. Taking this into account enables a more complex and nuanced analysis of the firm's external relations.

When combined with the *contribution and reward model* mentioned in Chapter 4, questions arise about how companies can reward stakeholders in a way that makes them contribute to the long-term survival of the company (Barnard, 1938; March & Simon, 1958). Thus, an organization will survive only as long as the contributions *from* stakeholders are sufficient to provide rewards *to* stakeholders necessary to maintain long-term contributions.

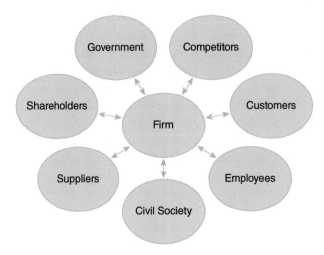

FIGURE 5.1   The stakeholder model (Freeman, 1984) (by kind permission of Cambridge University Press)

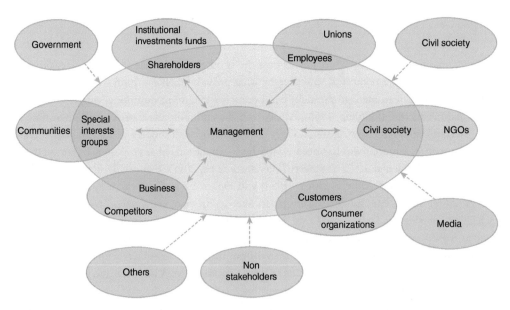

FIGURE 5.2   The refined stakeholder model of the firm (Fassin, 2009) (by kind permission of Springer Nature)

According to contribution–reward reasoning, the employee's behaviour, for example, can be explained by the perceived balance between contribution and rewards. Every employee (which is one type of stakeholder) contributes in a different way to the organization (energy, knowledge, skills) and in return receives rewards (salary, status, professional challenges). As long as the employee perceives that there is a balance between their contribution and rewards, the relationship is maintained. The model constitutes an *equilibrium* model, in which both the employee and the employer perceive that there is a balance, i.e. that the employee has a feeling that his or her contribution matches the rewards, which, in turn, from the perspective of the company, should correspond to the company's desire to compensate and retain its employees.

EXERCISE 5.1

Consider a modern university as an open system, and apply one of the stakeholder models discussed in the text above. Examine the role of five key stakeholders in terms of the contribution and reward exchange model. What are stakeholders contributing and how do universities reward these stakeholders so that the stakeholders maintain their relations to the university?

In what ways do you think the role of stakeholders to a university have developed during the last 10 years? Is there reason to believe that the role of stakeholders will change significantly in the coming years, and if so, how?

MINI CASE 5.1

Changes to fit the environment in the Western European Police

The Western European Police has faced different challenges over the years. After a period of stability in the 1950s and 1960s, the environment became more dynamic due to student rebellion, anti-war protests and terrorism in the 1970s and 1980s. The bureaucratic and centralized structures that fitted the stable environment were changed into a more flexible and technology-driven structure in order to achieve alignment with the new challenges. Around the turn of the millennium, yet another landscape started to surface. With open borders, globalization and new technologies (the internet and social media), the existing structures were once again

(Continued)

considered to be too slow and bureaucratic to deal with the new situation. The police faced a greater diversity of demands. In addition to dealing with local issues, they had to deal with the threats of terrorism, internet crime and organized crime nationally as well as internationally. In order to restore fit with these new external challenges, new surveillance technologies have been adopted at airports, train stations and other public locations, investigation technologies have been updated and cross-border cooperation between police forces has been strengthened.

Another quite significant change in many European police forces was the introduction of various management methods from the private sector (performance measurement, management by objectives and cost accounting systems) in order to meet the external demands of faster and more efficient procedures. These changes, however, severely clashed with internal factors and resulted in resistance from the workforce. In this regard, these methods clashed with the identity of many police officers who saw themselves as people 'serving the common good and fighting for security and justice' (Jacobs et al., 2013, p. 778). To adopt models from the private sector, which they considered to be primarily focused on selling and profitmaking, were unjustified and inappropriate. Many of the officers felt alienated by the politicians and consultants, who did not seem to differentiate between a police force and a private company.

Source: Jacobs et al. (2013)

INTERNAL ALIGNMENT

Viewing organizations as open systems is, however, as shown in the case above, not only a question of the organization and its relationships with its environment. It also involves considering the organization internally as a system, consisting of a number of subsystems that have to be aligned with each other in a way that enable internal consistency and preferably synergy, so that the organization as a whole becomes more than the sum of its distinct parts. In this context, an important question is what function the different parts – the organizational subsystems – have in relation to each other and to the organization as a whole. Are they organized appropriately – in a high degree of harmony or alignment – so that they achieve a certain degree of stability over time, or are they badly aligned, causing friction, conflicts or disruption?

A central assumption in systems theory is thus that the different subsystems are mutually dependent on each other, often as a result of how they have emerged historically. This means that a change in one organizational subsystem, for example a change in the organizational structure in terms of a vertical division of labour or a change in a recruitment policy, will impact the relations with many other organizational subsystems (such as power structures or organizational culture, for instance) due to their mutual dependency.

Based on this, it can be argued that even a seemingly limited change in an organization potentially can become a complex change with long-term and often unpredictable consequences. For example, a change in the vertical division of work tasks due to the introduction of new levels of decision-making (perhaps because of fast market growth or changes in the product mix) can weaken motivation among those that are not promoted and who instead perceive that another layer of managers has come between them and their previous managers. This in turn can deter people from taking the initiative and cooperating vertically, and also be detrimental to cooperation between different departments or functions, and potentially create breeding grounds for organizational cultural fragmentation. The latter can be a risk to the organization's renewal ambitions and further growth. A seemingly harmless structural adaptation to growth can thereby counteract the organization's ability to grow in the long term.

This exemplifies how an organizational change can result in the opposite effect than intended, due to a range of mutual dependencies that can be difficult to map out and analyze when one is in the midst of working out how to simplify decision-making. In other words, a change is never a matter of a simple 'quick fix' in terms of analysis, formulation, implementation and results, even if it might sound that way when somebody wants to encourage change.

REVIEW QUESTIONS 5.1

Recall	Within the open systems theory it has been common to view the organization as a living organism. List at least three characteristics of an organism that are used to understand organizational dynamics.
Explain	Explain the key ideas of the systems approach to organizations. Make sure that you include the environment in your description.
Reflect	Based on a systems approach to organizations, what do you think are the key managerial aspects to consider when embarking on change processes?

INTEGRATED ORGANIZATIONAL MODELS AS SITUATIONAL ANALYSES

One of the central points of a systems approach is that it enables descriptions of both organizational complexity and organizational integration. This promotes understanding of mutual dependencies between different subsystems – including both 'hard' and 'soft' dimensions as described below – in order to identify problems and develop measures and action plans. Thus, a study of a system means that one has to 'not only observe the structure, but also the processes, not only social but also technological factors, not only the "closed" organization but also how it interacts with its environment' (Blegen, 1968, p. 12). This is a typical socio-technical systems approach that can be developed and refined based on which and how many subsystems are included in the system, as well as its characteristics. Viewing organizations as systems, there are normally a few softer (social with process characteristics) and some harder (technical with systems characteristics) systems, as they are known, that usually appear in the models launched during the last 40 years. Beer and Eisenstat (1996, p. 598) provide the following as an example:

> The change process should be systems oriented. Organizations are complex and mutually dependent systems. [...] Strategy, structure, leadership and the character of the company's behaviour all need to be coordinated. In particular, coordination between the 'softer' elements, such as people, leaders and values, and 'harder' elements like technology, strategy and structure.

MINI CASE 5.2

Systemic view – the case of corporate sustainability

Following the discussion of viewing organizations as consisting of a variety of subsystems, the systemic perspective is still widely employed in order to understand complex environmental forces and their relevance for managing change (Lozano, 2015; Montano, 2018). For example, in a study on how to successfully integrate corporate sustainability (CS) in a corporation, Lozano (2015) emphasizes the importance of employing a systemic perspective on change management. This is a perspective that potentially facilitates a broader and more holistic focus on how to understand and manage sustainability. In particular, Lozano (2015) proposes that integrating sustainability in organizations means acknowledging not only the obvious and more technical elements, such as raw materials, processes and products, but also the softer issues, such as culture and people's attitudes: '...organizational changes for sustainability need to go beyond change in technology and management systems; they require changes in culture...' (Lozano, 2015, p. 34). Such a change process, it is suggested, needs to address individuals, groups and the company at large, as an organizational culture, also recognizing that thinking, feeling as well as behaviour need to be targeted. Lozano (2015) also recognizes a variety of internal and external drivers in this process, of which leadership is very important, but so too are organizational culture, moral obligations, customers, reputation, regulation and legislation.

Sources: Lozano (2015); Montano (2018)

Based on the systems view, a variety of organizational change models have been developed that build upon and express how different subsystems, both soft and hard, align together to create a whole (a system) with different types of relationships with the environment (a wider system). For example, Nadler and Tushman (1980) have developed an analysis model that describes organizations as separate systems, between which there must be alignment (congruence) for long-term survival (see Figure 5.3). The model is described in classic systems theory terms, such as input, transformation and output.

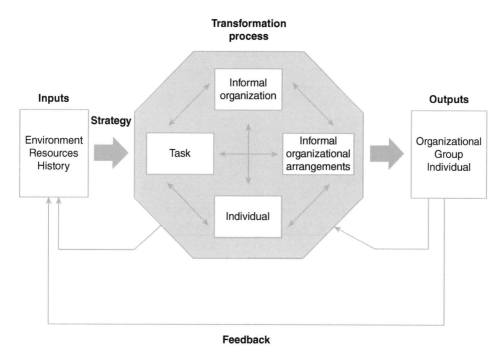

FIGURE 5.3 Nadler and Tushman's congruence model (1980)

In this version, *inputs* refer to external stakeholders but also traditional resources, such as capital, raw materials and people. The relevance of organizations' external environments gained much attention in the 1960s in studies demonstrating that the characteristics and pace of change had a significant impact on the organization in terms of tasks and responsibilities, i.e. vertical and horizontal differentiation, and the degree of formalization and decentralization. For example, Burns and Stalker (1961) demonstrated that organizations that existed in stable environments had more mechanical structures, while those in changing environments demonstrated more organic structures.

Transformation in the model describes how resources are utilized by the organization. They are represented as four elements in Figure 5.3: individuals and tasks as well as the formal and informal organization. Individuals are described in terms of knowledge and professional characteristics, among others. Tasks include its inherent characteristics, working methods and types of dependencies between different work tasks. Formal organization refers to the structure, incentive and governance systems and other formal relationships that structure work. The informal organization involves the social structure, politics, rumours and informal influence, i.e. relationships that informally influence organizational processes.

Finally, *outputs* are described not only in terms of how well the organization achieves its financial goals, but also how well the organization transforms its resources in terms of cooperation, human behaviour, communication, conflict management, absenteeism, and so on. Outputs are described in quite broad terms and also include results at group and individual levels, as well the organization's ability to deal with change. Thus, outputs should correspond to inputs and transformation – are we achieving what we intend to do?

EXERCISE 5.2

Consider an organization that you are familiar with (for instance, it could be a university, a bank, a shop or a café). Apply Nadler and Tushman's congruence model by suggesting what the various parts in the model could consist of in this specific case.

- Do you primarily find congruity or incongruity between the various parts? Discuss the implications of your findings.
- What do you think can be gained from applying such a model on an organization? How can the insights from such an analysis enhance understanding and possibly also support efforts to manage change?

The model should enable an analysis of how well both the overarching system and the parts or subsystems that are included in each element fit together. Consequently, it is not just a question of characterizing an organization in mere descriptive terms; it also involves an assessment of how well the parts are aligned to each other and, if necessary, suggest organizational changes that correct misalignments and inconsistencies. The model is very wide-ranging with the aim of being universal. One of the risks, though, is that its analytical value is limited to the obvious, such as that different subsystems are dependent on each other in complex and unpredictable ways, or that organizational change is difficult to manage.

As mentioned in Chapter 4, OD has been shaped in the direction of this broader open-systems view during the last 20 years, but there are also many other popular change models that draw on the open-systems idea. Some of these will be discussed in the next section.

EXERCISE 5.3

Briefly gather information about a contemporary organization by drawing on secondary sources such as the internet, newspapers and business magazines. You could, for instance, study IKEA, by searching for facts and figures presented on the company website. 'The testament of a furniture dealer' written by the founder Ingvar Kamprad, can give you further insights.

Analyze the organization with the help of an integrated organizational model and try to identify some of the more significant subsystems. These can, for example, involve:

Strategy – what position does the organization seem to have in its market or its industry? What competitive advantage is the organization striving for (e.g. low-cost or customer value)?

Structure – to what extent are work tasks and responsibilities formalized? What do the division of work roles, distribution of power and degree of formalization look like? Does it seem highly formalized and centralized or more flexible and organic?

Culture – are there any signs of salient or more tacit norms and values that characterize the organization?

Control – how are work and tasks coordinated in the organization? Is this accomplished with the help of bureaucracy and administration, culture and norms or by emphasizing results or output? Or is it a matter of technical control by standardized assembly-line production?

Analyze how the various subsystems are aligned or misaligned in relation to each other. Is there reason to suspect any mismatches between the subsystems? For example, is there a match between the internal culture and structure and the competitive advantage that the organization is striving for?

- What does your analysis suggest in terms of the need for and possibility to manage organizational change?
- What did you experience as the key challenges in performing the tasks of documenting and analyzing the organization according to an integrated organizational model?

REVIEW QUESTIONS 5.2

Recall	List a number of subsystems of an organization in a typical integrated organizational model. Make sure that you include hard as well as soft elements.
Recall	Briefly describe the meaning of the classical system-oriented concepts 'inputs', 'transformation' and 'outputs'.
Explain	Explain the purpose of using an integrated organizational model in a situational analysis.
Reflect	Do you see any limitations with using an integrated organizational model in order to diagnose organizations and their need of change?

INTEGRATED ORGANIZATIONAL MODELS AS SUPPORT IN CHANGE WORK

Some integrative organization models not only facilitate analysis of the change needs of organizations, they also aim to guide the change work. One such model that has had a strong impact was developed by Tichy (1983). An intention of this model is to highlight the complexity of change, and especially that one cannot implement changes successfully by simply focusing on what is called the technical system of an organization. Successful change work requires a broader view and should also include – the often neglected or marginalized – political and cultural aspects of an organization.

The model is based on three problem areas. One involves the *technical problems* – production, organizational structure, incentive systems – that occur as a result of a rapid technological development. Another involves *political problems* – issues of distribution stemming from questions of power and influence – as a result of external political developments in which distribution and power politics, such as participatory decision-making, increase in importance. The third area consists of *cultural problems* and the importance of managing norms and values that emerge as a result of a stronger focus on work ethics and the need to fulfil one's own ambitions at work.

Based on these premises, an integrated organizational model was constructed, consisting of three mutually dependent (sub)systems, one technical, one political and one cultural. Tichy compares this to three interwoven strands of a rope. From a distance, the three twines are inseparable, but to understand an organization more deeply each part has to be taken into account, and each part has to be managed during a change process. For each of these three systems, three sets of management tools were formulated that relate to different organizational components: mission and strategy, organizational structure and human resource management (HRM). Combining the subsystems and managerial tools by intersecting them in a matrix provide nine decision-making areas that should be taken into account during change work.

Managerial tools

Managerial areas	Mission and Strategy	Organizational Structure	Human Resource
Technical system	• Assessing environment • Assessing organization • Defining mission and fitting resources	• Differentiating • Integration • Aligning structure to strategy	• Fitting people to roles • Specifying performance criteria • Measuring performance • Staffing and development
Political system	• Who gets to influence mission & strategy • Managing coalitional behaviour around strategic decisions	• Distribution of power • Balancing power across groups of roles	• Managing succession politics • Designing and administrating of reward system • Managing appraisal politics
Cultural system	• Managing influence of values and philosophy on mission and strategy • Developing culture aligned with mission and strategy	• Developing a managerial style aligned with structure • Development of subcultures to support roles • Integrating subcultures to form company culture	• Selecting people to build or reinforce culture • Developing (socialization) to mould organization culture • Managing rewards to shape the culture

FIGURE 5.4 Strategic tasks in organizational change management. Based on Tichy (1983)

The matrix displays the complexity of change and, in contrast to traditional strategic planning – mainly focusing on the upper-left corner – it offers a significantly broader and more multifaceted view of what successful change work normally requires. We provide a short review below.

The *technical system* involves considerations that are conventionally described in the prevalent management literature. The mission and strategy area involves traditional strategic planning activities using classic analytic tools such as a SWOT analysis and formulation of the company mission. Another task in the technical system involves shaping the organizational structure and its relation to strategy in terms of alignment, sometimes referred to as 'structure follows strategy' (Chandler, 1962). The third task is about human resource management and involves matters such as the matching of personnel, roles and work tasks, and creating systems for performance evaluation.

The *political system* involves the formal and informal distribution of power, and the politics that accompany things such as resource allocation, promotions and appointments. Who is given the opportunity to influence missions and strategic direction? What are the political consequences of change? For example, what are the negative effects of strategic decisions on different people? Another aspect involves the horizontal and vertical distribution of power in the organization generally. What should one be able to influence at a division or headquarters level? How should one manage horizontal divisions of power, for example between the production and marketing departments? The third aspect of the political system, human resources, involves, for example, succession matters. Who is given the opportunity to make a career, and who is not promoted and offered a chance to advance? Human resources also include questions such as the incentive system and criteria for evaluating the employees' performance. The political system encompasses priorities that have political consequences and, accordingly, there are always individuals who will be disadvantaged by the decisions that are taken.

Within the *cultural system* three additional leadership tools are presented. Mission and strategy include influencing and controlling values so that they align with the strategy. The importance of developing a leadership style that is aligned to the structure is also described. For example, a project-oriented organization that demands deliveries to deadlines requires a more open, negotiating and conflict-ready style than a traditional line organization with clear hierarchy and traditional managerial command. It is also suggested that it may be important to develop subcultures that are aligned to different parts of an organization: within production there might need to be a cost-conscious culture, whereas in the research department it might be beneficial to have an open and innovative culture characterized by certain entrepreneurship. The division of labour normally also requires and demands strong and broad organization-wide coordination in order to prevent and counter organizational fragmentation. The cultural system can also be developed and fashioned with the support of human resource management tools, such as recruiting people who fit culturally with the norms of the organization; this is known as social fit as opposed to finding the right person from a mere technical competence or knowledge perspective. It is also possible to work with cultural matters internally by developing human resource programmes that train and foster people in the organization's core values.

A key point of the model is that organizational change work normally affects all the systems, and managers or change agents should try to acknowledge all the managerial tools as part of the change work. Similar to Nadler and Tushman's (1980) model, organizations are presented as complex entities comprised of several connected subsystems that it is difficult to manage in isolation from each other.

A lot of this sounds reasonable and fine, and many of these models can arguably help people to identify and recognize previously neglected but highly relevant connections between subsystems. At the same time, the models are abstract and probably not always easy to apply to local conditions that seldom adhere to general concepts and abstractions. Much of what is suggested within the different areas often requires great efforts of analysis, with uncertain outcomes in terms of what particular actions should be taken.

It should also be pointed out that even though organizational change is presented as complex, it is nonetheless reduced to boxes, cells and arrows, as in many other models, without regard for how people – often those targeted by change initiatives – experience and think about change. How do members of the organization experience the change in terms of status, respect, self-esteem, imagination and thoughts? How important are people's different experiences, wishes and ideas about what needs to be done for the change project, and how do these ideas, wishes and experiences substantially influence the process and the result of the change work? Technical aspects are often prioritized and the models become abstract and theoretical, and thus also insufficient and unsatisfactory when it comes to one of the most central elements in change work – people.

REVIEW QUESTIONS 5.3

Recall	Sketch Tichy's model of strategic change by pinpointing the 3+3 dimensions in the matrix.
Explain	Discuss what each box of the matrix represents.
Explain	In what ways can Tichy's model be seen as representative for a systems view of organizations and change?
Explain	What are the possible practical impacts of adopting the model?
Reflect	What boxes in the strategic change matrix would you say are most typical for how managers think about organizations and change?

INTEGRATED ORGANIZATIONAL CULTURAL MODELS

Culture is a central element in many models and approaches to organizational change. For example, in McKinsey's 7-S framework (Waterman et al., 1980), culture is one of the 'soft' aspects and is described as 'shared values' together with 'skills', 'staff' and 'style'. The 'hard' aspects, as they are called, include strategy, structure and system. Other authors have highlighted the importance of culture and make it the main focus (see Heracleous, 2001; Johnson et al., 2011). These models can also be divided into models that analyze the situation and models that discuss managerial action.

Situational analysis with culture in focus

Johnson et al. (2017) draw upon a metaphor – the cultural web – in portraying organizations as made up of seven subsystems including a central paradigm that acts as a culturally cohesive glue for the other subsystems (see Figure 5.5). The central paradigm consists of the basic assumptions about how the organization functions in its work environment. These basic assumptions form the backbone of the organization and are seldom immediately obvious to the members of the organization.

The paradigm is expressed through a number of subsystems:

- *Routines* are the historically accepted and habitual ways of working and general work procedures; this is often referred to as 'the way we do things around here'. These are often deeply rooted among people and can be seen as an expression of what is taken for granted in the daily organizational life.

- *Rituals* refer to procedures for promotion, recruitment, appointments, meetings or other relevant actions that reinforce the organization's routines and thereby further affirm the organization's basic assumptions or paradigm.

- *Stories and myths* are tales and narratives about the organization's development and history, especially historical events that people talk about for a long time afterwards. They may be about people who stand out for something positive or about somebody who has acted against traditions and thereby illustrated how one should *not* behave.

- *Symbols* refer to logotypes, trademarks, titles or other emotive representations that are drawn upon. This includes language and other expressions that illustrate what the organization stands for.

- *Control systems* include the forms of governance and control, incentive systems and the performance evaluation systems that are used and what they focus on.

- *Power structures* include the distribution of informal and formal power and influence on decision-making in the organization. These are also expressions of the organization's values or paradigm.

- *Organizational structures* are the formal and informal, horizontal and vertical divisions of labour in the organization and how they relate to what the organization stands for.

This model is intended to support analysis of, and reflection on, the existing organizational culture and how it is expressed in the different subsystems, as well as how well-aligned they all are to each other and the external environment. An objective behind this kind of analysis is to identify problems, and thus the potential need for change. The model's focus on culture illustrates both how central culture is and how it is expressed in other organizational subsystems. One of the ideas of the model is to highlight the mutuality between different subsystems that is not always obvious.

FIGURE 5.5   The cultural web. Source: Johnson et al. (2011)

The principle message in this integrated model, and the others presented earlier in the chapter, is that an organization can succeed over the long term, provided that alignment is achieved between the different internal subsystems as well as between the organization as a system and its external environment (customers and markets are for many organizations key stakeholders but it is necessary to form alignment with most of the stakeholders in the long run). The models can be seen as tools for analyzing organizations to identify any misalignments or opportunities for development. To this extent, they also facilitate an improved understanding of organizations as fields of stabilizing and undermining forces that were central to Lewin's model of organizations as a force field, discussed in Chapter 4. For example, which subsystems indicate a need for change, i.e. which forces are pushing for change? If one subsystem is changed, which of the other systems will then need to be changed in order to avoid resisting and obstructing forces? The above models can therefore enable an identification of the need for change and an assessment of how urgent any need for change is, based on the strength and relevance of the different forces.

Integrated model with culture in focus to support change management

Heracleous (2001) takes the cultural web one step further. He shows how it can be used as an analytical tool intended to examine the prevailing situation and additionally suggests a model for managing change. The model is proposed to enable a deeper understanding of the organization's dominating values and norms, and how these in different ways inform not only how the members understand and make sense of an organization, but also how they behave and organize their existence. This is expressed in elements like the choice of organizational form, incentive system, leadership and approach to human resources. The idea is that this understanding will facilitate the change work. The model includes the following five steps:

1. *Situational analysis*. Where are we now? What are our core values and common assumptions (often historically accepted)?

2. *Policy and strategy development*. In which direction should we develop? What is our strategic redirection or which organizational changes should we make? (This is linked to the internal and/or external triggers of change.)

3. *Consequences for the organization*. Which values have to be changed as a result of the strategic redirection or ideas regarding organizational change?

4. *Leading change*. How should the change be implemented?

5. *Monitoring and evaluation*. The cultural web should be built and evaluated regularly.

In this way, the cultural web and its different subsystems (routines and rituals, stories and myths, symbols, control systems, power structures and organizational structure, as well as the overarching paradigm) can be used both to analyze an organization's current situation (and thereby identify any need for change) and as a support for the actual change work – in other words, the implementation of the suggested changes. This is demonstrated in Mini Case 5.3, which involves planned change in a consulting firm.

MINI CASE 5.3

Organizational change in a consulting company in UK

Based on changes in the market of a global human resources consulting firm (i.e. external triggers), a need for organizational and strategic change was identified and change plans were made. A central ambition with the change was to encourage the consultants to work in teams rather than individually, which was no longer deemed to be aligned and consistent with market demands. To create an understanding of how the change should be implemented, an analysis of the existing organization was carried out with the help of the cultural web model.

The analysis showed that the suggested organizational changes (from individual work to teamwork) challenged several of the basic beliefs and values within the organization, including the belief that consultants work best and most effectively when they work individually. After further analysis it turned out that this belief was based on underlying assumptions about human nature, including a belief that humans are naturally individualistic, autonomous and prefer to work as lone rangers and entrepreneurs. The analysis also showed that there were underlying assumptions about a strong action orientation in which doing things was deemed important (as opposed to an orientation that emphasizes being or becoming). This action orientation was obvious in the requirements placed on the consultants. They were expected to deliver and generate results based on individual work. The underlying assumptions (self-motivated individuals who work autonomously and constantly deliver without any particular coordination with colleagues) were also apparent in the consultants' behaviour and organizational routines, such as the incentive system (which was individually designed), communication (which was informal), myths (consultants became role-models for others based on individual performance) and organizational structure (which was decentralized). In other words, individual work was celebrated, supported by stories and myths about individual heroes. Working procedures, recruitment processes and incentive systems were well aligned with the basic belief about the importance of autonomous consultants.

We see here how a change in one subsystem (from individual work/autonomy to teamwork) has consequences for other subsystems such as organizational culture, human resource management communication and the relationship between superiors and subordinates. The case is interesting because it is described as a successful case – they changed the individualistic culture and became more team-oriented. Success was attributed to the managers acting as leaders in terms of being clear about the direction of the changes. They organized the resource allocation in line with team norms and developed experts within several new areas. They also redefined the work procedures and work tasks, changed coordination mechanisms and developed new incentive systems. The company also developed new control systems for measuring team-based performance.

Source: Heracleous (2001)

Based on the study of the consultancy firm presented in Mini Case 5.3, Heracleous (2001) proposed that change work should be characterized by:

- Visible, active and clear leadership. In this case, the leaders are said to have acted as role models. Based on this, it is suggested that changes should be evolutionary, led by committed and politically and intellectually aware leaders.

- Participative planning. Those that are impacted by the change should participate in the planning of it. Here, working continually with local and smaller satellite projects in larger change projects is said to be important.

- Communication that supports understanding of the rationale for the change and its importance. Most employees are described as having this understanding, hence the lack of opposition.

- Development of knowledge and roles. Change agents that drive changes are said to have been important.

This case illustrates the importance of managing change in an evolutionary, planned and sequential manner. It is also clear that monitoring the change work closely is vital to increase understanding of the course of events. In this regard, this case differs from mainstream success stories that are often based on anecdotal second-hand material (e.g. Beer & Nohria, 2000). But even with more advanced data collection and analysis, there are still problems. In the case of the consulting company, it is difficult to draw any definite conclusions about the importance of visible leadership, participation, communication, knowledge and roles from the material presented. The suggested guidance is rather general and fairly vague. As an example, the material says that leadership should be clear, which, by the way, is what most lists of how to implement successful change say. But what does clear leadership really involve? The meaning of leadership should be clarified before it can be made visible. Does it involve leaders regularly showing up and spending time speaking to people? Or does it mean that leaders should charismatically show the overarching direction through an evangelistic speech? Is it a matter of taking control by making decisions, taking action and, if necessary, forcing people by authoritative means? In other words, does visible leadership mean that leaders should be more visible or is it their actions – their leadership – that should be more visible? Is it about frequency or about big and distinct actions? Similar questions can be asked about many of the other guidelines, such as what do they mean in different contexts?

EXERCISE 5.4

Assume that you want to know more about a specific organization's culture. Draw upon Johnson et al.'s (2011) reasoning and try to identify the organization's culture by analyzing its expression in a variety of other subsystems, such as organizational structures, control systems, rituals and routines, stories and myths, symbols, power structures.

For example, can we say anything about the organizational culture of Apple Inc. through our knowledge of some of the stories, myths and symbols that we often hear or see regarding that organization? Do the stories and myths about Steven Jobs, for instance, suggest anything significant about the organizational culture at Apple?

Taking another example, can we say something about the culture at Amazon by listening to the stories told by Jeff Bezos or analyzing his way of leading the company? Does knowing something about the rather tough management control systems employed by the organization tell us anything about the culture at Amazon?

- Can you distinguish a cultural paradigm?
- Would you say that the culture is strong or weak? Why or why not?
- What does the strength of organizational culture suggest about the possibilities of managing organizational change?

REVIEW QUESTIONS 5.4

Recall	Briefly describe the meaning of the 'cultural web' and its central 'paradigm'.
Explain	In what way(s) can an integrated organizational model be used to better understand forces for and against change (as described in Lewin's force field analysis)?

ORGANIZATIONAL CHANGE AS A SEQUENTIAL PROCESS

There are numerous models that advocate that organizational change should proceed through a well-organized sequence of distinct steps, known as *n-step models*. Some of these models have gained huge impact, both in academia and practice, but they have also been subjected to severe criticism.

N-steps models of change

The models often include a mapping of potential barriers and opposition to implementation, as well as some form of recommended leadership. As a generalization, most of these models express an underlying rationalistic template that involves following a number of phases in a linear manner: analysis, planning, implementation and evaluation. There is a certain amount of variation within the scope of these, however, even though there is hardly any substantial departure from the rational basic assumptions (see Palmer et al. (2017) for a summary of nine of these models). The number of steps varies but otherwise the models are very similar. Already in the 1970s, a Scandinavian organizational scholar, Rhenman (1974), developed a model that describes change work in four phases:

1. Articulate a vision of the change.
2. Identify the forces for change.
3. Identify the barriers to change.
4. Develop and use methods for conflict resolution.

In this version, articulation of the vision and leadership have a more prominent role compared with Lewin's model. Otherwise, it would appear that Rhenman, just like many others, both clinical researchers and authors of mainstream texts, was inspired by the OD schools of thought.

A model that has gained a lot of influence is Kotter's 8-step model ([1996] 2012a). The model was developed based on Kotter's own practical experience with change work and is not a result of a scientific study. The model was designed to anticipate the typical problems that occur in change processes. *Why transformations fail* was the subtitle of Kotter's first publication (Kotter, 1995). The basic message was that the listed problems all needed to be handled, otherwise the organizational changes would never be implemented, acquisitions and mergers would not create synergies, changes would take too long and cost too much or a quality programme would not deliver what it promised. The list of problems was later developed into a model of how the mistakes could be avoided (Kotter, [1996] 2012a):

1. *Establishing a sense of urgency.* Often, too much self-contentment is permitted – we are good as we are – when a change process commences, so organizations fail to communicate to others about the need for change. Two important aspects are therefore:
   - To research the market and competitor landscape
   - To identify threats and opportunities.

2. *Forming a powerful guiding coalition.* Seldom are organizations successful in creating a powerful enough steering coalition for change, and therefore they don't achieve momentum in the change work. Soloists rarely produce results in organizational change processes. So, one therefore needs:

- To put together a group that has a mandate to drive change
- To get the group to work as a team.

3. *Creating a vision.* The importance of vision is often underestimated, and organizations therefore fail to use vision as a source of inspiration and a driver for the change work. One therefore needs:

- To develop a vision that can steer the change work
- To develop strategies that make the possibility of achieving the vision apparent.

4. *Communicating the vision.* Failing to communicate the vision weakens the chances of keeping the change work alive. One therefore needs:

- To use all opportunities to communicate the vision and the strategy
- To let the steering group be the role model of the type of behaviour that is expected of all those impacted by the change.

5. *Empowering others to act on the vision.* All too often mental and structural barriers are allowed to block the power of the vision and therefore the momentum of the change work. People buy in to the vision but are then paralyzed by structural barriers. One therefore needs:

- To get rid of barriers
- To change systems that undermine the vision for change
- To encourage risk-taking and non-traditional activities.

6. *Planning for and creating short-term wins.* Many organizations fail to make the results of change visible as and when they occur, and thereby risk losing momentum in the change work. One therefore needs:

- To plan to highlight progress early in the process
- To highlight and reward those who achieve quick wins.

7. *Consolidating improvements and producing still more change.* Many people claim victory too early and therefore fail to embed the change work adequately in the organizational culture. It is therefore important:

- To use the credibility that comes with quick changes to intensify the change in systems and structures that are considered to impede the changes
- To recruit, promote and develop people who can implement the vision for change
- To revitalize the change work continuously through new projects, themes and people.

8. *Institutionalizing new approaches.* Organizations often fail to embed the change work in their organizational culture, so the conditions for long-term change are thereby not created. What is central here is:

- To create better results through customer and productivity-oriented behaviour, more and better leadership and more effective management
- To articulate the connection between the new behaviour and organizational success
- To develop the means for ensuring leadership development and succession.

EXERCISE 5.5

Consider the case 'No "Musical chairs" – or...?' in Chapter 2 (pp. 31–32) and answer the following questions:

- Based on Kotter's 8-step model of change, what could the managers have done differently?

Thereafter, critically examine the different steps in Kotter's n-step model of change:

- Discuss their significance – what they mean – and their relevance for actions taken in an organizational change process. Base your discussion on the case or some relevant change in a contemporary organization on your own experience from a change process.
- Discuss also in what ways you regard these steps helpful in terms of managing change? For example:
  - What does it mean to create a sense of urgency and for whom is it important to create such feelings? What do we hope to accomplish and are there any risks in trying to create feelings of urgency for organizational change?
  - What is a governing coalition in practice? Who is supposed to be involved in such a group and who is to be left outside? What risks are connected with creating separate groups for change that normally entails some division of work?
  - How can a vision to change be communicated to people who have a fundamentally different understanding from the guiding coalition in terms of what the organization stands for and thus should focus on?

In recent years Kotter has updated his ideas and rebranded the eight steps as 'accelerators' (Kotter, 2012b, 2014). The background to the changes, he explains, is that in times of hyper-competition and rapid change, the traditional way of working – hierarchy-based operations – will not be enough. Instead of working in rigid, finite steps, accelerators need constantly to be at work. Furthermore, a small guiding coalition will not be enough. Instead, a larger 'volunteer army' made up of employees (approximately 10% of the workforce) who understand the need for change and are committed to implementing it, should be driving change in the organization. However, the eight accelerators are almost the same as the eight steps, with slightly more emphasis on strategic and multiple changes. A key message of Kotter (2012b) is still that leadership is important and top management still plays a crucial role. They are the ones that launch and maintain the network, make sure that people they trust are recruited as volunteers, and acknowledge and reinforce a sense of urgency to change.

The popularity of Kotter's model ([1996] 2012a) is notable. The ideas were first published as an article (Kotter, 1995) and a year later as a book (1996). These two publications have been the most cited texts on leading change (during the 1978–2012 period) and have framed both the practitioner and academic debate on the topic (Hughes, 2016). One possible explanation of this impact could be Kotter's ability to package and convey the message (Hughes, 2016). The model is prescriptive and presented in an up-beat tone. It could also be that it appeals to the likes of consultants and practitioners, partly because many who have been involved in change processes – which includes most people in modern organizations – easily recognize the issues and suggestions for solutions that are presented. Many people have likely been involved in specific change projects that, for different reasons, have lost momentum and fizzled out, without delivering any real results. Many have also probably listened to grand visions presented by some charismatic manager who has momentarily instilled a desire for change, but once people go back to their daily routines, they suddenly realize that there are many difficult barriers to the changes being implemented.

N-steps models of change problematized

On a general level, the challenges Kotter ([1996] 2012a, 2012b) brings up appear to be as obvious as many of the solutions are. For example, it seems obvious that barriers to change should be removed if you want to change.

In the same way, it can be easy to embrace Heracleous's (2001) or anyone's list of steps to be taken to implement change successfully. It is largely a matter of simply doing the good things and avoiding the bad. Most probably agree that there are barriers to people's ability to take the initiative or to act, and that it can be good to remove those barriers that counteract change, but that is really fairly trivial. Such barriers can include things like formal structures that get in the way of employees' initiative, lack of knowledge, inappropriate incentive systems and recruitment principles, or bad managers that don't allow their employees to act in accordance with the organization's vision. In general, much of this advice sounds reasonable, but the issue is what they mean in practice. For example, what is good or bad leadership, as mentioned in point 8? Is a good leader someone who participates in the change work by talking to their employees about what is happening and showing interest in and a commitment to substantial development, or is it a person who keeps their distance, avoids communicating so as not to take over the change work and thereby reduce the motivation of those who are more involved in it? In the same way, one can ask what a supportive or obstructive structure actually means. Are fixed guidelines needed to support ways of cooperating and evaluating the direction of change, or is it better to have more flexible forms whereby one is expected to act and change without guidelines or structural support? A number of people suggest that vision can act as a support for action and encouragement, but vision is normally vague and fluffy in nature and may not always be so helpful to guide action.

As mentioned above, it is easy to accept the problems and solutions articulated in n-step models, but the expressions are often standardized, which limit their value. The question is what they mean and what relevance they have in a local change context. The models can be seen as 'reminder-lists', rather than providing a solid theoretical perspective that increases an understanding of the complexity of change and change management. Accordingly, the lists can occasionally help to structure some of the diagnoses and analyses in a change context, but they also risk distancing the change work from those on the receiving end (Alvesson & Sveningsson, 2015). How do we know whether employees feel inspired or even believe that the vision for change is serious? Who has not heard a manager, consultant or change agent talk about the importance of change only for the ideas and vision not to be followed up with action? Instead of mobilizing engagement, the risk is that frustration, irritation, cynicism or even opposition are evoked.

MINI CASE 5.4

A sense of urgency?

Structural changes in the UK healthcare sector is nothing new. However, the new strategy presented by the Chief Medical Officer (CMO) for England in 2002, was quite out of the ordinary. For the Public Health Laboratory Services (PHLS) it meant the most significant changes they had faced in over its 50 years of existence. From a managerial perspective, this radical change was necessary since there was an urgent need for change in response to terrorist threats, spurred by the terror acts of 9/11 in the US. The ability to efficiently respond to different types of potential future terrorist threats – biological, chemical and radiological – had become crucial. A grand strategy for combating infectious disease was thus introduced, where the key strategic idea was to take responsibility for managing biological, radiological and chemical threats to the public. In practice, it involved breaking up the current network of over 40 laboratories and transferring the surveillance and specialist laboratory functions and the remaining network to a newly created organization – the Health Protection Agency (HPA) – and merging it with the National Radiological Protection Board (NRPB) and the Microbiological Research Authority (MRA), among others. The HPA should have had a leading role in helping to prepare for the new emerging health threats. This change was supposed to take place within a year and affect around 5,000 employees.

From one perspective, there was an urgent need for change due to terrorist threats. Among employees in the organization, however, there was no widespread sense of urgency to implement the changes. Instead, many of the employees asked for the rationale of the changes to be better explained and made relevant to them specifically. There was an overarching strategic plan of 'Getting Ahead of the Curve', but for the people in the organization it lacked clarity, and they sought a more precise description of the vision, tailored to the needs of the audience.

What is shown in this case is that events in the environment (such as a large-scale terrorist attack) do not in themselves lead to a sense of urgency. It could of course have triggered certain ideas and been used as an argument for an organizational change in a certain direction – here focusing on specializing work functions – but other people might understand the situation differently and advocate a different sort of development. The government provided an overarching vision, but it was not enough for the employees, who asked for it to be made more relevant for them.

Source: Bamford & Daniel (2005)

Even though social and cultural aspects are mentioned as being important in several of the models above, they all emphasize some form of situational orientation (Dunphy & Stace, 1988, 1993) – the significance of the context often remains underemphasized. Organizational culture is often said to be the single largest cause of organizational change failure (Balogun & Johnson, 2005). However, organizational culture is often regarded as another managerial tool and many models are based upon a so-called variable view of culture, suggesting that organizations *have* cultures that can be changed and controlled. Culture thus becomes a variable with which to experiment and align with other subsystems (such as structure and control systems) (see the top half of Figure 5.6).

An alternative to this functionalistic tool view is to understand organizations *as* cultures. This implies adopting a more anthropologically-oriented view on culture, considering culture as a root metaphor (Smircich, 1983) – as a way of looking at the world (see the lower half of Figure 5.6). Viewing organizations as cultures suggests that other subsystems, such as leadership, structure and incentive-systems, should be understood as expressions of culture as they have been developed in a particular organizational cultural context. This metaphorical view of organizational culture acknowledges the relevance of paying attention to meanings and interpretations in order to understand organizational change.

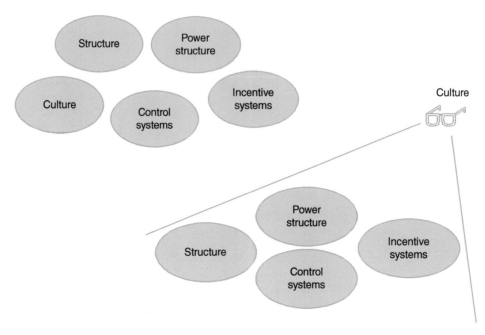

FIGURE 5.6 Culture as a variable and as a root metaphor

Recognizing the relevance of meaning and sense-making points at the importance of acknowledging how people understand and interpret change, rather than assuming that people's ideas about change are well-aligned with managers' ideas or visions for change, or that culture is something mangers can control (Alvesson, 2012). This involves a more process-oriented view of change, which we will discuss more thoroughly in Chapters 6 and 7.

EXERCISE 5.6

What do you think are the advantages of planning according to an n-step logic? Do you see any risks or problems with following an n-step logic? Would you follow such a recipe when driving a change project? Why or why not? Discuss this proposition in a small group.

REVIEW QUESTIONS 5.5

Recall	List the steps in any of the planning models that express a sequential view on organizational change.
Explain	Why are the n-step guides so popular among managers? Discuss.
Reflect	What contingencies or situations do you think typically create the most serious problem with applying an n-step model rigidly in a change process? Based on your arguments, in what ways can we work with these models in actual change work?
Reflect	What perspective of culture comes through in Tichy's model? Is the view of culture in the model limiting managerial thinking of change in any way?

SUMMARY

In this chapter we have focused on organizational change – either revolutionary or evolutionary – as being a result of more normative-oriented tool-based activities, whether as more distinct n-step activities and/or as articulations of, and work with, organizational design. This change work normally builds upon analyses of organizations and their relationships with the external environment in a broad sense, including a variety of stakeholders. These analyses are often carried out from a systems perspective of organizations and their environments, and are therefore focused on identifying the misalignments to be tackled with the help of organizational changes.

A systems perspective of organizations involves seeing organizations as living organisms in constant need of 'nutrition' from their environment to ensure long-term survival. Consequently, an organization must achieve a balance or fit between how it rewards those that provide 'nutrition' – the stakeholders – and what these require in order to contribute to the organization's long-term health. A systems perspective also means considering the organization as consisting of a number of different subsystems that should also be aligned to each other for long-term health and survival.

As stated above, analyses of organizations as organisms are intended to identify misalignments between different subsystems, as well as between the organization and its environment. This is considered to be particularly significant when the environment is complex, changing and turbulent. The identification of misalignments – for example, through analyses of gaps between where the organization currently is and where it wants to be in future, given developments and changes in the environment – forms the foundation for managing organizational change.

In addition to describing the systems perspective and models for analyzing the need for change, we also highlighted models for how change should be managed. The basic idea of these models is that organizational change can be formulated in a sequential and well-planned n-step logic and/or with the help of more organizationally-oriented design, the latter of which has a stronger focus on the different subsystems of the organization.

Organizational change in this regard is often a management-initiated drawing-board project in which it is assumed that change can be coordinated and led with the help of sophisticated analyses. A key problem with this assumption is that organizations and organizational changes are often difficult to manage. In particular, radical changes are mostly characterized by a high degree of uncertainty, which is connected to unpredictable changes in the environment. Yet what is important here is also that it is seldom known how people who are targeted by change initiatives interpret and make sense of things such as change plans, formulations of visions and strategies, etc. In change contexts it is therefore crucial to recognize and acknowledge local understanding, interpretation and sentiment. However, the models presented in this chapter often neglect much of the concrete and local organizational reality. A central question is what happens when ideas and initiatives of change are set in motion in real organizational change situations?

Another problem is that the models are often too abstract and propose things that are self-evident – that one should do the things that are good and avoid those which are bad. The models thereby become rather clichéd and banal, which reinforces the trivialization of the context in which they are intended to be applied. This limits some of the models' prescriptive (and descriptive) strengths.

 # KEY PRACTICAL INSIGHTS

What we can say about organizational change following this chapter:

1. Organizational change commonly comprises a certain complexity in terms of affecting many interrelated subsystems of the whole organizational system. Viewed from the perspective of systems theory, even a seemingly rather insignificant change often entails a range of both intended and unintended consequences because the organization consists of various more or less well-aligned subsystems. Even smaller changes, therefore, call for a broader organizational perspective – such as the systems view – in change work.

2. Integrated organizational models can be seen as diagnostic tools in that they enable a broader and a more complex view of the possibilities and challenges in managing change in organizations. This facilitates situating organizational change efforts in broader cultural, political and social contexts.

3. Managing organizational change normally means including organizational culture as a key element in the toolbox. Besides being considered a subsystem in itself – something that organizations have – organizational culture should also be acknowledged as a perspective or metaphor – something that organizations are. The latter suggests that the various organizational subsystems, and thus the organization in its entirety, can be seen as an expression of the organizational culture, sometimes framed as the cultural net.

4. N-step models of change can help in structuring change processes in well-defined phases and also provide a certain optimism about the possibility to accomplish change successfully.

5. However, n-step models do need to be approached with certain caution. While injecting a large dose of optimism about the manageability of change, the models in question marginalize many facets of change that often complicate the life of change agents.

CASE

Oticon – radically changing an integrated organizational model in the hearing aid industry

The Danish hearing aid company Oticon can serve as an interesting embodiment of an integrated organization. Oticon was founded at the beginning of the 20th century and had been successful for many years when strong competitors entered the hearing aid industry in the 1980s and threatened Oticon. Responding to the new situation in order to realign Oticon to the demands of the market, the company changed its vision, strategy and organization. In the process of radically changing the company away from being a traditional, departmentalized and bureaucratic business, they developed an entirely new and integrated organization, comprising major changes in most of the organizational subsystems. As stated in 1988 by the newly recruited CEO, Lars Kolind:

> The vision was to develop a truly knowledge-based company, which could make a difference in the form of a breakthrough in user satisfaction with hearing aids. This not only requires a creative combination of technology, audiology and psychology, but also a much closer cooperation between the different professionals involved in the actual selling, fitting and fine-tuning of the hearing aid to the needs of each individual user.

As this quote reveals, we can see how the company includes its customers as a key stakeholder. In approaching the customers and the market, upon his arrival, Kolind also reframed the business they were in, stating that they were not in the hearing aid business, but rather in

(Continued)

the business of making people smile. In terms of organizational structure, Kolind redesigned it radically by introducing the so-called 'spaghetti organization', a kind of team-based project organization that gave substantial freedom to project leaders to select their own team members (and allowed employees to refuse to be selected to a particular team). At the time of its change, Oticon was seen as one of the first knowledge-intensive and paperless organizations in the world (Peters, 1992). In terms of radical change initiatives, Kolind was also famous for prompting a dramatic reduction of the workforce, creating a 'lean team' and engaging all the remaining employees in development activities.

In order to form a strong organizational culture that aligned with the strategy of quality and innovation, the employees were encouraged to share the corporate values of trust, empowerment, open communication and respect for the individual. Rather than focusing on creating a relaxed culture, challenging goals and individual development were explicitly emphasized. In line with the strategy and vision, employees were encouraged to think the unthinkable and to challenge the status quo. They were also asked to challenge managers' views and to eliminate activities that did not add value to customers, who were seen as a key stakeholder in the near environment. To some extent we can see this as an effort to replace traditional management control with normative control, by enabling individual employees to identify with the organizational culture and identity.

In line with the idea of encouraging everyone to challenge the existing business state of affairs, symbols such as titles were also abolished and decisions were to be made by those influenced by them. In an effort to empower subordinates, Kolind introduced a new custom: 'When in doubt – then do it. If it works, it's good; if not, you're forgiven' and 'It's easier to be forgiven than to get approval'. Kolind clarified this by stating that:

> The employees' hidden resources are brought out so they can play together like an efficient football team where each individual knows the objectives and the strategy and can kick the ball immediately without having to look up the rules and ask why.

Kolind was not afraid to change traditional power structures by giving employees responsibility. From his time as a boy scout, he knew that good results could be achieved through cooperation and delegating responsibility: 'No one can resist confidence. That is the greatest thing a manager can give an employee, and it most certainly activates creativity.'

In addition to this integrated view of Oticon, there was the leadership exercised by Kolind himself. Not long after many of the strategic and organizational realignment measures were taken, the company began to show market and financial success, and Kolind was increasingly seen as a role model for how to turn around and lead – in terms of inspiration and ideas – a knowledge-intensive organization. As suggested by one of his employees when talking about Kolind's leadership in encouraging empowerment: '[O]ne of the really nice things about him … he is extremely good at letting people do the things themselves.'

Although much of this sounds impressive and illustrates successful alignment in organizations, a word of caution is required. It has also been suggested that the great idea did not work out as intended. Gradually corporate reality became more conventional, while Kolind continued to express his vision to an admiring business press. Also, many employees felt proud of the company, despite the mismatch between the claimed ideals and actual practice (Kjærgaard et al., 2011).

Sources: Döjback & Söndegaard (2004); Kjærgaard et al. (2011); Joost & Pim (2017); Larsen (1996); Peters (1992); B. Taylor (2018)

Questions

1. Characterize the strategic and organizational changes at Oticon by conducting an analysis of alignment between different organizational subsystems.

2. It is mentioned in the case that the traditional hierarchical control is replaced by normative control. What challenges do you see in trying to work with normative control in order to foster an environment of innovation?

3. What kind of leadership do you think is appropriate and significant in order to implement an atmosphere of confidence among the employees in an organization striving for innovation?

4. Can you think of any other organization that would benefit from implementing some of the organizational characteristics – downplaying hierarchies, implementing spaghetti organization, promoting employee to challenge managers, emphasizing innovation, exercising leadership as trust – the one at Oticon? Why?

 # FURTHER READING

Ackoff, R., & Gharajedaghi, J. (1996). Reflections on systems and their models. *Systems Research*, 13(1), 13–23.

Burns, T., & Stalker, G. (1961). *The management of innovation*. London: Tavistock.

Heracleous, L. (2001). An ethnographic study of culture in the context of organizational change. *The Journal of Applied Behavioral Science*, 37(4), 426–446.

Hughes, M. (2016). Leading changes: Why transformation explanations fail. *Leadership*, 12(4), 449–469.

Kotter, J. (2012) Accelerate! How the most innovative companies capitalize on today's rapid-fire strategic challenges. *Harvard Business Review*, 90(11), 43–58.

Lozano, R. (2015). A holistic perspective on corporate sustainability drivers. *Corporate Social Responsibility and Environmental Management*, 22, 32–44.

Scott, R., & Davis, G. (2016). *Organizations and Organizing: Rational, natural and open systems perspectives* (4th ed.). New York: Routledge.

THE PROCESS PERSPECTIVE: FOCUS ON INTERPRETATIONS AND UNDERSTANDINGS

LEARNING OBJECTIVES

When you have completed your study of this chapter, you should be able to:

- Describe and appraise the main characteristics of the process perspective.

- Explain the significance and relevance of the process perspective for understanding organizational change.

- Contrast the process perspective to the tool-based perspective in key dimensions.

- Explain how people's interpretation of change efforts and formulations can be understood in relation to their background, experiences, identity and profession.

- Recognize and discuss the key significance of acknowledging politics in change processes.

- Appraise how a process perspective can facilitate organizational change work.

At the end of the last chapter we touched upon organizational change as a process, although within the framework of a systems approach focused on management-driven change. We also emphasized that there are various shortcomings with the systems models as they marginalize the social and cultural contexts in which changes take place. The organizational context in which change occurs, and which is also the subject of change, is considered in an instrumental way – as a system among other subsystems that has to be managed and controlled. The central premise in that approach is that it is possible to plan and predict organizational change. The change work is typically described at an abstract and neutral level, and circumstances that are often the most difficult to work with during change processes are neglected. The latter concerns people's understandings and interpretations of the change work and the importance of the social, cultural and political contexts in which these interpretations arise and are intertwined.

As we also saw in the last chapter, prescriptive, tool-oriented studies primarily focus on how change should be carried out, but neglect to describe what happens in practice when plans are put into action. However, successful organizational change is not simply about the ideas, intentions and well-formulated plans that are created by senior organizational management. It is also, and maybe even more so, a result of the local interpretations that occur during interactions between the members of the organization, members that are expected to put the plans into local operation in a meaningful manner. How these people interpret the situation will affect their subsequent actions, and in turn to what extent managerial change plans will be implemented.

One of the central characteristics of the process perspective is the interest in how employees perceive, interpret and understand a change situation (Jabri, 2012; Weick, 1995). Instead of focusing primarily on management and their change ambitions, we now widen the lens to also include other members of the organization and what happens when change plans are implemented and meet the organizational reality. A specific focus is on how those impacted by the organizational changes experience and look upon the situation: How are change plans received? What do the change plans mean to those targeted by change initiatives? How do organizational members consider the new situation? A key idea here is that the practical result of an organizational change process is dependent on people's interpretations. In order to take this into account, we now take a more descriptive and understanding-oriented perspective of the course of events.

Furthermore, organizational change is not necessarily initiated from the top. Beyond what happens in relation to the officially formulated change plans, continuous adjustments, modifications and local adaptations also occur in organizations, with potentially long-term consequences for the organization and its strategy. A process perspective attempts to portray more carefully and in detail what happens during change work, not only in centrally formulated and initiated attempts at change, but also in emergent organizational changes.

We start by describing the origin and emergence of this perspective, which can generally be seen as a counter-reaction and criticism of the tool-oriented perspective. We then outline the perspective's defining features. In the remainder of the chapter, three descriptive, in-depth process-oriented studies are discussed in more detail. Prolonged case descriptions are followed by discussions about what conclusions and practical insights can be drawn from these.

ORIGIN AND EMERGENCE OF THE PROCESS PERSPECTIVE

The basic ideas of the process perspective can be traced back to the situational theory within organizational research. In particular, Woodward (1958) and Burns and Stalker (1961) are considered to be significant authors (Dawson, 2003). Their contributions to change theory include empirically oriented and content-rich portrayals of change processes in practice. In these descriptions, power is brought into the picture, such as the importance of political game-playing, rhetoric, alliances and negotiations in organizational change processes.

Child's (1972) central focus on the individual as a change agent with the capacity to make strategic decisions is also highlighted as a significant contribution to the understanding of the dynamics between stability and change. Here, it is argued that besides structural and contextual determinants, people – with intentions and agency – also influence change and development. The view of organizational change as a political process was thereby developed, as was the view of individuals as active parties in an organizational context. A more dynamic view of organizations emerged in this way, both in terms of how the relations between the individual and the organization (and its context) were understood, and in terms of how the relations between change and continuity were considered.

A dynamic and integrated view of change processes

One of the most significant initial contributions to the process perspective was Pettigrew's study of the company ICI (see Mini Case 6.1). In contrast to earlier studies on organizational change, his study stands out in its long-term focus on how change historically came about as a result of political processes.

MINI CASE 6.1

Organizational change and strategic development

At the British chemicals company ICI, organizational change efforts, initiated already in the 1960s as a response to environmental triggers and pressures to change, were ongoing for pretty much most of the 1970s. These and other incremental change efforts slowly

(Continued)

produced a strategic change that became apparent in the 1980s. The change process was characterized by countless individual interpretations, decisions and actions at different levels and in different departments and functions. Among other things, it involved interpretations of internal change initiatives, plans and actions, as well as interpretations of the market development, the economy and politics. These interpretations were seldom well coordinated with each other in all-encompassing formal and rational organizational analyses. Organizational analyses took place but were seldom coordinated between different groups of managers and other employees or between the different divisions of the larger organization. Interpretations and actions were influenced by the backgrounds, ambitions, interests, professional profiles, organizational seniority, sense of departmental belonging, etc., of those involved. Those in charge of or otherwise involved in the change processes manoeuvred and plotted in a highly bureaucratic and politically very conservative organizational context and organizational culture. It was a context where various means of power – resources, the 'right' language, shared understandings of the organization and its environment – were mobilized in committees, among consultants, in investigations, work groups, informal project groups and other forums as people attempted to undermine the existing state of the organization (and subsequently its strategy) in order to legitimize change.

Source: Pettigrew (1985)

Among other things, the ICI case illustrates the political aspect of change processes and the importance of creating legitimacy and an ideological platform among key actors involved in the change work. Pettigrew (1985) also highlights how people tried to influence the beliefs of others, for example about an organization's history, need for change and future prospects. One particular political instrument of power brought forward is the use of symbolism, which includes reference to organizational myths, stories, narratives and dogma. The importance of managing meaning and the general significance of the cultural and interpretative dimensions in organizational change is thus highly underscored (Smircich & Morgan, 1982). This does not rule out that elements of classic rationality in terms of analyses and plans can have an effect, but they are subject to political and cultural influences that create a more complex and symbolic change process. All in all, Pettigrew provides, both vertically and horizontally, a more integrated and complex portrayal of change processes. Vertically in the sense that different levels – individual, group and organization as well as social, economic and political factors – are related to each other. This is sometimes referred to as a multi-level or several-layered analysis that places organizational change processes in a broader macroeconomic, social and political context. Horizontally in the sense that changes in a wider time context – as a result of past, current and future projections – are considered.

MINI CASE 6.2

Puma vs Adidas – a tale of two brothers

The fierce competition between the two sport brands, Puma and Adidas, illustrates how individual factors can have significant impact on the undertakings at a group and organizational level. It also shows how the past can be intertwined with the present – an old quarrel between the founders seemed to have influenced the development of the two companies for decades.

Adidas and Puma were founded in the late 1940s by two brothers, Adolf (Adi) Dassler and Rudolf (Rudi) Dassler, respectively. The brothers initially worked together, but a family quarrel spurred them to each establish their own brands. Both companies were founded in the small German town of Herzogenaurach. The dispute between the two brothers turned into a fierce rivalry between the companies. Their rivalry even came to divide the citizens of the town – people either belonged to a Puma or an Adidas family depending on where the parents worked. As a result of this, Herzogenaurach became known as 'the town of the lowered gaze' since the residents had developed a habit of glancing down at the shoes of people they met in order to early on establish to what side they belonged. This habit even lingers on today among the older generation. According to Mayor German Hacker, 'if someone comes in through the door, your gaze still wanders to their shoes'.

The conflict and rivalry have over the years spurred the development of the companies. In a constant competition to be faster, better and bigger than the other, these two businesses have grown into world-renowned brands. Adidas was ahead in terms of technical know-how, but Puma, with a stronger sales force and ability to adapt, has played catch-up. It could, though, have been their intense focus on each other that made them slow to react to the competition from Nike, which now dominates the athletic footwear industry.

The two camps in Herzogenaurach remained as long as the brothers lived (to the end of the 1970s). Both Adidas and Puma are now public limited companies and no longer in family ownership.

Sources: Ahktar (2013); Schwar (2018)

Pettigrew (1997) has presented five principles that are necessary to take into account in understanding organizational change as an emergent process, i.e. recognizing the importance of context and that changes occur incrementally as a process of events evolving over time:

- *Embeddedness* – Social processes are deeply embedded in their context, and both the inner and outer context of the organization needs to be taken into account when studying organizational change. The inner context relates to the structural, political and cultural environment of the organization and the outer context includes macro dimensions, such as the economic, social and political milieu of the firm. Changes can occur at several different levels simultaneously, and can relate to each other in different ways. Therefore, change processes should be studied from different levels of analysis.

- *Temporal interconnectedness* – Organizational change processes do not take place in a vacuum and should be studied as being linked to the past, present and future. It is crucial to understand the history of the organization, specifically how people comprehend and view the past. Through people's understandings of what has happened, the past becomes active in the present, and can be a key factor in the shaping of the future.

- *Action and contexts* – Both actions and contexts need to be considered. It is not a matter of focusing, and thereby reducing, the processes to either actions or context, but rather to understand the dynamics between the two. Actions take place in (and are constrained by) the context at the same time as actions (intentions and agency) shape the context (see Giddens, 1979).

- *Holism* – In order to take the three previous principles into account, one needs to aim for a holistic rather than a linear and singular explanation of the change course of events. Instead of searching for one grand theory, a more comprehensive, in-depth analysis and a search for multiple, interconnecting conditions that can explain the development should be undertaken. In particular, longitudinal case studies are suggested.

- *Processes and outcomes* – If the processes can relate to the results that emerge, it is an advantage. Demonstrating a clear connection between processes and outcomes can anchor the study of organizational change by providing a focal point. However, emphasis should not solely be on the outcome, as both the processes and the outcomes are important, i.e. how processes lead to and shape a variety of outcomes.

Taken together, these principles stress the value of broadly recognizing the content, process and context of change, thereby also acknowledging its complexity and dynamism in time.

This way of understanding change has been enormously influential and has been drawn on in numerous studies of change over the last three decades (see Mirfakhar et al., 2018; Sminia, 2016; Todnem et al., 2018). For example, Mirfakhar et al. (2018) explicitly draw on the framework of content, process and context in a review of empirical studies of the factors that influence the successful implementation of HR practices. For example, in terms of content, they show that elements such as user-friendliness are highly important, but also that the characteristics of HR practice, such as its degree of complexity, matter too. The latter suggests that a performance appraisal may be more difficult to implement than salary information. Next to the content, they also show the relevance of the process – in this case the actions by managers, HR professionals, etc. – for the implementation of HR practices. They discuss elements such as training, incentives, planning, the clarification of roles and communication. These actions are shown to take place in different kinds of contexts, such as the broader macro context (industry, national culture), the meso context (organizational culture, existing policies) and the micro context (the abilities and power of HR professionals). Their review also reveals the importance of time dynamics, as contextual conditions tend to continuously change, which impacts on the implementation of practice. Mirfakhar et al. (2018) conclude that their dynamic view is consistent with Pettigrew's view of change in terms of acknowledging both structure (context) and agency (actions) in time.

EXERCISE 6.1

Conduct a short analysis of an organizational change process that you have experienced or that you have read about in secondary sources. This could be a small and seemingly insignificant change, but one which had unforeseen or unrecognized consequences for the organization. Apply two or three of the principles that Pettigrew formulated for the purpose of understanding change.

In what ways are the principles helpful in getting a more in-depth understanding of the change process? Appraise the value of the principles from a managerial perspective.

EXERCISE 6.2

Translate Pettigrew's (1997) five principles for studying change from a process perspective into practical managerial insights. In other words, how can Pettigrew's principles improve our understanding of how to manage organizational change more successfully?

The process perspective as a reaction against the tool-based perspective

Another important component in the emergence of the process perspective was the growing criticism directed at tool-based change theory (Dawson, 2003). This criticism was often formulated against a background of in-depth case studies which described how organizations changed and developed in real life. Pettigrew has been a key figure in this critical approach, repeatedly emphasizing that much of the traditional and prescriptive change literature omitted and trivialized the historic, processual and contextual circumstances, and thus were of less practical value (Collins, 1998).

More broadly, there are three main lines of criticism of the tool-based perspective that can be discerned among process scholars. First, the belief that it is possible to formulate universal recipes for managing change is criticized, as these trivialize the significance of the context and therefore the organization's cultural, political and historical circumstances (Pettigrew, 2012). Of course, culture, politics and power are also sometimes discussed in classical texts, but they are then often reduced to tools for managing and controlling change (see for example, Heracleous & Langham, 1996; Tichy, 1983). Further, by treating organizational change as a process that occurs during a limited period of time, the organization's history and traditions are pushed into the background and sometimes obscured (Dawson, 2014). Second, the somewhat clichéd tone of much of the popular change literature is also questioned as it trivializes the inherent complexity of change processes. As we mentioned in the previous chapter, much of the content sounds intuitively good, but perhaps does not say much more than that one should do the things that are good and avoid those that are bad (Alvesson & Sveningsson, 2015). Complex change processes are thus often reduced to banalities and platitudes with hardly any descriptive and prescriptive relevance. Third, normative change literature has been accused of overstating the possibility of managing and controlling change processes (see Collins, 1998; Dawson, 2003). Optimism about the possibility of controlling changes from a managerial level, which is prominent in many of these models, may explain their popularity. The problem, however, is that their simplified and idealistic managerial focus implies that complex and unpredictable change processes are thrown out of the spotlight, and, by extension, these models say very little about what happens in practice.

Process-oriented studies of change can be understood to be a reaction against these failures.

REVIEW QUESTIONS 6.1

Recall	Briefly explain some of the key ideas that have influenced the origin and emergence of the process perspective.
Explain	Describe three areas of critique of the tool-based perspective raised by the proponents of the process perspective.
Explain	Explain why viewing change as an (emergent) process does not necessarily imply the application of a process perspective on organizational change.
Reflect	Compare the process perspective with the tool-based perspective and think about why the tool-based perspective seems to dominate in so much of the practitioner-oriented literature about change. Why is it that, considering what we know about the complexity on change today, the tool-based perspective still appeals to many of those actively engaged in change processes?

THE PROCESS PERSPECTIVE – DEFINING FEATURES

Simply put, change as a process means that change is seen as a result of people's daily communication, discussions, decisions and actions. It may often be the efforts of top management that instigate organizational changes to adapt in the business environment, but it can just as well be initiated by others in the organization. For instance, organizational change processes can be fuelled by political power struggles between departments, regarding which interests should be prioritized in conjunction with new product development, or by a group's or an individual's attempt to launch an alternative view of how the organization should innovate or strategically develop. A central premise is that organizations are viewed as being in a frequent state of change.

Organizations as an ongoing accomplishment

The process perspective of change has its roots in social constructionism (Berger & Luckmann, 1966) and can be related to what Weick (1995) labels *sensemaking*. Organizations are here viewed as an ongoing accomplishment; in other words, something that people continuously create, recreate and maintain beliefs about while making sense of what is going on around them. From this perspective, it is less interesting to talk about the organization in and of itself (as a form of well-defined objective entity), and more interesting to focus on people's views and assumptions. These views and assumptions are created in interaction with others, which the term *social* constructions suggests. It is therefore primarily the shared, rather than individual, understandings that are in focus.

A driving force behind social constructions are people's 'efforts to create order and make retrospective sense of what occurs' (Weick, 1993, p. 635). Instead of assuming that people live in an objective, 'ready-made' reality, it is emphasized that people try to rationalize what is going on – in acts of sensemaking – by infusing meaning into their experiences. By doing that, understandings of reality are created and sustained.

Taken together, this means that interpersonal interactions are central, as it is through communicating with each other that people give meaning to what is happening around them. And it is in these types of processes the organization is created, maintained and sometimes changed (Brown et al., 2005). For example, the meaning and consequences of formal work procedures, work conditions or lines of reporting are formed by the communication and talk that occurs in relationships between people in a workplace.

Through the process perspective, then, organizations are considered to be frequently changing as people continuously try to comprehend formal organizational procedures and initiatives (change attempts, guidelines from the head office, lines of reporting, structures, and so on) by reflecting and communicating with each other. Individuals interpret what is happening, and might also try to control and influence other people's interpretations by proclaiming and arguing for the validity of their point of view. They thereby frequently contribute to adaptations and changing views about specific elements, such as work methods, leadership, procedures and problem-solving techniques. Thus, organizational change is understood as an ongoing process that takes place in relationships, wherein sensemaking is central (Jian, 2011; Thomas et al., 2011). This is referred to as organizations being in a state of continuous change (Tsoukas & Chia, 2002; Weick & Quinn, 1999).

REVIEW QUESTIONS 6.2

Reflect (a) Imagine an acrobat posing and holding his/her balance on a high wire. Would you primarily describe what the acrobat is doing in terms of stability or movement? Make a note to yourself and then continue reading the text below.

Both answers are possible. You could consider the acrobat as someone standing still, thus describe what the acrobat is doing in terms of stability. Or you could focus on the continuous but minor adjustments the acrobat makes in order to hold the position and thus describe the acrobat as being in constant motion.

(b) When you answered question (a), did you imagine the acrobat being far away or close to you? If you imagine the opposite, would you then give a different answer?

(c) Relate this thought experiment to how organizations are seen (as stable by some and in constant flux by others). What conclusions can you draw from this comparison?

The process perspective takes a close-up view on organizations and considers change to be the result of the various decisions, the communication and the actions that are carried out daily by employees at different levels (not uncommonly at a local operational level) and within different functions and various capacities. Proponents of this view of change believe that if one regards organizations from a distance, they can occasionally look fairly stable, but upon closer examination of what actually happens every day in organizations, one sees that they are more frequently changing.

Organizational change seen from a process perspective can derive from formal ambitions and plans as well as originate informally from people and social processes within the organization, such as for instance political games or struggles for resources between different departments, disagreements over priorities, or different employees pushing for a change in work methods or better working conditions. Change is, in other words, not necessarily seen as a result of formulated initiatives from the organization's management or particular senior managers. On the contrary, change can occur as a result of evolutionary and long-term processes, as Tsoukas and Chia (2002, p. 580) propose: 'Change occurs naturally, incrementally and inexorably through "creep", "slippage" and "drift" as well as natural "spread".' Taking this into account, our view of formal change attempts needs to be expanded; formal change initiatives can lead to a realization of plans but they may also lead to stability that is maintained or even reinforced, depending upon how the plans are received and acted upon (Alvesson & Sveningsson, 2015).

Focus on interpretation

The processual perspective of change places great emphasis on understanding how people interpret and understand the situation, and it thereby becomes valuable to follow change processes over time. To avoid becoming lost in the complexity, Dawson (2003) proposes paying attention to the three dimensions of politics, context and content, and to consider the mutual exchanges between them. This can involve examining the following: How do the members of an organization view the scope of a planned change? From their perspective, what is it that is going to be changed? For them, is it important that the change happens? In Chapter 2 we discussed different ways of labelling a change initiative. The point here is to remember that a change in itself does not have certain objective characteristics but that people *attribute* different properties to it. Even when it is a matter of the organization's internal and external context, as we raised in Chapter 3, it is the different actors' *understanding* of the context that is in focus. Internal and external contexts are often the subject of varying interpretations, which in the end can result in disagreements and conflicts. A process perspective recognizes and appreciates the existence of diverse and sometimes conflicting portrayals of an organization. Conflicts might be about an organization's current status and/or what can justifiably – or not – be changed given the organization's future visions and ambitions. There is seldom one unambiguous version of events that everybody agrees on and that can become a cohesive foundation for a shared commitment to change. One of the things that defines process studies is their openness to this diversity, and their interest in how the people involved in a change process view and react to the change events.

EXERCISE 6.3

Consider the case below and answer the following questions:

- Have you experienced or do you know of any cases where people at different levels of an organization interpret and describe the situation at hand profoundly differently?
- From a managerial point of view, what potential risks do you see with this kind of divergence in interpretations?

CASE

Extensive vertical collaboration and team-spirit, or...?

During an organizational change in an Australian manufacturing company, there were diverging accounts on the current status of the vertical collaboration. At least three competing versions could be distinguished:

The managers described the organization as 'very much a work-together team' and emphasized that they were heading towards being a 'world-class operation', pointing out that the people of the organization would be world class too.

The supervisors, on their part, did not agree that the organization was a collaborative team. For them, the role of the managers was to inform the workers about what was going on in the company and to make sure that they were updated on what decisions were made. According to the supervisors, the managers needed to communicate more to all employees and not only with supervisors and leading hands.

The employees emphasized that the mass media version on the current state of the organization was not correct: 'It's not like what you read in the papers'. According to the employees, the managers got all the recognition at the expense of the workers, who did not get their share of the limelight. This perception, too, was clearly at odds with the 'working together' version of the organization held by the managers.

Source: Dawson and Buchanan (2005)

Focus on politics

It is common for processual studies to take into account the existence of organizational politics, even if not all of the authors express this point as strongly as Dawson (2003), who believes that organizational politics should be a central part of change studies. A political view of organizational change assumes that the objectives of changes are never obvious or unambiguous in terms of how people view them. Thus, an organization's management team cannot implement change solely by communicating a change plan based on traditional, rational reasoning. Rather, a political perspective recognizes the existence of a pluralism of interests and different actors' desires to push their own interests using different means of power. Instead of assuming a harmony of interests, the spotlight here is on friction, tensions and conflicts in change processes. In this regard, organizational change involves negotiating, convincing, persuading, building alliances and legitimacy, mobilizing resources, threatening, scaremongering, promising and other activities that are part of the political game (Pfeffer, 1992). It is not uncommon for this to be accentuated at the beginning of change projects, when plans are being formulated and there needs to be agreement on future priorities and resource allocation (Pettigrew, 1985).

A process perspective is interested in politics both within and outside the organization and highlights how people mobilize the means of power to push their own more or less conscious interests and ambitions.

MINI CASE 6.3

Public power struggles at Volkswagen

Sometimes political struggles in organizations are made public, as in the power play at the very top managerial levels of Volkswagen. The former chairman, Ferdinand Piëch, had a long history of winning power struggles, and had been involved in the German company for over two decades. He was known to be a demanding and mercurial person, both in his role as the chief executive and later on as the chairman of the supervisory board. When he declared, in an interview with the German magazine *Der Spiegel* in April 2015, that he was distancing himself from the CEO, Martin Winterkorn, many expected that Winterkorn did not have many days left in the company. It was not the first time Piëch had used this tactic of undermining someone in public. However, in this case, Winterkorn refused to go. He sought and managed to gain support from a broad majority of the supervisory board, which voted five-to-one in his favour. Instead it was Piëch who had to resign. The public explanation from the deputy chairman of the board was that 'Ferdinand Piëch has made an enormous contribution to Volkswagen and the entire automobile industry. [...] The developments of the last two weeks have, however, led to a loss of trust between the supervisory board chairman and the other members, which in recent days has proven to be impossible to resolve.'

Less than six months later, the political struggle entered a second round. In September 2015 it became known that Volkswagen (and later also a number of other car makers) had been trading cars that had been rigged in order to cheat on diesel emission tests. This time it was Martin Winterkorn who had to resign, even while claiming that he 'wasn't aware of any wrongdoing'. In 2018, Winterkorn, and other executives, faced criminal charges in the United States, while Piëch declared his innocence by claiming that he had already discussed the dieselgate problem with Winterkorn in February 2015.

Sources: Ewing (2015, 2018); Schmitt (2017)

Change work always involves priorities and considerations that benefit or disadvantage different individuals and groups, who can then be expected to mobilize energy and power, negotiate priorities and defend themselves against what they perceive to be threats to their own positions and interests. Politics infuse organizations, for example through company priorities and the allocation of resources, and are a result of historical political disagreements, conflicts and negotiations (Pfeffer, 1992). Even if a historically institutionalized form of politics is not always very salient in regular business, it is often highlighted and stressed in change situations when uncertainty and ambiguity increase. This uncertainty can revolve around resource allocation, strategies, positions or people's career prospects, all elements that generally trigger a lot of reflection for people, upon themselves and their capabilities as well as their own work situation (Buchanan & Badham, 1999; Maitlis & Sonenshein, 2010).

REVIEW QUESTIONS 6.3

Reflect	Can you think of organizational change situations where often-valued elements, such as openness, transparency and inclusiveness, become problematic with regard to the ability to achieve the change?

In sum, the process perspective involves creating an understanding of the complexities and occasionally chaotic circumstances that real-life organizational change is about. It involves making organizations understandable, and that includes the full spectrum of issues that planned attempts at change give rise to: opposition, political processes, negotiations, political games, ambiguity, the diversity of the environment, misunderstandings in communication and everything else that is part of the ordinary (and occasionally not so ordinary) daily life of an organization.

EXERCISE 6.4

Consider the case below and answer the following questions:

- In what ways can a transformation of the perceptions regarding a change initiative (including the perceptions of the key change agent) be favourable for the new senior manager and his change team? Discuss from a political perspective.
- Do you see any potential risks with attempting to change a prevalent understanding of how the company has developed?

CASE

From hero to villain

In a small Australian manufacturing company undertaking technological change (see the previous example too), the managerial group initially described the organizational change process as a success. The senior manager who was driving the changes initiative was portrayed as being a charismatic leader who had played an important part in steering through the change process. The managerial account of the change initiative, however, altered fundamentally when a new senior manager was appointed. The newly arrived manager and his team revised the initial version of what had happened in the company. The technological changes that had previously been labelled a success were now described as a major problem that needed to be tackled. The earlier version of the charismatic leader of change process was replaced with a narrative of incompetence. In other words, shortly after the senior manager was replaced, the understanding (or at least the common story told) of his contribution transformed him from a hero to a villain.

Source: Dawson & Buchanan (2005)

REVIEW QUESTIONS 6.4

Recall	Identify three key characteristics of the process perspective.
Explain	Describe what it implies to take a political view of organizational change.
Explain	What does it imply to think about the organization being in a state of continuous change?
Reflect	Assess and reflect on how a detailed analysis of the (potential) receptions of a particular change proposal can improve its chances of success? Consider how those targeted are likely to make sense of the change ideas on the basis of their experience, background, profession, etc.

INSIGHTS INTO ORGANIZATIONAL CHANGE PROCESSES

As described, much of the traditional literature within organizational change is often normative and focused on models that primarily support managerial governance and control of the change process. In contrast, in this section we present a number of descriptive studies providing more intimate and detailed examinations of organizational change processes. The ambition is to support a more in-depth understanding of change dynamics and, in turn, a more realistic and reflective attitude towards change management. Specific focus will be on how those most closely involved understand events, what dynamics can be discerned and what can potentially throw a spanner in the works of managerial change ambitions and plans.

Bringing understanding into the picture

The process perspective stresses the value of starting from how those people who are involved in, and impacted by, the changes experience the situation. A key point that has been repeated is that we cannot assume that plans are implemented according to how they are formulated. In contrast, as with all change attempts, plans are interpreted by those who are involved in the change, based on their personal experience, background, interests, desires, dreams, hopes and identity. So one needs to acknowledge that both those who initiate the change and those who are subject to the plans interpret the proposed change and the situation in a variety of ways. For example, it is difficult not to see attempts at change as a way for an organization's management to appear active and decisive every now and again. How is it otherwise possible to explain and understand all the energy that goes into formulating and communicating change ideas, compared with the energy spent on following up implementation, how it is received and the outcomes? Most attempts at change fizzle out anyway.

It is therefore important to follow up the course of events during change initiatives, and not to consider the targets of change – the people at the receiving end – as peripheral, inactive parties or potential trouble-makers who are expected to try to counteract the change. Such people do exist, of course, but the point of this orientation is to try to understand how different people and groups of people think and feel about the attempted changes in terms of how they interpret them more broadly (Helms-Mills, 2003). In the process perspective, employees are not considered as just passive recipients of change (that change will happen independently of them), but rather as active actors who participate in creating and shaping developments by the very act of trying to make sense of them (Balogun, 2006).

It is not uncommon for recipients of change to be blamed for change failures, and usually this is done by classifying people who are not embracing change initiatives as resisters (see more on this in Chapter 9). Managers also tend to be subjected to blame. For instance, they can be accused of poor communication, hypocrisy, unclear messages, fluffy articulation of the organizational change, or using complex and ambiguous language about change, and so on. An alternative way to understand the unforeseen consequences regarding change attempts – from the process perspective – is not to be too quick to attribute blame to different parties, and instead to show an interest in how messages are interpreted in the local organizational context. Organizational changes often impact a lot of people, and since these people normally have different experiences and interests, it is not strange that ambiguities and disagreements occur. In the end, these can turn the change process into something that looks completely different from the often rather well-oiled change machinery expressed in the more prescriptive and tool-oriented literature (Alvesson & Sveningsson, 2015).

The idea of the process perspective is to paint a picture of organizational change in a rich, animated and more insightful way, so as to create a better understanding of change processes in practice. This can, in turn, provide valuable insights on how change work can be managed in a more productive manner. A way to do this is to 'unpack' or open up a change process into different analytical phases – background, strategy, formulation of change, implementation, reception, interpretation, results – and to pay attention to how people experience the different phases in the process (see Alvesson & Sveningsson, 2015).

Central to the process perspective is that everybody involved, not just management, are taken into account as potential influencers of the process and are viewed as active sensemakers. Managers as well as employees can contribute to keeping the change work alive by actively engaging in the work and in praising its ideas, in the same way as they can oppose it by not engaging in the work or actively counteracting the initiative.

Below, we present three cases on organizational change dynamic and in turn discuss: (1) how different worldviews led to clashing interpretations and tension between (groups of) people; (2) how divergent interpretations led to unpredicted consequences; and (3) how informal sensemaking affected a change process.

Different worldviews and diverging interpretations

MINI CASE 6.4

A coordination attempt that resulted in fragmentation

After a merger of two global pharmaceutical companies (studied by one of the authors), the senior management, together with an international consulting company, initiated a change attempt in order to increase organizational standardization in the two companies.

(Continued)

They formulated new central guidelines for financial control and reporting between the head office and the local research units as well as new work procedures of many work roles. The new guidelines were documented quite extensively as formal instructions and standards – in paper and in digital versions – so that all organizational members could be part of the process. These written and digital documents also contained procedures for vertical reporting (between the global organization and local levels of R&D) and instructed that the local R&D managers were to implement these guidelines in local research units. In order to achieve this form of change – increased standardization of reporting procedures and work roles – the local site manager at a large research site presented the new guidelines at a meeting with other local R&D managers, where they discussed what needed to be done to implement the central guidelines.

At the meeting, a discussion almost immediately opened up about the meaning of the concepts in which the new guidelines were expressed and the specifics of the new work roles. What did the guidelines actually mean and what did the newly formulated work roles entail in terms of concrete ways of working? In spite of the ambitions of the central administration to specify the guidelines and roles through detailed documentation that everyone could be part of, they were perceived by the local managers as being abstract, unclear and arguably very detached from the reality in which they were intended to be used. At the meeting, the local managers tried to make sense of and determine what the central guidelines would mean for them, but concluded that they could not be meaningfully translated – or subsequently implemented – into their local setting. Instead, people were greatly frustrated and irritated that the guidelines and principles had been developed centrally without any regard for or recognition of the local realities in which these managers operated. As far as the local managers were concerned, the central guidelines were a remote and unrealistic drawing board project, detached from the complex local organizational world. As a result, the standardization efforts that aimed to form an aligned coordination based on shared guidelines produced increased distance between central and local levels due to different assumptions and worldviews.

The case presents a rather typical situation expressing how company management, central administration and consultants live in a world of analytical concepts, in contrast to the local actors, living in a world of demands for concrete deliverables and material results. The world of analysis and concepts is clean and flawless, with strict and almost universal definitions of concepts and terms, in contrast to the local world's complexities and deficiencies. The latter seldom matches the definitions of the former, which is why opposition and clashes between the two worlds often occur in change processes when people interpret change suggestions in fundamentally different ways.

Divergent interpretations and unpredicted consequences

Simply basing assumptions (about change dynamics) on one's own logic or sphere of understanding – perhaps especially if one lives in a world of concepts and abstract reasoning – often provides very limited insight on the dynamics of change processes. It is important to consider that change initiatives driven by top management can take alternative routes than those planned and lead to several unpredicted consequences (as in the following Case) if people involved in the process do not share basic viewpoints.

EXERCISE 6.5

Read the case below and discuss the following questions:

- What types of unexpected consequences do you think this change process could result in?
- If you were in a senior managerial position at the company, how would you have carried out the meeting aiming to align the diverging viewpoints?

CASE

Divergent understandings of 'open and honest communication'

A change initiative at an international finance company ran into problems that can be traced back to divergent views of the change process by senior managers and the employees 'on the floor'. The divergent interpretations were due to the differing logics that groups of people had developed within different work contexts and parts of the organization.

The senior managers primarily expressed an economic and financial logic. Against the backdrop of a consultant's report about the organization's high costs and increased competitive situation, a change plan was formulated that involved acquisitions and cost reductions through restructuring, aimed at maintaining a high share value. The assumption was that these changes would make the company more attractive on Wall Street and raise share value.

(Continued)

The latter was seen as important as it would make it more difficult for someone to buy the company. The changes, it was argued, were needed to give the company the chance to control its own destiny (by preventing a takeover). The changes were in other words justified by managerial claims that the company had no choice but to adapt to the market conditions, even though the significance placed on the share value as the main factor allowing the company to control its own destiny can be questioned.

The company policy on how this plan should be communicated to employees stated that nothing should be said until decisions had been made on what would actually happen: 'We will tell you what we know when we know it ourselves.' None of the employees was to know about anything before it was decided, and thereby, according to the managers, done and agreed. From the management perspective, this was considered to be open and honest communication. They thought it would help prevent rumours and gossip. In other words, they made a distinction between management and other employees in terms of access to knowledge: managers know best and make decisions without further dialogue and others, those less-knowledgeable, are allowed to be enlightened once the right path has been chosen. The logic and fundamental assumptions of the senior managers, which were expressed through their formulated plans and communications standards, reflected classic Taylorism, which emphasizes that managers are responsible for the thinking and others are responsible for the doing (the implementation of the thinking). However, the employees constructed a completely different version of the change initiative.

As so often is the case, the employees existed in a more concrete, action-oriented world (as opposed to the managers' text-oriented, abstract world), which was characterized by obligations, work methods and routines. It was a local context in which the different documents had to be understood and made meaningful. Accordingly, the central directives were understood against the backdrop of the employees' local sphere of understanding, which were partly built upon previous experience of changes and interaction with the senior management. Based on this reasoning, open and honest communication meant that employees should be strongly involved in the decision-making process, rather than (as now) only being informed about decisions after the fact.

Given the company's history of lifetime employment and employee loyalty, the employees regarded the senior managers' proposal as a betrayal of the company values, as they believed that the loyalty they had shown the company was not being returned. They also felt that the proposal was unfair. Cuts in employment insurance, closing of the library and reduced overtime compensation only affected the employees. These interpretations contributed to the emergence of a counter-culture among the employees, which later reinforced divisions between the groups.

To counteract the division and bring the two worlds together, a meeting was organized for everybody. The objective was to increase integration and alignment of the views of the proposed changes. However, the meeting did not allow for any dialogue or negotiation about what needed to be done, and instead typically only functioned as a platform for managers to justify their views on the changes. For example, one of the employees asked a common question in this type of situation about who would do what; in other words, how certain ideas would be implemented in practice. The senior manager's response referred to documents that actually did not provide much concrete guidance, which very clearly illustrated the different worlds of the individuals: the senior managers' abstract world versus the employees' concrete and action-oriented reality.

Source: Jian (2007)

It is hardly surprising that the meeting between the two parties, referred to above, was not successful. It could have been an opportunity to discuss and examine the managers' and the employees' divergent understandings more closely, but no time was allowed for this. In contrast, the managers stuck to their mantra that they would only inform employees about matters once they knew about them themselves, i.e. once the decisions had already been made. Issues of loyalty and unfairness also came up during the meeting, but the senior managers did not use this as an opportunity to find out more or discuss whether there were alternative solutions or other ways of looking at the changes. In short, the meeting merely served to lock people into their existing positions and to intensify the conflict.

Jian (2007) highlights three unpredicted consequences of this change work. First, trust between the senior managers and the employees diminished, which consequently further under-mined the chances of productive dialogue and future changes. Second, the change work created a substantial amount of stress, primarily among the employees, who saw themselves as victims. Third, productivity decreased during the entire period of the change process. The senior managers were preoccupied with trying to anticipate and prevent rumours and gossip, and many meetings had to be held to repair relationships between senior managers and employees. The employees, in turn, were preoccupied with trying to understand the uncertainties surrounding their own job situation.

This study illustrates that the 'recipients' of a change process should not be seen as passive executors of change plans, but rather as active change actors in that they interpret and reinterpret plans based on their own concrete situation. This means that the original intentions and objectives need to be reformulated in a dynamic relationship of tensions between those who initiate the change and those who implement it. Thus, the study shows that change work is not only a result of the intentions of management – teleological change – but also a result of tensions in the interpretation of the change between management and employees – dialectical change (Van de Ven & Poole, 1995). Both those who formulate changes and those who are expected to implement them should therefore be seen as change actors, to the extent that they all participate in forming the change process in different directions. Both management and other employees have intentions for the project, based on their own interpretations and interests, which cause tensions throughout the change process and lead to results that diverge from the original intention of the managers. Both groups of actors influence the change project so that it ends up being somewhat ambiguous and unpredictable (Brown, 1998).

From a practical point of view, one can say that classic Tayloristic or more current managerial assumptions about effective change management have clear limitations. Based on Jian's study, it would seem wiser to be more open about how a change process develops in terms of work and results. To reduce polarization and increase integration between people and groups (in this case, to increase vertical integration), it seems important to create conditions for employee participation, open meetings and forums for discussion and negotiation about change initiatives and work. Rather than issue orders and control change work, it can be beneficial to bring protests and assumptions into the open and encourage broad and open dialogue. Jian's study also proposes that managers should participate in the change process to increase the chances of integrating divergent understandings and converting tensions into productive energy.

Before rounding off, we would like to encourage critical reflection on how the case is presented. The example 'Divergent understandings of "open and honest communication"' describes the different logics in a polarized way: it is the managers' understandings against the employees'. Or it is 'those that cause problems' against 'the innocent victims'. However, it is important not to take for granted that there is harmony within the groups; differentiation and disagreements can occur within these groupings. We also want to stress the value of taking everybody's role into account and thus not highlighting (or blaming) the actions of one actor in a partial way.

REVIEW QUESTIONS 6.5

Recall	Recall the key characteristics of the teleological and dialectical views on what drives change.
Explain	Describe why the process perspective is more in line with a dialectical rather than a teleological view on change.

Informal interpretation processes

In change contexts, one group that is not visible in the above example is the middle managers. They are often expected to act as a link between the senior leadership and those on the floor. Middle managers are often those who initiate the implementation of an organizational change programme, and are therefore often seen to have an important role as the interpreters of the change initiatives and aims (Huy, 2002). In the next example, Mini Case 6.5, we look more closely at how informal sensemaking among middle managers impacts a change process.

MINI CASE 6.5

Informal sensemaking among middle managers

The senior management in a recently privatized organization initiated an organizational change process that involved splitting one organizational division into three new divisions, one Core division and two support divisions – Maintenance and Services. The underlying ambition was to achieve a cultural change – to enhance a more business-like way of working. The structural change was aimed at encouraging the development of a more business-like approach through internal markets and customer relationships between the divisions. A key vision was increased professionalism. An idea was that this change in the long run would make it possible to reduce costs and at the same time maintain quality and increase the workers' customer orientation.

A design team consisting of consultants and senior managers provided the change plans. The main recipients of the change – the middle managers – were expected to implement the change and work out the details themselves without the daily involvement of the senior managers. The change plan involved new structures, systems, roles and areas of responsibility, although with the overarching idea that it was 'business as usual' throughout the entire change process. The structural changes were meant to contribute to cultural change, and the implementation included communication and workshops in order to ensure that everybody understood the vision for increased professionalism.

During the change work, the middle managers tried to interpret and understand the change initiative through interactions primarily with colleagues and other managers at the same level. This lateral process was very informal in nature; it took place not only in meetings but also in informal conversations and included – as usual – rumours and gossip about how the change would work. Against the backdrop of the previous divisions being equal in terms of status, and there being a high level of cooperation between co-workers, a new understanding soon emerged among the managers in which the new structure involved competition and an 'us and them' mindset. This led to tensions between the divisions as people increasingly thought in terms of boundaries between the divisions. For example, employees wanted to protect their own business by not unnecessarily sharing knowledge with the other divisions.

The senior managers had not predicted this. As the change process continued and the interactions developed between the middle managers through conversations, stories, rumours, disagreement and negotiations about who should do what, the situation worsened. In addition, a number of other problems arose, partly as a result of a lack of clarity about roles and responsibilities.

A year after the implementation had begun, cooperation had improved between the divisions, but an 'us and them' mindset remained. Customer service was also reported to have

(*Continued*)

deteriorated. One particular issue in this change work was caused by the notion of 'business as usual', which many people believed aggravated the situation as they could not run their own business area as they used to due to the cuts that had been carried out as part of the change process.

Source: Balogun & Johnson (2005)

What is central in this case is the significance of the horizontal sensemaking that occurred between the middle managers in their attempt to understand the change plan. These informal sensemaking processes shaped how the change was interpreted and subsequently effected the (unpredicted) results of the change work. The point is not that such sensemaking takes place, but that it contributes to initiating new and unplanned changes. One important lesson is that these types of unplanned changes are not only the result of vertical processes (poor change formulations or unclear and ambiguous roles) but also, and above all, due to horizontal processes. Horizontal or lateral communication is often more informal than vertical communication, and is therefore often more effective in terms of shaping interpretations and understanding of complex change initiatives. This informal communication is both verbal (spoken communication) and non-verbal (for example, a lot can be read from people's actions, gestures and body language). The horizontal communication was also significantly intensified in this case due to the relatively limited involvement of the senior leadership in the change work, and it consisted to a large extent of rumours, gossip, stories about progress and other people's behaviour and opinions of the change work (also see Labianca et al., 2000).

The case also illustrates the difficulties in trying to control and govern cultural change by implementing structural changes that involve roles, structures and formal areas of responsibility (also see Beer et al., 1990). One of the problems with many of the change models is that they typically don't include informal processes. It is not enough that senior management has a plan that involves the structural and the cultural dimension of the organization (in line with the integrated organizational models in the previous chapter). A key issue is how the changes are received, and people's thinking, feeling and acting are not a direct result of anybody's words or decrees. Balogun and Johnson (2005, p. 1596) write: 'The outcome of an intervention by senior managers in one component cannot guarantee a corresponding change in another component since the outcome of that intervention is mediated by informal inter-recipient sensemaking processes.' In their study (which Mini Case 6.5 is based upon), they provide a more differentiated view of organizational change than the previous examples by emphasizing another group of actors, the middle-level managers, and the interactions between them.

Similar to other processual studies, this study expresses a certain amount of scepticism about the ability of management to implement organizational changes in line with the objectives and plans made. As in Jian's study (see the case on 'Divergent understandings of "open and honest communication"' above), we here see how interpretations by the different actors about what has to be done give rise to a more dialectic (as opposed to teleological) change process with uncertain and ambiguous outcomes. A senior management team seemingly has power over the formal shape of an organizational change, but alternative interpretations and stories limit its effects. Balogun and Johnson (2005) suggest that managing change rather involves supporting the processes of interpretation and understanding of those involved so as to achieve a more aligned view of the change work. They advocate that energy should be spent on creating a shared view of what the change should result in, and the relevant limitations for what the change work should not include, rather than managing details. In practice, this suggests that it is clearly beneficial to be actively present in change work in order to be able to influence interpretations of the changes. Balogun and Johnson seem generally to suggest a more integrative view of change work, thereby avoiding an all too strict division of labour between those who formulate and those who implement.

Interpretations and identity work

Change processes usually involve far more employees than senior management teams and consultants. As discussed above, middle managers often play an important part in change processes. Not seldom they are comprised of a fairly large and heterogeneous group of people at several different decision-making levels and with different needs and responsibilities, which makes it reasonable to assume there is a variation of interpretations and views of change initiatives. Additionally, often the human resources departments, with a variety of people in different capacities, such as competence development people, recruitment and career experts, and change facilitators, have a central role in change processes too, as messengers and communicators of change, and also as support for those implementing the change work. Then of course there are all the other employees who, during radical changes such as a culture change, are the 'recipients' of the change attempt. Radical changes are often intended to change the actions and thinking of large groups of employees, and these people can interpret the change work in many different ways, depending on their education, department, profession, previous experience of change, roles, and not least how they view themselves – their identity (cf. Alvesson & Sveningsson, 2015).

Also, the outcomes can be subject to diverging views. The variety of perceptions of the impact of the change work is not as uncommon as one might think and to investigate what 'actually' happened is often very difficult. To 'objectively' determine the variety of achievements of those involved in a change process, no matter how lengthy and inclusive the list may seem, tends to be tricky as there is an endless variety of interpretations of the process and of the different participants' activities and accomplishments. Even the very first step – to agree on what criteria or ways to measure the impact – can be very difficult. Ambiguous situations, with a diversity of interpretations of the impacts of the change, can provide room and an opportunity for those participating to maintain a positive self-identity. At the same time, divergent views can be reproduced as a result of the identity work of the people involved in the process. By attributing credit for what was done and blame for what was not done in a way that casts oneself and one's group in a favourable light and subsequently reproduce an attractive self-identity, can, as a side-effect, fuel diverging understandings of reality.

Sensemaking is not primarily about finding the most accurate or true version. It is rather about crafting a plausible account about what has happened (Weick, 1995). What is plausible for one group can be implausible for others, depending on already existing beliefs (Weick et al., 2005). Furthermore, since the story only needs to be sufficiently plausible, there is scope for people to make sense in a way that also contributes to a positive identity construction.

In particular, in certain work contexts – characterized by high levels of ambiguity, boundary positions, project work, diverse identification and loyalties (such as in knowledge-intensive organizations in general and consultancy work specifically) – the attribution of credit and blame often becomes a key theme, not only in relation to organizational politics and attempts to gain material and status benefits, but also as material for identity constructions (Alvesson, 2004). The ambiguity of the actual or substantial impact of a change project can in these contexts be understood as a 'resource' that makes it possible for the people involved to adopt various evaluation criteria, which opens up multiple versions of successes and failures, which in turn can facilitate identity work. Moral and evaluatory aspects are often central here. Identity work is not only about reproducing coherence, stability and distinctiveness, but can also include claims to moral superiority and character. A certain version of a particular course of events, involving crediting and blaming oneself and others, potentially drawing on publicly available blaming-templates and stereotypical understandings of groups of people, can in other terms be understood as a key resource for identity work.

EXERCISE 6.6

Search secondary sources (reports, mass media, articles in business magazines, the internet, etc.) for an organizational change effort that is known to, or seems to, have failed in some sense. Perhaps it has drawn negative publicity. Examine the key reasons for the failure, as stated in the gathered sources, and discuss them by drawing on relevant concepts and theories in this chapter. To what extent could the reasons for failure have been avoided with a more in-depth understanding of the process of organizational change? Was the failure more or less unavoidable?

EXERCISE 6.7

Many organizational change efforts contain a well-formulated plan and values about what the organization wants to achieve, such as greater customer orientation, the highest quality products/services, establishing a culture of innovation, leading change, etc. Although many of those involved in the change process would agree that such values sounds good, and that it is the right way to advance for the organization, it is also often the case that not much happens in terms of actual change. Based on a process perspective, how can this be explained?

REVIEW QUESTIONS 6.6

Explain	In the process perspective, employees are considered as active contributors, rather than passive recipients, of change. Explain what this implies.
Reflect	What do you consider to be managerially challenging when trying to apply a process perspective to change in a real-life situation? What contingencies is important to consider when assessing the extent to which a process perspective is beneficial for the change work?

SUMMARY

In this chapter we have emphasized how the process perspective of change means seeing change as something in progress that occurs more or less continuously as people create, communicate and interpret and reinterpret plans and ideas about what has to be done. A simple division between formulation, implementation and reception is therefore somewhat misleading in terms of understanding the process of change. Change plans are reformulated by those who are affected by them through continuous interpretation and reinterpretation among themselves and with others. Thus, people's communication, dialogue and behaviour have consequences for how change comes into being and is played out in organizations. This contributes, of course, to an image of leading and governing change that is much more complex and difficult than many of the more tool-oriented models depict.

Considering organizational change as a process means being focused on and interested in understanding how the individuals that are involved in the change perceive and interpret the change. Furthermore, it requires a profound and thorough knowledge of the entire course of events, not just formulations and intentions but also how these changes are received and their results. Upon closer examination, it appears that many attempts at change fail to achieve their original objectives and intentions. Those who initiate and embark upon organizational changes, the senior managers and other actors of change, often present completed organizational changes as successful and as having achieved the intended results, but some of these claims should be taken with a pinch of salt. A lot of energy and time is often spent on talking about the need for changes and formulating plans and strategies for change and development. However, some of the work stops with these plans and (managerial) wishes as people do not have the energy or even the interest in seeing changes through to the end. Some of the work therefore fizzles out, and perhaps the most important part of the changes, the results, fail to come through. One of the reasons for this is that leaders often initiate changes primarily to exhibit decisiveness and that they are in charge, rather than to achieve real change – people want to appear progressive, capable and in control. In turn, this indicates the significance of conceptualizing change attempts and change plans in terms of the social, cultural and political contexts in which they occur.

We have also seen that when regarded more closely, change is more or less a frequent phenomenon that occurs through people's continuous understanding about day-to-day events in organizations. Here, interaction between people is important and communication is central to this. In talking about – considering, evaluating and interpreting – change, change is constructed as a social phenomenon based on how people experience events in organizations, irrespective of whether it refers to a concrete and explicit change plan or not. Communication about change does not necessarily refer to a specific item, such as a change plan; rather, it can be a general conversation about the need for change, for example. Nor is communication reserved for certain (formal) occasions; instead, it occurs constantly in organizations. Informal communication is easily trivialized but can be very important for those involved in a change process in terms of how they perceive things, which can lead to symbolic and material consequences for what actually happens. It can also contribute to immediate intellectual changes in those who communicate, potentially with consequences on actions. For this reason, the value of dialogue is increasingly referred to in change contexts.

In the next chapter, we look deeper into interpersonal communication by focusing on the significance of language and stories.

 ## KEY PRACTICAL INSIGHTS

What we can say about organizational change following this chapter:

- Relying on rational planning – a central tenet in the tool-based perspective – as a way of accomplishing successful organizational change is too simplistic and idealistic.

- Solely following n-step models may complicate matters and obstruct successful change since complexity and unintended consequences are not fully taken into account.

- Managing a change process is normally facilitated if the cultural, social and political contexts of change are acknowledged as inherent characteristics of the change process rather than simple managerial tools. These are aspects that are normally marginalized or trivialized within the tool-based perspective.

- Managing change calls for an understanding of the local context in which it occurs. Too abstract ideas about change may be seductive but can also cause confusion and distance from the local reality that may trap and ultimately block the most well-formulated change plan.

- More than anything else, organizational change involves people. Those who are involved in change processes are all in some sense co-producers of change and need to be recognized as active sensemakers rather than passive receivers of simple communications and messages. Be attentive to the way change ideas are received.

- Managing organizational change requires considerable understanding of people's ideas and representations about the changes. This involves recognizing their motivations, commitments, identity, ideas about change, etc.

- Managing change processes often entails an active presence and constructive dialogue with those involved in the change process. Even if this occasionally produces frustration and more lengthy change processes, it often also reduces resistance or negligence.

- An active presence by those instigating change efforts – managers and change actors – normally creates trust and mutual confidence in the change processes. Trusting relationships are vital in change processes, especially considering that change often brings uncertainty and anxiety.

- Conflicts and power struggles are an inherent part of organizational life and tend to be accentuated in times of organizational change. Do not expect there to be a harmony of interests. Organizational change work tends to involve negotiation, building alliances, mobilizing resources and other types of political games.

CASE

Global Pharma Ltd – the ambiguous results of change work

After a recent merger between two global pharmaceutical companies, senior organization management decided to consolidate a variety of support functions within the R&D department in order to try to cut costs and enhance the overall corporate efficiency of the newly

(Continued)

formed Global Pharma Ltd. To realize this, Global Pharma engaged a global consultancy firm that specialized in management consulting and had experience of working in the pharmaceutical industry. Subsequently, the project was developed into a medium-sized business process re-engineering of support services. This involved standardizing routines and centralizing support services – finance services (payrolls, travelling expenses, etc.) and property issues – among the various R&D sites that were located in different parts of the world (mainly in Europe and the US). As such, the re-engineering change project represents a very common route for contemporary organizations: the increased standardization and centralizations of support services in order to try to increase savings and economic performance. In the business press, the change was regarded as necessary in order to realize the increased profit expectations and promises made to shareholders before, and as the rationale of, the merger.

It was, however, more or less impossible to come to an unambiguous conclusion about the results of the change project in economic or organizational terms. Consultants and client managers involved in the project expressed fundamentally different views of the outcome and how it had been achieved.

When it came to questions about the results of the project, and whether it was a success or failure, one of the consultants suggested that millions had been saved from the project (a success). Although not really an organizational result, the consultants also evaluated the project in terms of improving their own image. On this matter, the project was described positively, in that the consultants involved had managed to create a favourable impression of themselves in the eyes of top management (also a success). However, other consultants mentioned that the client had had to pay large consultancy costs without any substantial result (not a success).

Among the client managers, one spoke of weak deliveries but that his own intervention had spurred some savings (some success). Another manager talked about cost-cuttings although he could not specify any of them (probably some success), and yet another client manager talked about the lack of any substantial results (no real success) but referred to a well-received formal presentation to senior organization management (a success). Also, one of the client managers evaluated the result in terms of image improvement among the senior managers. Moreover, one consultant and two managers argued that some substantial effects were achieved. However, this was contradicted by other consultants, who indicated limited accomplishments. Furthermore, the consultants claimed that the client had confirmed that they did a good job. This in turn was confirmed by one of the client managers. In contrast, however, two other client managers talked about having problems with the consultants and emphasized their own role in getting the consultants back on track.

Taken together, two opposing standpoints could be distinguished.

The *consultants* involved in the project argued that they had achieved a positive result in the change project. They suggested that the difficulties in reaching a completely successful outcome – problems of an unrealized change potential – were due to the client. The unrealized potential was attributed to the lack of drive and confusion among the client managers, who were seen as morally degraded and unable to deliver and drive the change process. The consultants also blamed the client for not following up and implementing their high-quality proposals. In particular, the consultants expressed their own drive, consistency, knowledge and ability to manage the radical changes. They also indicated that they were clear, professional, active, and results-oriented for the long term. These accounts corresponded to how the ideal consultant is typically described: as rational, professional, decisive, well-trimmed, results-driven and change-oriented. In contrast, the client was described as being unclear, passive, unknowledgeable and inefficient, which is also in line with a stereotypical image of the client as someone who is spoiled, soft, irrational and incapable of running a competitive business.

Interestingly, the *client managers* told similar stories, although with an inverted view of who was to be credited for the positive achievements and who was to blame for the failure to realize all the potential and promises of the project. The client managers said that they initiated the change process and displayed firmness in an unproductive and chaotic situation (caused by the consultants). They managed to take the lead, faced the difficult situations and stood straight, and displayed character and order in contrast to the consultants, who were described as unreliable, greedy, too theoretical and potentially chaotic. The client managers also emphasized their own key role in managing the process – the consultants left on their own did not lead to success. Rather, they were the realistic ones, who undertook straight and firm leadership. The managers' descriptions consisted of several typical elements of what it means to be an ideal manager (working with consultants). Being a manager implies being tough, down-to-earth and acting like a sheepdog, i.e. exhibiting determination and consistent and directive management and being the senior ones in charge of junior people. The clients emphasized that they confronted the inexperienced, unreliable and confused consultants. Such descriptions were in line with a stereotypical view of consultants as excessively commercial and slick but incapable of understanding company specifics and with no serious talk and ability to ensure delivery.

Questions

- How did the consultants construct themselves in respect of the client?
- What function(s) do you think the portrayal of the client had for the consultants?
- How did the client managers construct themselves in respect of the consultants?
- What function(s) do you think the portrayal of the consultants had for the client mangers?
- The constructions expressed rather stereotypical views of the client respectively the consultant. Why do you think stereotypical images were invoked?

FURTHER READING

Go online to access free and downloadable SAGE Journal articles related to this chapter at **https://study.sagepub.com/sveningsson**

Alvesson, M., & Sveningsson, S. (2015). *Changing organizational culture*. London: Routledge.

Helms-Mills, J. (2003). *Making sense of organizational change*. New York: Routledge.

Kunda, G. (1992). *Engineering culture: Control and commitment in a high-tech corporation*. Philadelphia, PA: Temple University Press.

Mirfakhar, A., Trullen, J., & Valverde, M. (2018). Easier said than done: A review of antecedents influencing effective HR implementation. *The International Journal of Human Resource Management*, 29(22), 3001–3025.

Rouleau, L. (2005). Micro-practices of strategic sensemaking and sensegiving: How middle managers interpret and sell change every day. *Journal of Management Studies*, 42(7), 1413–1441.

Sminia, H. (2016). Pioneering process research: Andrew Pettigrew's contribution to management scholarship, 1962–2014. *International Journal of Management Reviews*, 18, 111–132.

Todnem, R., Kuipers, B., & Procter, S. (2018). Understanding teams in order to understand organizational change. *Journal of Change Management*, 18(1), 1–9.

Watson, T. (1994). *In search of management: Culture, chaos and control in managerial work*. London: Routledge.

Weick, K. E., Sutcliffe, K. M., & Obstfeld, D. (2005). Organizing and the process of sensemaking. *Organization Science*, 16(4), 409–421.

Ybema, S. (2010). Talk of change: Temporal contrasts and collective identities. *Organization Studies*, 31, 481–503.

VIDEO

Go online to view video clips related to the key themes discussed in this chapter at
https://study.sagepub.com/sveningsson

THE PROCESS PERSPECTIVE: THE IMPORTANCE OF LANGUAGE

LEARNING OBJECTIVES

When you have completed your study of this chapter, you should be able to:

- Discuss the role of language as not only representative (describing reality) but also constitutive (shaping reality) and the implications this has for organizational change.

- Describe how the dynamics of conversations in organizations can play a key role in change processes.

- Compare and contrast monologic and dialogic communication.

- Discuss how employee storytelling can influence organizational change processes.

- Appraise storytelling as a way for change agents to manage change.

- Understand the meaning of the concept discourse and explain its relevance for understanding change.

In the previous chapter we introduced the process perspective by highlighting its focus on people's interpretation and understanding of change processes. In this chapter we continue our focus on the process perspective by looking not only at how people understand organizational change, but also the prerequisites underpinning this understanding. We covered this to a certain extent in the previous chapter in the discussion of sensemaking related to basic assumptions and identity constructions. We also touched upon political facets of change. However, we now turn our attention to language and its significance for how people think, feel, talk and act during change processes. Our ambition is to discuss in more depth the factors that influence and inform people's sensemaking by focusing on the importance of communication, stories and discourse.

During recent years, research in organizational change has focused on the importance of language in change. This involves capturing both how change occurs through daily interactions and how language and communication can be central in managing change. In this context, language is not only seen as an instrument for expressing thoughts and ideas, but also as something that forms and constitutes thoughts and ideas. Literature in this field is largely descriptive, but we note that tool-based approaches are increasingly popular. Thus, we include both theories aimed at increasing an understanding of change processes as well as discussions about how language can actively be employed to achieve change. The concepts introduced here are often also important for critical analyses of change, which is why this chapter also constitutes an important foundation for the next chapter.

This chapter discusses organizational change in relation to communication, stories and discourse, one after the other, with the idea of successively increasing the level of complexity.

COMMUNICATION, CONVERSATION AND ORGANIZATIONAL CHANGE

It is not new to say that communication is important in organizational change; indeed, it is a recurring theme in organizational literature, albeit with different areas of focus. First, let us repeat what we have said in previous chapters regarding communication. The classic managerialism – such as Taylorism – stresses the importance of assigning and communicating what each and every employee should do, through detailed job descriptions. The Human Relations approach highlighted that communication is paramount for motivating and engaging personnel. Based on the latter, Barnard emphasized that communication with employees is one of the most important tasks for the senior management. The Organizational Development tradition highlights the value of creating open communication, and many authors stress the importance of describing and conveying the core ideology (Cummings & Worley, 2009). Heracleous (2001) further emphasizes the importance of communicating the rationale for the change and why it is vital in order to avoid opposition, and Kotter ([1996] 2012a) encourages change leaders to use all opportunities to communicate the vision for change and the strategy to achieve it. What stands out among these approaches is communication: through communication, a message is conveyed; through communication, understanding and commitment can be created; and by means of communication, resistance is likely to be reduced. In this chapter we will go beyond this view of communication and look at communication and language as performative. This implies considering that communication as such creates organisational change (Ford & Ford, 1995): the way we talk about the world frames our understanding of it and our shared basic assumptions are formed, sustained and changed through various forms of communication with others. Change from this perspective thus occurs within communication rather than the other way around.

Communication and the use of language are therefore not merely considered as neutral reflections of an objective reality, but as acts that have a potential sensemaking power. A particular use of language frames a situation and highlights it from a particular perspective; it can strongly influence people's understanding. In other words, language enables a certain way of making sense of and understanding the world.

Conversations as drivers for change

From this performative perspective on communication, change is seen as a phenomenon based on and driven by language. Ford and Ford (1995), who were early advocates of this approach, believe that change processes develop in the form of four types of conversation:

- Initiative conversations (starting a change)
- Conversations for understanding (generating understanding)
- Conversations for performance (getting into action)
- Conversations for closure (completing the change).

The content of these can vary, as can their sequence and tone. For example, change-initiating conversations can arise in informal situations (e.g. in small gatherings in the canteen) and be discussions about how work conditions can be improved (e.g. how to manage complaints from customers and clients). They can also derive from formal statements from the company CEO, for example regarding a plan for expansion into new markets that has organizational structural consequences such as reporting relationships and delegation procedures. Depending on how these conversations develop, they can shift into the next phase (generating understanding), in which people try to comprehend the situation by making sense of the problems facing the organization and alternative ways to approach them, or move directly to the performance phase if the initiating conversations are themselves very convincing. Or the proposal can be rejected, in which case the conversation moves towards closure. Performance conversations are action-oriented, where directives and requests are made as well as promises to accomplish a specific result. Conversations for closure, in turn, consist of declaring the change process to be over. The work as such may be finished (or not even initiated!), but this type of conversation asserts and shapes a common understanding of completeness and closure. It usually consists of a declaration of what works or does not work, including an acknowledgement of the new possibilities lying ahead.

The premise is that specific conversations can generate specific aspects of change (Ford & Ford, 1995). Thus, a stalled change process can be understood as a stalled conversation, or as a conversation that has not changed in form and therefore not been able to proceed to a new phase. From this perspective, all aspects of change are seen as something created and established through communication. The environment and external change triggers are thus not understood as given, objective facts. They are rather seen as created and anchored in initiative conversations and conversations for understanding. From this point of view, achieving change primarily involves generating new conversations. It is therefore important to ensure that the conversations support the purpose or objective set and that the intentions of the change are well aligned with the type of language used. For example, if the purpose is to create a flatter organization with increased employee influence, the language and the way in which the change is communicated should align with this intention. In other words, primarily communicating directives and decisions made by senior managers would probably be counterproductive in terms of generating understanding and not be recommended in this example.

EXERCISE 7.1

Recall a situation when you have taken part in one of the following: an initiative conversation, a conversation for understanding, a conversation for performance (action-generating) or a conversation for closure. This can be related to something very small, such as a change in how work is performed. The conversation could have been triggered by some unfavourable work conditions, such as ineffective reporting relationships, a lack of formal feedback routines, a lack of managerial recognition or an unfair evaluation of work efforts. It could even be a matter of an unproductive work atmosphere or a lack of social activities among employees.

How would you characterize the changes that followed this specific type of conversation?

It is, however, not only change that is created through communication. People also create and convey an image of themselves, and this work with identity and image does not necessarily go hand-in-hand with communication related to change ambitions. For example, a manager's ambition to be perceived as powerful and decisive might clash with change intentions to mobilize and increase employee influence. The opposite may also happen. A change actor who wants to be perceived as a good and democratic manager might avoid distinct and direct language and thereby fail to communicate urgency with adequate energy and power in situations where this is required.

EXERCISE 7.2

Consider the case below and discuss the following questions:

- What type(s) of conversation(s) do you think his speech could encourage?
- From a performative view of communication and change management, what kinds of important managerial challenges related to communication still need to be handled?

CASE

Elop's speech to employees at Nokia

As a newly appointed chief executive at the Finnish telecom company Nokia, Stephen Elop gave a speech in which he warned the employees that they were 'standing on a burning platform'. Throughout the speech he continued to draw upon the metaphor. Below are extracts from the speech.

> [...] we have more than one explosion – we have multiple points of scorching heat that are fuelling a blazing fire around us.

> For example, there is intense heat coming from our competitors, more rapidly than we ever expected. Apple disrupted the market by redefining the smartphone and attracting developers to a closed, but very powerful ecosystem. [...]

> And then, there is Android. In about two years, Android created a platform that attracts application developers, service providers and hardware manufacturers. [...] Google has become a gravitational force, drawing much of the industry's innovation to its core.

(Continued)

Let's not forget about the low-end price range. In 2008, MediaTek supplied complete reference designs for phone chipsets, which enabled manufacturers in the Shenzhen region of China to produce phones at an unbelievable pace. By some accounts, this ecosystem now produces more than one third of the phones sold globally – taking share from us in emerging markets.

While competitors poured flames on our market share, what happened at Nokia? We fell behind, we missed big trends, and we lost time. At that time, we thought we were making the right decisions; but, with the benefit of hindsight, we now find ourselves years behind. [...]

How did we get to this point? Why did we fall behind when the world around us evolved?

This is what I have been trying to understand. I believe at least some of it has been due to our attitude inside Nokia. We poured gasoline on our own burning platform. I believe we have lacked accountability and leadership to align and direct the company through these disruptive times. We had a series of misses. We haven't been delivering innovation fast enough. We're not collaborating internally.

Nokia, our platform is burning.

We are working on a path forward – a path to rebuild our market leadership. When we share the new strategy on February 11, it will be a huge effort to transform our company. But I believe that, together, we can face the challenges ahead of us. Together, we can choose to define our future.

Sources: Arthur (2011); Ziegler (2011)

Monologic and dialogic communication

When managing change, it can be valuable to differentiate between monologic and dialogic communication (Jabri et al., 2008). A monologic mode of communication involves information transfer from one part to another (such as from the top to the bottom of the hierarchy). It is about shaping messages with the aim of convincing other people to accomplish what the speaker wishes. This is a top-down or classic authoritarian view of how change is achieved without any substantial participation from those who are impacted by the change. They are seen only as recipients who are supposed to get the point and agree. A problem that we also raised earlier is that this communication mode overlooks other people as active actors and their abilities to participate substantially in the change process. This ignorance in turn risks alienating people and generating resistance.

In contrast, a dialogic mode of communication invites alternative viewpoints into the conversation and those impacted by the change are expected to participate as active co-authors (Ford & Ford, 1995). The idea is to encourage several different perspectives to meet, and thereby try to achieve a more diverse change process in which different experience is acknowledged and becomes a substantial part of the change initiative (Jabri et al., 2008). Rather than being specified in advance, the change ambition, according to this communication, remains open for discussion and further specification along the way.

Dialogic communication seeks to achieve real rather than false consensus. The latter can arise in situations of monologic communication when people avoid raising a conflicting opinion so as to avoid disturbing the social order or appearing as complaining or retrogressive. People officially agree with what has been said and the need for change, but feel alienated and are neither interested nor eager to contribute to it. So they delay expressing their dissatisfaction with the change programme until they become affected by it themselves (when they are expected to change something, such as work methods or routines, or become active in the change process), and then resist by not complying or by sabotaging the change. This is one reason why change programmes that are characterized by a great deal of monologic communication often have unpredicted and undesired consequences. As the one-way communication from above meets other ideas and experiences, it may spawn unpredicted interpretations and actions. Accordingly, it is difficult to manage and control results and developments, even in carefully designed change programmes. Conversations that have a more dialogic nature can thus be a way to generate more coordinated and effective changes. In order to achieve it, however, change agents need to move beyond the idea of change as a ready-made product that should be communicated and instead focus on facilitating dialogues. On this matter, Jabri et al. (2008, p. 681) encourage change agents to ask themselves whether 'the people in their organizations are the objects of communication or subjects in communication'.

EXERCISE 7.3

Consider a situation where you have:

a. Experienced and appreciated monologic communication
b. Experienced but disliked monologic communication
c. Experienced and appreciated dialogic communication
d. Experienced but disliked dialogic communication

Discuss these situations among your fellow students and compare your ideas. What conclusions can you draw from this exercise?

REVIEW QUESTIONS 7.1

Recall	Contrast dialogic and monologic communication in terms of organizational change.
Explain	What does it imply to look at language and communication as performative?
Explain	How can acknowledging the significance of conversations in organizations facilitate in understanding organizational change?
Reflect	What contingencies (e.g. related to the workforce characteristics, size of the organization, industry, growth phase, degree of emergency) do you think are relevant to take into account when deciding whether a monologic or dialogic mode of communication is the most appropriate to pursue in a change process? Can you come up with any counter-arguments?

STORIES AND ORGANIZATIONAL CHANGE

One way to approach organizational change is to investigate the creation and significance of stories. The premise for this tradition is that people's interpretation and sensemaking of events within organizations often takes the form of storytelling or narrative (Brown et al., 2009; Collins, 2018; van Hulst & Ybema, 2019). Usually, people create more or less coherent stories about how they understand and see a historic turn of events and existing events in organizations, and it is productive to examine these stories more closely as they express and form people's sensemaking (Brown & Humphreys, 2003).

Stories can mean many different things, and in some cases include all sorts of things, such as anecdotes, folklore, tales, myths, legends, jokes, case studies, reports and other statements. In change contexts, a more limited view of stories is usually referred to as a portrayal of happenings that occur one after the other, generating a somewhat coherent sequence of events. A coherent sequence of events means that the story portrays a starting situation, and then the happenings that change the starting situation and, through those, the formation of a new state, i.e. a portrayal of an organizational turn of events in terms of what happened before, during and after (Czarniawska, 1998). Stories are, however, more than a description of chains of events. They also describe the context in which the action occurs, portray how different factors influence each other and include explanations for actions, such as people's interests and motives.

Gabriel (2000) elaborates on four basic types of stories:

- *Tragic stories*, which present the main character as a non-deserving victim who experiences unmerited misfortune. Tragic stories typically invoke feelings of sorrow and compassion and maybe also resentment or fear.
- *Epic stories*, which are about the hero who manages to achieve a noble victory and success, making the reader feel pride or admiration. They can also evoke a nostalgic mood.
- *Romantic stories*, which have a love object as the main character who experiences the trials and triumphs of love. The key message is that love conquers all, evoking feelings of kindness and sympathy.
- *Comic stories*, in which the main character is a fool or a deserving victim who comes across justified misfortune. Comic stories evoke laughter and feelings of scorn.

These four are presented here as theoretically distinct types, but in practice they might overlap because the stories that are told are often hybrids, such as the tragicomedy.

Taking a narrative perspective on organizational change, i.e. paying attention to the stories told in and of the organization, implies that accounts are constructed and told by someone, as opposed to them being purely descriptive and neutral portrayals of organizational events and happenings. Stories form more or less disputed constructions that are infused with meaning and some kind of message, which can be more or less explicit. A story projects one version of a complex and often multifaceted course of events. Taken together, we will refer to stories as 'accounts of sequenced events, with plots that weave together complex occurrences into unified wholes that reveal something of significance' (Brown et al., 2009, p. 324).

We make no distinction between the two concepts 'stories' and 'narratives', since they are often intermixed and used on a broad basis (see Brown et al., 2009). Some authors refer to the 'narrative' concept and others use the concept of 'stories' when discussing the same phenomenon. In order to avoid confusion, we primarily use the concept of 'stories'.

We primarily discuss storytelling in terms of sensemaking and sense-giving, and discuss stories as a way to access and better understand organizational life.

EXERCISE 7.4

What function(s) can a story like the one of the burning platform (see the Case above and Mini Case 7.1) play in a change process?

MINI CASE 7.1

The story of the burning platform

The very first part of chief executive Stephen Elop's speech at Nokia (see the Case on p. 179) took the form of a short story:

> There is a pertinent story about a man who was working on an oil platform in the North Sea. He woke up one night from a loud explosion, which suddenly set his entire oil platform on fire. In mere moments, he was surrounded by flames. Through the smoke and heat, he barely made his way out of the chaos to the platform's edge. When he looked down over the edge, all he could see were the dark, cold, foreboding Atlantic waters.

> As the fire approached him, the man had mere seconds to react. He could stand on the platform, and inevitably be consumed by the burning flames. Or he could plunge 30 meters into the freezing waters. The man was standing on a 'burning platform,' and he needed to make a choice.

> He decided to jump. It was unexpected. In ordinary circumstances, the man would never consider plunging into icy waters. But these were not ordinary times – his platform was on fire. The man survived the fall and the waters. After he was rescued, he noted that a 'burning platform' caused a radical change in his behaviour.

Storytelling as sensemaking

Storytelling is often driven by a personal interest and an ambition to understand what change is about and how one will be affected personally (Bies & Sitkin, 1992). To the extent that people experience changes as worrying and unpredictable, storytelling can help to clarify the change process. In such a case, storytelling has a therapeutic function and can contribute to the development of a more optimistic view of the change. The process of trying to comprehend change can thus influence people's attitude and position towards change (Reissner, 2011).

Conventionally, people try to make sense of what events entail and mean for them by crafting stories that fit and resonate with their existing worldview. Therefore, it is not uncommon that people create and tell stories that challenge and contest proposed changes in some way, in particular change ideas that do not align with their prevalent beliefs (Buchanan & Dawson, 2007; Degn, 2016).

Uncertainty about the consequences and outcomes of a change programme can give rise to active sensemaking (Brown & Humphreys, 2003; Heath & Porter, 2019). It can, for instance, imply attempts to make sense of where one stands in relation to the change and to reflect about one's identity as well as one's relationship to the organization. Above all, radical change processes can give rise to great uncertainty and worry, and create a breeding ground for more profound questions about how people view themselves and their relationship to work, work teams, the department or the broader organization. This applies to groups of employees as well as individuals. During organizational change, groups can also create stories about who they are and what they stand for – the group's or the organization's identity – in contrast to what they perceive the change to represent or involve (Sörgärde, 2006). During acquisitions and change situations, it is not uncommon for members of the organization to create clear and distinct identities that often contrast sharply with what they perceive other organizations stand for (Kleppestø, 1993).

Stories about what one really values and treasures (e.g. stories about the greatness of a certain working method or a special spirit in the organization) can also be a way of expressing distinct local values and beliefs that employees perceive to be under threat in times of change. In these situations, nostalgia can be a prominent feature (Gabriel, 1993). Nostalgic stories are often romantic stories about how things used to be, in contrast to the distressing present. The stories of the past then become selective and idealized, as a description of a lost paradise where everyone was friendly and nice and the organization accomplished great things (Ybema, 2004). Nostalgic stories can help employees maintain a sense of continuity and keep historical images of the organization alive. In times of change, they can therefore function as both a shock absorber, reducing anxiety and stress by reassuring employees about what the organization 'really stands' for, and an antidote to change, conquering new ideals and alternative stories of the future (Reissner, 2011).

MINI CASE 7.2

The new appraisal system at Glenrothes Colliery (part 1)

In Glenrothes Colliery (pseudonym), a large multinational mining company in Australia, the CEO decided to implement a performance management system for underground coal miners.

(Continued)

The decision was made without consulting those involved locally. The initiative was met with extensive resistance, even before the first round of appraisals. The first round of performance reviews was followed by a noticeable drop in workforce morale and performance. The relationships between the parties involved were severely strained. Storytelling among miners became more intense than usual as they tried to make sense of the change initiative and protect their collective identity. A number of nostalgic stories about how it used to be in the good old days were told. In particular, they portrayed a past characterized by friendship, humour and solidarity among the workers, in which they supported each other in dangerous conditions and the work morale was high. According to the miners, this atmosphere had been eroded by modern performance initiatives implemented by managers. The past was fun, but the humour had gone. Now 'everything is so serious'.

Source: Dawson & McLean (2013)

Neither depictions of the history, the course of events of present changes nor the outcomes should blindly be considered as objective facts, but rather just as stories constructed by a person or people based on direct or indirect experiences, motives, intentions, career ambitions, background and identities. Stories often contain elements of politics and the exercise of power, which the complexity within organizational change allows for (Thurlow & Helms-Mills, 2015). It is often difficult to unequivocally determine the outcome of an attempted change, and many people want to construct a positive outcome of their own efforts, even if the change as a whole is perceived to be less successful, as could be seen in the case about the consultants and clients in Chapter 6 (Alvesson & Sveningsson, 2011a). The same change process can thus be described as anything from a success to a failure (Buchanan, 2003).

Impression management tends to be a central element in change stories. It is normal for people to want to highlight their own role in the process if the change is judged to have been successful, and to downplay their significance if the project is seen as unsuccessful (Maclean et al., 2012). Furthermore, people promoting organizational change may tell positive stories about previous changes in order to mobilize others towards future changes. Here the point is that every change, whether historic or ongoing, can be portrayed by many different people who all shape their own story. As such, a series of change events can always be portrayed (and thereby influenced) by many voices with different objectives, experiences, ambitions, interests and identities. In change contexts, it is difficult, if not completely impossible, to reach an authentic or true version of a series of events that everybody involved can agree on (Alvesson & Sveningsson, 2011b; Czarniawska, 1998).

MINI CASE 7.3

Two types of stories of the past at Courier

The 160-year-old family-owned newspaper production and publishing company Courier (pseudonym) had been undergoing major changes. Among other things, they had diversified their business, introduced new technology and decided to move from being a local to a national newspaper. The changes were followed by a period of increased profits and sales. Thereafter, readership figures dipped. At the same time, the fifth-generation CEO was retiring and the first non-family CEO was appointed.

Two different types of stories of the past emerged during the time of these changes. On the one hand, there were stories of paternalism, portraying the organization as a family- and community-oriented firm. For instance, there were stories of how the owners of Courier would support their employees in difficult times. One story that was often told was about the situation during the war, emphasizing how the company remained loyal to the employees, even in the most difficult of economic times (O'Leary, 2003, p. 690):

> During the war, because of the shortage of newsprint, the number of pages in the paper was reduced down at one stage to a single sheet and they couldn't use the linotype machines because they were run on gas [...] but do you think that the family would let people go? Of course not, they found things for the staff to do – mending bicycles and such [...]

The reasoning behind these stories was that people who loved their organization were more likely to be loyal and do a good job. These kinds of romantic stories of the golden past were used as a way to resist the changes that were underway, emphasizing the need to hold on to the traditional values of loyalty and commitment which were being undermined by the changes.

On the other hand, there were stories of false paternalism which satirized and ridiculed the old ways of working. A key focus in these tragicomic stories was portraying a dysfunctional workforce who drank too much (O'Leary, 2003, p. 692):

> [...] there's the story about the young lad who fell asleep under the stacking machine after a night of drinking. The next morning, they found him there and when someone tried to wake him, he said, 'Mam, phone work and tell them I'm sick.'

The stories revealed how alcoholism was widespread. Through these stories, a sense of false paternalism was evoked since managers who turn a blind eye to this type of addictive and dangerous behaviour are not very caring. The key storyline was that the changes were necessary: the organization had to become more professional and responsible than it had been in the past.

Source: O'Leary (2003)

The value of listening to stories

A storytelling perspective on organizational change focuses on how people talk about change processes and how past experiences are linked with the present situation and their visualized future. This can involve how people speak about the reasons for an organization's need to change, or why it should not, or it can be stories about change processes themselves or the results of different attempts at change. Paying attention to these stories can give a more in-depth understanding of how employees interpret and subsequently relate to change processes in organizations, and in turn provide important insights for managers about the possibilities of embarking on and implementing organizational change (Beech & Johnson, 2005). Stories can provide insights into the experiences of those who feel threatened by the change and particularly how and why people feel the way they do (Jabri, 2012).

In this endeavour, it is important to take into account that sensemaking takes place more or less continuously. During more extensive and revolutionary change attempts, storytelling usually intensifies as it becomes more urgent to comprehend what is happening. Expressed experiences of change should, however, not be seen as static accounts since they can be reinterpreted and retold in the light of new experiences of change. Stories of the past can therefore tell us more about the present than the past.

Dawson and McLean (2013) distinguish between four types of stories:

- *Retrospective stories* – stories that look back at what has been. Usually these stories have existed for some time in the organization. They are often told with a clear beginning, middle and end.

- *Present change-oriented stories* – stories focused on the here-and-now that reinterpret the past in order to understand the present and project what the future may look like in comparison. These stories challenge the status quo.

- *Present continuity-oriented stories* – stories focused on the here-and-now that attempt to create a continuity between the past, the present and the future.

- *Prospective stories* – unfinished stories of the future that are told to make and give sense to disruptions, uncertainties and opportunities.

All these types of stories can be present in an organization undertaking change. The point is not to clearly separate them nor elevate any type over another, but to be aware of the variety of stories and how stories of the past, present and future are intertwined.

MINI CASE 7.4

The new appraisal system at Glenrothes Colliery (part 2)

The stories told among the miners at Glenrothes Colliery as a result of the changes in performance appraisals show how the past, present and future can be intertwined with each other. It also shows how stories of the past and future can be told in order to influence the present.

First, there were the retrospective, nostalgic stories of the past that were told by the miners (as described in part 1, in Mini Case 7.2). These stories gave romantic accounts of a workplace characterized by friendship, humour and solidarity among the workers. Second, there were other types of stories told in the organization, including: present change-oriented stories told by managers trying to challenge the status quo; present continuity-oriented stories in which miners resisted change and reasserted their situation by relating to historic happenings; and prospective stories told by miners predicting a tragic future if the change process continued.

The managers in their stories attempted to question the present. They emphasized the need for change and promoted the benefits for miners to undergo regular performance reviews as well as changes in their ways of working. The miners, on their side, resisted these change initiatives and told stories about occurrences that portrayed managers as not having respect for miners:

> A boss who has been here five minutes will come down and ask you something. You will tell them, but they take absolutely no notice, walk away and do whatever they want to do anyway, even though we have been working on the job for 20 years. (Dawson & McLean, 2013, p. 214)

This kind of story reproduced a notion of 'us' and 'them' by showing how the well-intended miner was insulted by the ill-informed, disrespectful manager who failed to listen and take advice from the ones with long experience. The story could therefore be used to justify their actions in the present, such as resisting the new performance system and not listening to managerial opinions in appraisal interviews. Their reasoning was that if managers were ill-informed, their performance ratings could not be accurate and reliable, and in turn not worth considering.

The miners also told stories of themselves as hardworking employees (in the past as well as in the present), thereby upholding continuity in their collective identity: they were, and had always been, hardworking. In turn, tragic stories of the present could be told in which the miners portrayed themselves as victims of serious mishandlings in the performance reviews, in which the managers criticized them for being lazy (which could only be false accusations because of their industrious identity, as reproduced in the other stories). The stories of injustice further enabled the miners to sustain a shared understanding of what it meant to be a miner and to oppose attacks on this understanding. The new appraisal system, which was intended to alter the view of expected behaviour and work performance, could therefore be resisted by miners through stories reproducing themselves as hardworking and managers as ill-informed.

The storytelling was thus not only a way to make sense of the changes, they also served to shape the change as well as their own identities. Furthermore, the ongoing present was interpreted by referring to a reinterpreted past and an anticipated future.

Source: Dawson & McLean (2013)

By focusing on the diversity of voices, managers of change can gain a more insightful picture of what happens in organizational change. This makes it possible to move beyond the stated and official beliefs, values and stereotypes (as in the case of the consultancy work discussed in Chapter 6) and instead approach the beliefs and values that actually influence and govern the change process and outcomes in practice. Also paying attention to alternative voices provides an opportunity to discuss change with the people whose work role and work are impacted by the change (Jabri, 2012).

Moving beyond the formal and management-sanctioned stories and taking the informal every-day stories into account normally allows a more qualified understanding of organizations and change dynamics. Stories that also provide insights into how employees think and feel can be obtained. Paying attention to different parties' stories can also generate openness towards and commitment to change processes. Simply, the act of listening can impact on engagement and a willingness to participate in the changes. It makes people feel recognized and acknowledged, and feel that they have a say. Listening can, in other words, be seen as an effort to empower people.

Storytelling as sense-giving

> At times of change, organizational members will construct an interpretation of events and the implications for them (sensemaking). The senior management of an organization cannot prevent this process occurring, but they can seek to have a major influence on the interpretations that are arrived at by presenting their own constructions of events (sense-giving). (Dunford & Jones, 2000, p. 1208)

Storytelling can be an effective way of sense-giving. It can mobilize individuals and groups for (and also against) change initiatives. In this context, it becomes especially apparent that stories are more than neutral descriptions of change. Stories and storytelling are here seen as an integral part of ongoing change processes. By participating in storytelling, people's understanding of a situation is formed (and potentially also their behaviour): What kind of organization are we and what do we stand for? What is important and distinctive about us? Does the organization work as it should, or is it in need of change? In which case, what kind of change would be appropriate? Important to note is that the impact of change stories is partly contingent upon the storyteller's ability to provide an engaging and convincing account (Dunford & Jones, 2000; van Hulst & Ybema, 2019).

MINI CASE 7.5

Storytelling in business

Organizations that see storytelling as crucial for their business occasionally hire people to work as storytellers, hence the job title 'Chief Storyteller', which is becoming increasingly popular, particularly in the US.

Steve Clayton is Microsoft's Chief Storyteller and manages Microsoft's Image and Culture team. They work to shape an understanding of the company internally and externally by capturing and sharing stories about the company. A key ambition is to transfer the view of the company as old-school to one that is world-changing, by telling stories about how their technology has impacted people's lives. Clayton is, for instance, spreading the story of how the Skype translator made it possible for him to talk to his Chinese mother-in-law for the first time and how Microsoft's technology has improved farmers' yields in India.

At Nike, all senior executives are titled Corporate Storytellers and are expected to tell the story of the founder Phil Knight, who sold running shoes out of his trunk, or how the co-founder Bill Bowerman got the idea of moulding soles in a waffle iron when eating waffles for breakfast in the past. Stories of past heroic acts are told to inspire future innovations.

Sources: McMenemy (2018); Schawbel (2012); Smyth (2018)

Stories about a weak market, business or customer orientation are probably the stories most frequently used to justify a certain amount of change and direction decided by top management (Doolin, 2003). In Chapter 3, we described the triggers for change and used the example of a global pharmaceutical company that tried to establish a story about weak business-orientation as the reason for a lack of progress in product development (see the Case on pp. 72–73, entitled 'Change as a result of trends'). The story was supposed to work as a trigger and justification for an increased business orientation and the strengthening of the managers' power and influence of the research and development processes. However, a critical examination of the company's history showed that there was significant ambiguity about the reasons for the lack of progress in the R&D work, so the proposed business orientation appeared to be a very weak foundation for the proposed changes.

Change agents commonly try to justify changes and facilitate implementation by creating stories about earlier successful changes, and present them neutrally, as part of the organization's history. There can be more or less dramatic stories about the company's traditional inclination for change, formulated with a view to mobilizing commitment. But there are often counter-stories, sometimes pure horror stories, aimed at thwarting change. For example, to undermine an ongoing change process, it is not uncommon for employees to point out that they have worked a lot with change in the past and never noticed any substantial result from all the efforts. As such, stories about change constitute part of the current change process as they can function as a tool to accomplish control (which is intended to either promote or thwart a certain development).

Stories aimed at clarifying and strengthening identities at different levels can also constitute a significant part of a change process. It could, for instance, be employees who distance themselves from management and their proposed changes with the aim of appearing more professional and as serious people who protect the company's origin and core. In this context, it is important to acknowledge that identity constructions often involve people portraying and viewing themselves not only as distinct in relation to others, but also as superior in key ways. Then change actors who represent the polar opposite to the identity constructions of employees might be devalued or smeared by employees who want to enhance their own preferred and lauded identity construction (Sörgärde, 2006). It is therefore important for managers to pay attention to identity dynamics and make efforts to support the development of new or modified identities in line with the new direction of the organization. If identity dynamics are instead dismissed as being solely 'resistance to change', they are unlikely to be properly addressed (Beech & Johnson, 2005).

EXERCISE 7.5

Consider the case below and discuss the following questions:

- What function(s) do you think the stories of 'the democratic company' and 'the big betrayal' played for the developers?
- How do you think their storytelling affected the implementation of the organizational changes?
- What would you recommend the managers to do?

CASE

Reactions to change – stories about uniqueness

A management-initiated attempt to reorganize a medium-sized Swedish IT company – referred to as AlphaTec – from a function-based organization to a divisional-based one ran into strong resistance from the employees who were affected by the proposal. The company management were very surprised about the opposition as they assumed that the change was a natural and necessary step in the development of the organization. As part of their resistance, the employees used stories about the company's origin to argue against the change and how it was being managed. The stories provided support for their view that the managers were behaving immorally, as they were abandoning one of the company's underlying principles. There were two recurrent stories in particular: the story of 'the democratic company' and the story of 'the big betrayal'. The story of the democratic company can be summarized as follows:

> It is us, the IT developers, who started and built this company, not the managers and accountants. As such, AlphaTec is the employees' company. We, the IT developers, are moral shareholders. We should therefore be part of the decision-making process, and the managers cannot control us.

This storyline stressed that AlphaTec was distinct from other companies where developers do not have much influence. AlphaTec belonged to the employees, which is why the managers had no moral right to control them.

The second story, 'the big betrayal', was a more developed version of the first one. It had a tragic undertone and can be summarized as follows:

> AlphaTec is a special company, it is the employees' company. We, the IT developers, were part of starting and building this company. Then a load of managers came along – the 'tie-wearers' – and destroyed everything that was special.

The powerful opposition to the proposed change can be understood in light of these two story-lines, which painted a picture of a very special company. Despite the fact that the company had grown substantially and was no longer a small company where all the decisions could be taken during a coffee break with everybody gathered around, the story of the small democratic company had a strong hold among the employees. The general understanding was that every-body could be part of decision-making and that the best argument always won in key debates, rather than the argument of a manager. In conjunction with the reorganization, the developers expressed profound disappointment about not being allowed to be part of the decision-making.

Source: Sörgärde (2006)

This case illustrates a situation in which a romantic story of the past and a tragic story of the present became a key element of the change process. The stories enabled the developers to reproduce a certain image of the company by referring to how the company was founded. Both elements of group and organizational identity work can be seen here: the stories portray the developers as the key actors of the company (the moral owners), whose voice should be taken into consideration, and the organization in turn was pictured as a very special company where the best argument should win, not necessarily the argument of the manager. In the light of these stories, the company management and their change actions could appear as out of place, and even immoral. The stories also undermined the authority of the managers, by presenting them as a group of people with no moral right to drive the suggested change, which had both significant implications on the change process at hand in that it functioned as a way to mobilize opposition, but also in the long run since it fuelled an averse and suspicious attitude towards the management.

By telling the story of how it all started, the developers reminded each other of what kind of a company AlphaTec 'really was' and how it should be run.

Of course, only certain stories become influential and have a wide impact on perspectives. Normally, it is more resource-strong individuals whose stories get more air-time in different contexts – company descriptions, annual reports and media – and become more dominant in the organization. However, these stories are not necessarily shared with all those involved in change situations, nor do they necessarily influence the views of the organizational members. Other people who have a decisive informal standing based on professional background or experience can have at least as strong an influence with their stories. Change processes can thus occasionally be seen as somewhat of a battleground between different stories. As such, as a participant in or observer of changes, listening only to one story provides very limited insight about the change course of events (Buchanan & Dawson, 2007).

In addition to the status and credibility of the narrator, there are other factors that influence which stories dominate. Stories that appear factual and that are conveyed in an appealing way are more likely to gain traction (Ng & De Cock, 2002). Above all, stories that fit with existing understandings take root more easily.

EXERCISE 7.6

List as many arguments as you can for and against the following proposition:

When managing change, it is important to present hard facts and a clear and logical plan in order to convince employees of the necessity of organizational change. A softer approach, focusing on conversations and storytelling, is rarely needed to get the change happening.

Stories, legitimating strategies and plausibility

Stories that gain specific foothold in organizations and become a dominating narrative are often those that people experience as plausible, i.e. stories that resonate with people's experience and expectations – expectations which in turn are influenced by the specific cultural, social and discursive context (Thurlow & Helms-Mills, 2015). These contexts both set the limits and enable sensemaking among people who search for plausible meanings for change events and change initiatives. The plausibility of change stories is related to how well the stories resonate with individual and organizational identity as well as the organizational culture (as in the case of the IT developers above). Plausibility is also related to how well the stories are consistent with previous experiences of change, the legitimacy of the proposed changes and also to what extent the change facilitates existing work projects (cf. Weick et al., 2005).

An important aspect for change actors when trying to create plausible stories among those targeted by change is to employ what is sometimes referred to as 'legitimating narratives', i.e. stories that are seen as valid and genuine in some sense. Thurlow and Helms-Mills (2015) discuss five forms of legitimating strategies: normalization, authorization, rationalization, moralization and narrativization:

> Normalization is described as a form of authorization whereby events or actions are constructed as normal or natural; authorization refers to legitimation related to the authority of laws, customs or individuals who hold some type of institutional authority; rationalization references actions based upon specific knowledge claims that are accepted as relevant or 'true' in a given context; moralization strategies are constructed by referencing specific value systems; and narrativization refers to the processes of situating the action within a relevant or accepted storytelling framework. (Thurlow and Helms-Mills, 2015, p. 249)

These legitimating strategies represent a possible list of rationales that can be drawn upon by change actors in order to try to manage or lead the change process in terms of enhancing its plausibility, something that may reduce resistance and conflicts and boost the possibility for shared meaning about the change process.

MINI CASE 7.6

Legitimating strategies in a community college

A change process in a community college in Eastern Canada was initially triggered by a governmental report suggesting that the college had serious problems. In particular, the operation of the college, such as its performance measurement, programmes and accountability were claimed to be insufficient. The government report also advised that the college developed its educational programmes, enlarged enrolment, and aligned itself more strategically with the industry and government. The assessment came as a shock for the college. Based on the recommendations, the newly recruited CEO launched a strategic re-orientation plan for the college. The key idea was that the college should change from being a vocational college

(Continued)

offering occupational training to become a more complete community college offering schools of business, communication, applied arts and health services. This transformation implied a change in organizational identity, culture, leadership and organizational structure.

The CEO of the college was seen as a key actor in the change process. With a working-class background and from a rural area, the CEO was described as a charismatic and confident leader. He had early on formulated a vision stating that those from more disadvantageous and rural parts of Canada should have access to a college community education of national calibre, declaring that: 'Part of the reason I took the job was I felt that there was, if you like, a fundamental wrong that had to be righted.' This represents a strong moral conviction that was drawn upon in many of the stories told by the CEO:

> Because of the anomalously slow development of college education in this province, it was accurate to say that simply by virtue of having the misfortune of being born in this province, you had access to fewer post-secondary applied education opportunities than if you had been born in any other province in Canada. And I just thought that was fundamentally wrong.

The vision was also closely tied to successfully securing government funding, which made it possible to renovate facilitates and extend educational programmes. The securing of the funding was seen as a major success for the CEO and for the college. This achievement became part of the storytelling and enhanced legitimacy of the change, especially at a time of governmental cutbacks for universities in general in the region. In particular, the college could be promoted as a legitimate post-secondary player in the region.

The story that came to dominate most was that of a college shifting identity from a 'vocational high school' to a 'national calibre college'. The stories drawn upon by the CEO were seen as highly plausible and gained a strong foothold in the college. Indeed, the whole change process was closely tied to the CEO and his vision for the change process. A restructuring of power from principals and campus administration facilitated his influencing power. A growth of the central office gave the CEO important access to those individuals who had a lot of decision-making power and who were communicating to the various campuses of the college. The passionate belief of the CEO was also contagious throughout the whole organization and seemed to have motivated many of the other employees.

Source: Thurlow & Helms-Mills (2015)

In this case we can note how the CEO draws upon the moral and authoritative strategies of legitimation in particular. These forms of legitimation seem to have had a powerful impact on how people made sense of the changes in terms of plausibility. Normalization through the government funding was also quite important. No counter-story emerged in this case, as the story promoted by the CEO resonated well with people's experiences and identities, and represented a broadly shared view of the change process. We can see here how legitimation strategies, which enhanced the plausibility of the stories told which in turn fuelled sensemaking processes, can be powerful managerial instruments in change processes.

The case also suggests that legitimation strategies are ongoing in change processes and not just something that change actors should think of when initiating a change. This is especially important when considering radical change processes, where people can feel that organizational identity and stability are undermined and threatened, and subsequently the new stories may need time to gain a strong hold.

EXERCISE 7.7

Find an organization (using secondary sources) that has recently been involved in a radical and preferably controversial organizational change process. It needs to be controversial to the extent that the change process included conflicts and clashes between different participants about the need for or direction of change. Analyze the statements and comments made about the change and identify any storytelling among those participating in the change. What reasons and motives can be identified behind the storytelling and what different interests and assumptions may lie within these?

REVIEW QUESTIONS 7.2

Recall	What does the concept 'story' refer to in the context of organizational change?
Explain	What roles can stories play for individuals in change processes?
Explain	How can storytelling influence organizational change processes?
Reflect	Why do you think the elements of stories have gained such a strong momentum in understanding change in recent years?
Reflect	Adopting a narrative perspective on organizational life, what method-related advice would you give to students about to design a study on organizational change process based primarily on semi-structured interviews?

DISCOURSE AND ORGANIZATIONAL CHANGE

Discourse has been a popular concept in the social sciences for more than two decades and is seen by many as being central to understanding reality as socially constructed. In this context, we see organizational discourse as ways of talking or writing about a phenomenon that also create and shape (constitute) the phenomenon in question. More specifically, discourse is seen as a set of related concepts and expressions that frames and influences how people understand a certain aspect of the world (Watson, 2006). Discourses are expressed and reproduced in academic as well as popular management literature, in speeches by practitioners, politicians and consultants, and in other influential media (daily newspapers, business magazines, films) and everyday communication.

Adopting a discourse perspective implies paying attention to how various forms of language use – in texts, images or speeches – express and contribute to shaping understandings of leadership and organizational change management. For example, Sveningsson and Larsson (2006) highlight a leadership and organizational change discourse that express an understanding of the leader and change as being decisive for the success of organizations.

At the same time as discourses shape and form people via their influence on how events and situations are comprehended, discourses in turn are shaped and formed over time by people's use of them. Put differently, discourses are expressed in stories, rhetoric, metaphors, humour and irony, which in turn arise and take shape in interpersonal interactions (Grant et al., 2004). Production (publishing a text or making a speech), reproduction (in interaction with others) and consumption (e.g. identifying oneself as a change actor) of discourses is sometimes referred to as *discursive practice* (Grant & Marshak, 2011; Hardy & Phillips, 2004). Or as Tsoukas (2005, p. 98) states:

> A discursive practice is the norms-bound use of a sign system directed at or to achieving something. [...] Rather than looking for abstract representations in the mind, from a discursive point of view one looks for patterns in the use of words. The rules governing the use of words – the grammar – are discernible in how people account for themselves and others – in how they use discourse.

The popularity of the discourse concept in modern social sciences can mostly be traced back to French philosopher Michel Foucault's critical studies of the emergence of the social and humanistic sciences (Foucault, 1976). These sciences are seen not only as the progressive development of neutral and objective knowledge of society and humans, but also as a new form of exercising power, and is intimately connected to the emergence of the modern disciplined individual. The concept of discourse makes us aware that the social and humanistic sciences are also about power and politics, through the disciplinary effect on thought, actions and identity that knowledge can have. Assimilating and identifying oneself with certain knowledge – for example, varieties of strategy or leadership – means allowing oneself to be disciplined by knowledge, and thereby becoming subject to a power that one can later reproduce in speech and actions (Knights & Morgan, 1991). The link between power and subjectivity is central in many discourse analyses (see Casey, 1999; Willmott, 1993).

The concept 'discourse' has only had a minimal impact among consultants and practitioners, and it seldom appears in their work. Most consultants probably consider the commercial potential of the concept to be somewhat limited compared with more business-like concepts, such as knowledge management and leadership. For many practitioners, it is likely the difficulty in making the concept tangible and concrete that has contributed to it being rather overlooked. However, the concept has been used in numerous studies of organizational change, mainly for descriptive analysis but also prescriptively. Below we discuss how it can be used to improve understandings of organizational change.

REVIEW QUESTIONS 7.3

Recall	What does the concept 'discourse' mean in the context of organizations?
Reflect	Why do you think that discourse has had a relatively low impact among practitioners and consultants in understanding organizational phenomenon such as organizational change?

Levels and influence of discourse

In order to comprehend what discourse analysis means, it can be useful to differentiate between different types of discourse and different levels of analysis. We can talk about discourse analysis at a *micro level*, focusing on the language use of individuals, at a *meso level*, focusing on a group of people (such as a department or project group), at a *macro level*, where discourses address dominant expressions in an organization and at a *meta level*, which includes discourses at a societal level (see for instance, Grant & Marshak, 2011). We will primarily consider the last two in this book.

At a broad *societal level*, discourses are often abstract in nature, such as statements about change being good (which politicians often claim), and offer no further specifics. For example, consider Barack Obama's way of speaking about change as 'Yes we can', or, more recently, Donald Trump's 'Making America Great Again', which has been distributed and replicated in other contexts. Indeed, the promotion of organizational change is one of the most dominant trends among organizational researchers, consultants, practitioners and mainstream writers

(Abrahamsson, 1996; Helms-Mills, 2003). It appears in a broad range of literature, at conferences and seminars as well as in newspapers and magazines. Management trends, popular concepts and other institutional forces create a host of demands and expectations on organizations, but many of them are abstract, without any relevance for the processes and outcomes of businesses. Furthermore, many popular slogans and fashionable concepts often clash with existing organizational discourses. Adopting them might generate organizational hypocrisy (Brunsson, 2006). A critical interpretation of these may help to prevent people from embarking on a change project in an unreflective way simply to appear progressive and competent by following the trend.

At an *organizational level*, organizational discourses might consist of organization-specific and more local ways of talking about (and understanding) organizational practice. For instance, that the organization is flexible and open to change or that the organization needs to be agile due to the continuous technological development and fierce competition on the market. Organizational discourses are often made up of local interpretations and expressions of broader meta-discourses. Even if there is a dominating discourse in an organization about how people should work to achieve their goals, organizations are usually full of many different discourses that compete and sometimes clash with each other. People have their favourite discourses based on their interests, goals and convictions about what organizations should do to be successful. Some people emphasize productivity and cost-efficiency – a production discourse – while others believe that quality and differentiation – a market discourse – is the route to success. A dominant organizational discourse is thus always at risk of being challenged by alternatives.

The performative aspect of discourses

As previously discussed, discourses not only express understandings, they can also influence and shape opinions, identities and political agendas within organizations. In those cases, discourses are said to be *performative* in the sense that they frame how people perceive organizations and the importance of change (Hardy, 2001). A traditional interpretation of discourse, according to Foucault (1976), implies viewing people – their thoughts and actions – as being influenced and controlled to a great extent by structures such as knowledge, institutions and trends. Based on this rather deterministic view, organizational change can primarily be viewed as a result of determining external forces.

However, the view of discourse as highly determining and powerful – or muscular (Alvesson & Kärreman, 2000) – with a large and unequivocal, almost complete, impact on people has been supplemented with a stronger focus on interpretation, understanding and purpose (Garrety et al., 2003; Grant & Marshak, 2011; Newton, 1998). In terms of what causes organizational change, as discussed in Chapter 3, we can say that the teleological aspect has also become more prominent in the context of discourse. The basic assumption, then, is that how people express themselves, think and act is to some degree influenced by discourses, but hardly in an unequivocal and undistorted way. Rather, it is a question of influence, which is formed by how people relate to and understand discourses according to their personal background, education, interests, ambitions and identity, among other things (Garrety et al., 2003; Spicer & Sewell, 2010). A local adaptation and adjustment of socially overarching and broad discourses occurs based on organizational contingencies. In local organizational interaction, for example in talk and conversations about organizational change, ideas, expressions and reasoning from meta-discourses might be used, but these usually arise on the basis of organizational contingencies and in competition with other established discourses. The background, interests and ambitions of the individuals involved also influence the local formation of organizational discourses.

For example, talk about the need to change due to external circumstances (so-called 'change or die' reasoning) can be understood as a broad organizational change discourse from the meta-level (see also the later discussion in Chapter 8). Based on this generally established discourse, local stories are formed about the need for change in the local organization. The meta-discourse, and also the local discourses, becomes the basis or starting point for the rhetoric that managers and other employees draw upon in order to drive change projects. Similar to stories, discourse use also has a legitimizing function: by referring to an established discourse, arguments can gain strong buy-in and thereby be understood as acceptable. This is why changes are often justified through reference to external factors, even though other factors, such as personal objectives and interests or career ambitions, may have at least as much influence (but might be seen as less legitimate).

REVIEW QUESTIONS 7.4

Recall	What is meant by discourse at an organizational and a societal level, respectively?
Explain	Explain in what way discourses can be performative. What are the possible implications of performative discourses for managing change?
Explain	Discuss the value of considering organizational and societal discourses when driving organizational change processes.

Discourses and politics

In line with the process orientation, a discursive understanding of change is generally accompanied by a political view of organizations. The usage and reproduction of discourses at a local organizational level often involves persuasion, power pressure and negotiation about the meaning of the phenomenon, by different people with different backgrounds, interests and ambitions (Hardy & Phillips, 2004; Thomas et al., 2011). This often leads to a certain amount of disagreement, conflict and local power struggles that mostly result in a discursively accepted view of the organization and the change being established, which becomes the dominant way of seeing the organizational reality (Hardy, 2001). This can be a matter of the classic disagreement between a market orientation and a production orientation.

Organizations can be understood as political systems in which parties push for their own objectives and interests by, for example, mobilizing discourses to create or enhance the legitimacy for or against a proposed change. Subsequently, change actors should not regard discourses as merely neutral and unpolitical ideas that stand outside power plays and organizational politics. For example, although being very popular and, for many, taken-for-granted, discourses, such as having a 'knowledge orientation' or a 'service orientation', can also be seen as expressions of the exercise of power because they also 'demand' – more or less explicitly – certain individual and organizational subordination in terms of thinking and acting. Social and organizational discourses that are drawn upon in order to push for organizational change are linked to different interests, with implicit priorities and resource allocations.

EXERCISE 7.8

Contemporary organizations quite routinely express in public the value of change and acknowledge – in formal statements, symbols, official talk, etc. – that they are change-oriented in terms of being open, adaptive and flexible. It is also common to talk about and stress the importance of learning, innovation and development. The opposite – glorifying stability in terms of being more closed, rigid and less adaptive – doesn't have the same value in the business community. Arguably, talking about maintenance and continuity seem to be old-hat in terms of what is the right and fashionable thing to say. But is this also the case when investigating what is happening in practice?

Based on your own experience of an organization or by using secondary sources, critically analyze and review how the organization seemingly only paid lip service to the idea of being an adaptable organization.

Discuss why some organizations maintain a public stance of being change-oriented and innovative while not actually applying these ideals in practice. Do you see any possible risks in doing so?

Managing change and discourses

Members of organizations can mobilize and use discourses in communication with others in order to position themselves in the organization (Garrety et al., 2003). In practice, this is accomplished through talk and conversation – i.e. in discursive practice – in which members of the organization use and apply certain expressions and concepts, and thereby also try to create and establish a certain understanding. The way in which we reason about change with others might produce the change in question, even if this is limited to the local interaction between just two individuals. As we discussed in the section about conversation, a local and limited dialogue about change can create new thoughts and views. Even if the conclusion of the conversation is that there is no need to change – that stability is good – this can comprise a new thought. And even a limited conversation can at least potentially lead to broader legitimization in the organization and have broader organizational consequences (Thurlow & Helms-Mills, 2015). To what extent this occurs depends of course on the content of the discourse and how it aligns to other discourses, the strength and legitimacy of the alternative discourses, the organizational situation, the legitimacy of the person speaking and the status of the interaction and communication in question (Garrety et al., 2003).

MINI CASE 7.7

Discourses with differing content

Change in the dominant organizational logic – in terms of conceptions, norms and actions – at the Australian TV company ABC during the course of a few decades illustrates how centrally positioned people used and locally modified broader discourses in a way that enabled them to push for their own interests. When viewed over a longer period, it might look like certain discourses – for example, that 'ABC should be rooted in the traditional Australian culture' – have been stable and important for the organization. However, a closer examination of what 'Australian culture' meant shows that it has varied a lot over the years, depending on who was interpreting its meaning and what organizational logic they were interested in establishing. Over the years, different groupings have pushed different organizational logics for ABC, such as nationalism, multi-culturalism, neo-liberalism and globalization, with the consequence that the very broad discourse 'Australian culture' has had a wide variety of contexts and meanings. Latterly, it has involved everything from the importance of Australia's European heritage to cultural diversity and heterogeneity. Put another way, 'Australian culture' can mean many different things to many different people, depending on the background and interests of the people interpreting it. We can see here how dominating actors shaped discourses in order to push their own interests. This can be referred to as *discursive agency*.

Source: Spicer & Sewell (2010)

In line with a discursive view of change, Grant and Marshak (2011) developed an integrative framework consisting of seven dimensions, which highlight the importance of language and communication in how people generally view and understand organizational change and the possibility of achieving it (Figure 7.1). The framework summarizes the value of using a discursive perspective for understanding organizational change for both academics and practitioners.

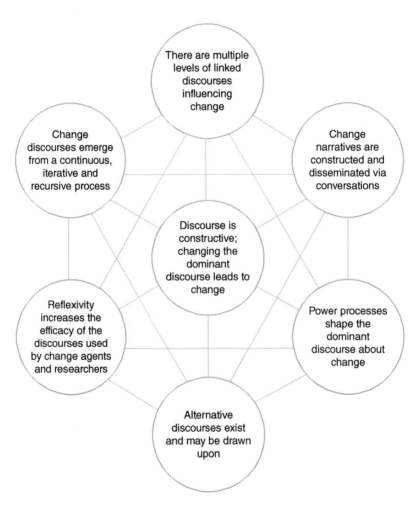

FIGURE 7.1   Discourse and organizational change (based on Grant & Marshak, 2011)

A central idea is that people's understanding and view of organizations and organizational practice is created, maintained and changed through discourses. Discursively anchored talk and conversations about change influence how we see change, in terms of whether we think it is something desirable or necessary, which in turn potentially impacts how we act.

The first dimension is about trying to identify *discourses at multiple levels* in order to understand, lead and sometimes prevent change. In change contexts, there can often be a point in trying to identify the relationship between different levels and, for example, to place local discourses in a wider context, or to understand how important it is to deal with meta-discourses – such as corporate sustainability or globalization – at the organizational level (Fairclough & Thomas, 2004).

In discursive practice, *stories* are central, which is highlighted in the second dimension of the model. Here, they are comprised of coherent stories about the organization that can be drawn upon and used either to push or prevent change (Alvesson & Sveningsson, 2011a; Brown, 1998). As we have previously discussed, during organizational change, narrative work in practice involves capturing and shaping daily conversations and stories to increase the chances of achieving a desired change.

It is further pointed out that discourse and *power* are considered to be mutually dependent, which is why it is unwise to disregard elements of exercising power from a discursive perspective (Hardy & Phillips, 2004). As discussed earlier, organizations can be seen as political arenas in which different parties push their own or their group's agenda, and drawing upon established discourses is an important way of creating legitimacy for one's point of view. In order to drive change, change agents are encouraged to identify key figures within the organization and to try to influence their conversations so that they support the change, or to create forums for identifying different interests and holding discussions connected to discourses that are strongly cemented in the organization.

What people perceive to be real and true in organizations can be understood as social constructions that are created and established through discourses. However, this seldom occurs without conflict and battles. Organizations usually contain many different, and sometimes opposing, discourses. Rather than ignoring these contradictions, it is often better to identify them, with the aim of establishing greater participation and thus more effective change (Ford et al., 2008; Gabriel, 2000). Acknowledging *alternative discourses* normally improves the prospect of innovation and radical change.

As a change actor, it is important to try to be aware of the discursive resources one uses in communication and conversation. *Reflexivity* is therefore desirable. To successfully implement a proposed change, one often needs to adapt one's language and expressions depending on the audience (Czarniawska, 1998). It is also important to recognize the importance of dramaturgy, symbolism, impression management and other influencing means. It can also be important to maintain openness in change situations and thereby be flexible towards alternative discourses and viewpoints. This can be particularly crucial in the introductory phases of change attempts where there is normally more room for creativity and a greater tolerance of ideas.

Discourses drawn upon and visible during organizational change *are changed in a continuous, iterative and recursive process* in terms of the meaning and content attributed to them. It is therefore important to try to understand how discourses surface in organizations and to be open to consider change as an ongoing process comprised of sudden changes often with uncertain out-comes. When considered as a process, change is more uncertain and complex, but not necessarily beyond the possibility of managerial control.

The last and interlinking dimension highlights the performative dimension, i.e. that discourse is *constructive*; by changing the dominant discourse, change can potentially be achieved. From a discursive perspective, change actors are encouraged to focus on understanding and changing interaction in terms of communication between people. It is important for the change actor to view changes as continuous and iterative, and often without any clear start or ending. A discursive orientation implies involving oneself in the ongoing conversations and communication of every-day organizational life and to try to manage these in the desired direction. This requires presence as well as understanding and sensitivity, partly for the interaction between people, and partly for the meaning of the concepts and terms used in that interaction.

In summary, a discursive orientation involves an interpretative effort in the study and management of change. This requires great focus on the constructive nature of language and thus its importance in the production and maintenance of – and challenges around – organizational change and its management. Conversations and communication are shaped by discourses, but discourses are also shaped by conversations and communication. It is there-fore vital to be aware of communication and conversations and the discourses expressed therein, and also how one can participate in these in order to achieve organizational change (Marshak & Grant, 2011).

MINI CASE 7.8

Highlighting an alternative to a traditional masculine discourse in a cultural change

In a large industrial plant in Australia, characterized by masculine values – tough and laddish – with a classic hierarchical top-down management defined by technical knowledge and rational decision-making, an organizational change programme was initiated in the context of inter-nationalization. The ambition was to move away from the masculine values and develop the emotional side of the organization, to facilitate flexibility and increase the level of relationship orientation. A cultural change was designed that placed a particular emphasis on changing the managers' views of themselves – their identity – in relation to the organization, partly with the help of performing personality tests to stimulate self-reflection. The idea was to get rid of the tough management approach and instead acknowledge and recognize the value of feelings such as spontaneity, uncertainty and doubt, and the more personal aspects of their identity. An open and flexible culture was desired in which it was acceptable and even valued to express feelings. Behaviour which before the cultural change process was seen as deviating from the norm would now be emphasized as the new normal and would be explicitly rewarded in terms of promotion, for example.

The personality tests were partly intended to enable people to recognize and appreciate the emotional aspects of their personalities. They were carried out using the Meyer-Briggs Type Indicator (MBTI), an instrument for self-insight, personal development and reflection on how one functions in groups and in dealing with other personalities. The test is built around four dimensions (personality preferences) that are combined in different ways so that the person can be positioned in one of sixteen personality types, as they are known. Each type contains different preferences in thoughts, feelings and behaviour.

When viewed as a discourse, the strict categorization of people into a personality matrix with defined personality types can be seen as a form of discipline. If this test and others like it are taken too seriously, then we are talking about the power of discourse exerting control over the people taking the test. The rather strict categorization of people into types can thus be conceptualized as subjecting individuals to a disciplinary power matrix. In the organization studied, however, the MBTI discourse appeared to have opened the group to alternative ways of behaving. Based on people's interpretation of and response to the test, it appeared to provide them with a tool that facilitated reflection about their identity and their relationships with colleagues. This does not, however, suggest an absence of power, but rather a more diverse and differentiated power.

Through the tests, some of the employees learned that their emotional orientation was not itself wrong, but simply deviated from the traditional taken-for-granted masculine discourse, the status of which could now be questioned and relativized. This contributed to increased self-esteem and self-respect and even pride among many of the employees who had previously felt left out. Some of the employees continued to work on their identity as a result of the personality test, reflecting on interactions with other people and new work experiences. The feeling of being a bit of an outsider within the organization thus decreased for some of the employees, which also contributed to a change in the organizational culture towards more openness.

But the tests also resulted in other outcomes. For some employees, a changed understanding of themselves led to them avoiding certain work tasks as they suddenly realized that the tasks were incompatible with their personality profile. This was later used as an excuse for a lack of cooperation and even a refusal to do some work tasks that they were expected to perform. Acknowledging the emotional aspect of their personality did not achieve any change in those cases; instead, it undermined the attempt at change. For some

(*Continued*)

employees, the personality tests were more identity-neutral and had no real significance for their identity. Some people perceived them to be irrelevant for their work and almost a source of irritation.

Consequently, the personality test discourse led to very mixed results, depending on how the employees related to and interpreted them. Rather than having a uniform and strong impact, in this case we can see how the discourse had a variety of influences, depending on people's interest, experience and background. Even though the overarching result was uncertain in terms of a broadly changed organizational culture, the MBTI process contributed to some extent in changing the power relationships of the organization by partially modifying the perception of what was seen as normal behaviour in the organization.

Source: Garrety et al. (2003)

As a whole, the example in Mini Case 7.8 illustrates how people actively work with discourses and continuously reinterpret them according to new experiences. It also demonstrated the importance of discourses on identity work, to the extent that it holds any relevance at all (cf. Alvesson & Lundholm, 2014; Sveningsson & Alvesson, 2016).

REVIEW QUESTIONS 7.5

Recall	What does 'discursive practice' refer to?
Explain	What is the key message of Grant & Marshak's integrative framework on discourse and organizational change? Discuss how it can be used to support efforts to manage change.
Reflect	Can you identify any discourse that you have used frequently? Reflect on the possible implications of this usage.

SUMMARY

Language is central for both understanding and managing organizational change. From this, it follows that awareness of communication, stories and more or less established forms of expression – discourses – are central in change processes. In this chapter we pointed out three aspects of language: conversations, stories and discourse.

Language sets the framework and conditions for different conversations that are central to the course of change events. Through a particular use of language, an organization appears in a certain light, which influences how people consider the organization: as in need of change or not. In this way, language influences people's sensemaking of and commitment to different issues. The importance of the role of communication in change processes can partly be explained by reflecting on how conversations can aid in initiating change, creating understanding and thus mobilizing commitment and facilitating implementation.

Stories comprise another aspect of language, and they provide insight into how people create meaning – understand – and manage change processes. Through stories (of the past, present and possible future), people's understanding of the organization is shaped. In other words, understanding stories provides insight not only into sensemaking generally, but also into how people relate to stories and how they are used to mobilize a reason for and direction towards changes (sense-giving). Stories are also normally tied to how people create and shape their identities and their efforts to exercise impression management.

A third important concept in this context is discourse, the verbal and popular expressions that people use and draw upon in order to create purpose, to drive and control change processes and also to position themselves (form their identity). The concept of discourse places a focus on how different forms of expression influence people in terms of what is important and crucial to address and change. Many organizational changes are the result of fashion and trends, which are not necessarily always the most appropriate choices. By understanding references to environmental triggers and other external demands as discourses, people may become aware that organizational change is not always a result of rational consideration. Rather, it can be about poorly thought-through attempts to imitate with the idea of appearing competent in the eyes of others. In other words, the concept of discourse enables a more critical position towards organizational change, which we will develop more explicitly in the next chapter.

 KEY PRACTICAL INSIGHTS

What we can say about organizational change following this chapter:

- Language is not merely a simple and neutral way of communicating intentions and decisions about change directions but is something that creates change as such since language facilitates and shapes our understanding of the world in a certain and particular light. The use of language (in terms of words, phrases, expressions, etc.) can thus be understood as a means of framing an organizational situation or event in a certain way that has a potentially powerful impact on meaning and sensemaking.

- Conversations can be seen as a key driver in change initiatives, influencing the process in different directions. Managing change can thus be understood as creating, supporting and transmitting conversations that facilitate the change ambitions, such as (depending on the current phase) conversations initiating change, facilitating an understanding the need for of change, performing respectively concluding change.

- Change processes following a dialogic communication logic commonly involve recognizing a multitude of voices and facilitating a more open and transparent process in which employees are invited to join. In contrast, a monologic mode of communication shuts out alternative voices and thus risks resulting in increased silence, employee detachment, disengagement, resistance and even sabotage.

- Storytelling in and about change processes is important when managing change. Changes normally entail ambiguity and uncertainties that trigger intensive sensemaking in those involved in and targeted by changes. This sensemaking often takes the form of stories that have a variety of different purposes, such as relieving anxiety and uncertainty, maintaining identity and self-esteem or confirming organizational continuity (which is often challenged in change processes).

- Social, organizational and individual identity are key themes in storytelling as they relate to how people understand and view themselves and their organization in terms of distinctiveness, coherence, continuity, status and esteem. Managing change processes is thus facilitated by an understanding of the role of storytelling in identity construction.

- Storytelling can be a powerful way to influence meanings and thus to undertake organizational change. Stories that are in line with established discourses in the organization and are told by a trustworthy speaker (from the listeners' point of view) have a better chance of gaining a stronger hold than others.

- Established ways of talking and expressing organizational realities – so-called discourses – often have a powerful impact on how people understand organizational change and its different elements, such as its triggers, dynamics and manageability. Beyond merely representing an objective reality, discourses are thus said to contribute to the shaping of organizational reality. Considering discourses at the organizational level – can therefore provide important insights into organizational dynamics.

- Organizations are normally framed by a number of alternative discourses – concerning its orientation, values, norms, identity, etc. – which compete for attention and recognition; not the least in relation to the need for and possibilities of accomplishing change.

- Managing this multitude of discourses is normally facilitated by adopting a reflective attitude, which essentially means that one is willing to consider what might be wrong with established ways of talking and framing organizational reality, including one's own. Thinking critically – that is, scrutinizing and problematizing conventional discourses in terms of assumptions and consequences for organizational change and considering alternatives – is key.

CASE

Three stories of organizational change

Stories can be used for different purposes and stories told in an organization do not necessarily resonate with the official one. This case is a collection of three different stories from different organizations, but they share the following features: they are all told in parallel to the official stories but they do not fully resonate with the official narratives and they are all employed by organizational actors to make sense of organizational change. They are stories about (1) 'the good old days', (2) deception, and (3) influence.

Story of the good old days

A British automotive supplier, Engineering Ltd, went through a radical technological and structural change process during the 1980s and 1990s. The official story about the change process has an epic and heroic flavour to it, explaining how the company developed from a failure to become a world-class organization in its industry. The story describes a difficult past as being a real crisis which was overcome by transformational changes, in particular relating to manufacturing, where robotic technology and new world-class techniques were introduced, as well as quality management. It is a very affirmative story, of a problematic past, a period of transition and a bright future.

One of the employees, Mary, tells the positive story. First, she describes the technological development with excitement and explains how amazing it was to see how the modern production technology worked. However, the second part of her story is somewhat different in the sense that it paints a nostalgic picture of a past that is rather common in change processes. Among other things, she says that:

> All this part [of the plant] here was built on while I was working here […] but it was always in my mind that it wasn't getting bigger too quick and then I thought […] it's people who're making it bigger, the management. You still thought 'is it getting too big too quick?' […] It went from a small friendly place to still being friendly, but you didn't know the people, you couldn't say hello […] you passed people and you didn't know who they were. (Reissner, 2011, p. 599)

The later part of the story expresses elements of doubt about the new orientation as it does not provide room for the old and smaller community where everyone knew each other, the more family-like organization. The loss of the family feeling was something others in the organization expressed too. For instance, people talked about how in the past they addressed

(Continued)

each other with their first names (senior managers too), helped each other out and organized social events, like day-trips and table tennis during breaks. This rather generalized image of how good things were in the past was typically not challenged by people in the organization. Even newcomers who had not experienced this period of the company's history retold the story of the golden past with its emphasis on relationships and the Engineering Ltd's family feeling. There were, in other words, two types of stories being told, one about the successful change, in line with the official version of the transformation of the company, and one about the good old days, acknowledging some kind of stability and continuity of values in spite of the transformation.

Questions

- Why do you think the official story – the transformation from the problematic past to the bright future – was not fully accepted and retold by Mary?
- What function(s) do you think the story of 'the good old days' had for Mary?
- How do you think the telling of the nostalgic story of the past affected the present (in particular, the organizational culture)?

Story of 'deception'

Sometimes change stories emerge around themes related to power play and identity, and may be sensitive to talk about. This is illustrated in one of the main steel producers, Steel Corp, in South Africa, which underwent radical organizational change after the end of the Apartheid era in the 1990s. Both economical and institutional factors triggered radical organizational change. Economically, the company faced increasing international competition and embarked on radical restructuring programmes, including cost-cutting and massive lay-offs. At the same time, the company also faced increasing pressure to comply with the institutional demands of the government's employment equity (EE) programme, which required that the demographics of the organization should reflect the demographics of South Africa. Following this demand, Steel Corp needed to promote black or Asian employees to managerial positions, while also demoting or laying off white managers who had historically been in a majority of the managerial positions. Transforming itself into a modern business that reflected the social demographics at the managerial level represented a radical change of the organizational culture. In order to facilitate this, white males in their 50s were encouraged to accept redundancy, thereby enabling black and Asian workers to take their positions, according to the employment equity programme. At that time, unemployment in this specific age group was high and new employment was hard to find. The change process was, in other words, a seemingly sensitive issue for the white males who were required to leave their managerial positions.

Damian is part of the group of employees who risk losing their jobs to EE candidates. He is a white manager in his late 40s. Damian reasons, in the first part of his story, that the EE programme is good: 'Employment equity, I think, makes good sense; there's no doubt in my mind about it.' He also critiques Steel Corp by questioning whether it has implemented EE successfully, and concludes that they have not done so – 'not at all'. 'The company just across the road has come so much further', he says. On the one hand, Damian is telling a story of EE in line with the official version, indicating that he has accepted the situation and is pro the changes, even though Steel Corp has not done enough. Other employees also highlight that the organization has not done what it could in terms of EE: it has not been the top priority in the firm. Interestingly, there is no indication in Damian's story that these changes will be a threat to him, even though he has seen others who have had to leave and he doesn't know if he will be next.

In the second part of the story, Damian explains the lack of development in terms of EE by claiming that there aren't enough people in the community where the company is located, white or black, who can be employed in those roles and that, drawing on what the company formally states, black people don't want to move to the community where the company is located. Based on this, the new situation, with the demands of EE, is not so threatening for Damian. However, Reissner (2011) suggests that these statements are factually incorrect as there are many unemployed people in the community who form a large pool of capable people who can potentially be hired by the company. There is indeed at real threat to Damian. Consequently, part of Damian's story doesn't seem to be a representation of factual conditions.

In this case, the unspoken stories as well as more private conversations need to be taken into account. Hardly any of the white employees officially state that it is hard to find qualified black workers to fill the positions, but informal conversations seem to reproduce the polarizations between black and white workers and these conversations are infused with elements of racial superiority, where blacks are described as lacking skills and experience. These opinions are in one sense taboo, but nevertheless they seem to be part of the undercurrent in the company.

Questions

- Why do you think Damian accepts the official story that EE is important and should be implemented?
- What function do you think the other part of the story played for Damian, where he gave the impression that there is a lack of candidates for managerial positions like his own?

(*Continued*)

Stories of influence

Stories of change are sometimes used as a mechanism of power in that they can substantially influence how people make sense of changes in the context of their work. This can be illustrated in Northern Steel, one of the largest steel makers in Russia. Founded in the 1940s, the plant had been part of the heavy industry system of the Soviet Union. Since the breakup of the Soviet Union, the company has radically modernized itself according to Western principles and ideas of how to manage a company. It has been privatized and diversified as well as been subjected to strategic and operational changes. Crucial for this development has been a variety of educational initiatives in which managers have been encouraged to study for an MBA in the UK and frontline employees have been supported to study how steel operations are managed and organized in the West.

Following this development, many employees were extremely proud of working for the organization and many seemed to hail its progressive culture. Most significantly, a key figure and a kind of hero in this development was its CEO, Mikhailov. It has been suggested by many of the employees that he has never been wrong in any of his judgements and people seemingly find it difficult even to imagine anything to the contrary. He is thus seen as a 'beacon of stability' among most of the employees, which was obviously important in terms of reducing organizational anxiety and uncertainty.

The official version of the new ways of working draws a lot on the traditional collective orientation of the plant – as a place where success is achieved together and everybody plays a part. Many employees express gratitude and pride in working for this reformist organization. However, the inclusiveness of the development is contested by some in the organization and listening to Eve making sense of the changes paints a more complex picture. Eve is a member of staff in her 40s. She has an engineering background and more than 20 years' service at Northern Steel, most of the time within HR. While maintaining that professional development in terms of education is important for Northern Steel, she also says that women in their 40s are excluded from such education, which they need to progress to senior management. She attributes this exclusion to Mikhailov, who once said that women over 40 can't contribute anything to the organization. She says that:

> There's more opportunity for development now, which we didn't have in our time. [...] Training's important because [our CEO] said once that women over the age of 40 couldn't do anything in the organization. That was a long time ago, maybe 10 years. Back then, obviously, I wasn't 40 yet and I thought 'what's that about?' But now I am that age I think that basically he was right. Simply living your life and communicating with a small circle of people, you already miss out a lot. There's no development. I think that a reduction [in our ability] might even start because you've got experience and you don't worry about things you've got to learn.

This is a story that opposes the official story of inclusiveness and opportunities. As a woman in her 40s, the doors are closed for her and she can't get into the training programmes for senior managers. The second part of the story seems to explain why she is still fine with it. What is particularly notable, though, is that the tension between her initial beliefs of career development (seemingly in line with the official version of the company) and her current experience of lack of opportunities seems to be resolved (made sense of) by a 10-year-old story told by Mikhailov about women over 40. We do not know in what context or with what arguments the original story was told (Eve did not even agree with it at that time!), but it could still be used as a sensemaking device for her. In other words, she engages in a story that explains her complacency with regard to her own (lack of) career possibilities. The story is built upon Mikhailov's saying, as well as her own reflections on her limited view of the whole organization. Her current work experience thus seems to be highly influenced by Mikhailov's statement, a man who is regarded as never being wrong.

Questions

- In what way could Eve's story be understood as identity work (i.e. as efforts to uphold a certain view of herself)?
- Why do you think Mikhailov's old saying made sense for Eve? Try to consider a broad range of answers.

 # FURTHER READING

Go online to access free and downloadable SAGE Journal articles related to this chapter at **https://study.sagepub.com/sveningsson**

Special issue on Storytelling and Change (2009). *Organization*, 16(3), 323–462.

Beech, N., & Johnson, P. (2005). Discourses of disrupted identities in the practice of strategic change: The mayor, the street-fighter and the insider-out. *Journal of Organizational Change Management*, 18(1), 31–47.

Boje, D. M., Haley, U., & Saylors, R. (2016). Antenarratives of organizational change: The microstoria of Burger King's storytelling in space, time and strategic context. *Human Relations*, 69(2), 391–418.

Boje, D. M., Oswick, C., & Ford, J. D. (2004). Language and organization: The doing of discourse. *Academy of Management Review*, 29(4), 571–577.

Gabriel, Y. (2004). Narratives, stories, texts. In D. Grant, C. Hardy, C. Oswick, & L. L. Putnam (eds.), *The Sage Handbook of Organizational Discourse*. London: Sage, pp. 61–79.

Rouleau, L., & Balogun, J. (2011). Middle managers, strategic sensemaking, and discursive competence. *Journal of Management Studies*, 48(5), 953–983.

Suddaby, R., & Foster, W. (2017). History and organizational change. *Journal of Management*, 43(1), 19–38.

Van Hulst, M., & Ybema, S. (2019). From what to where: A setting-sensitive approach to organizational storytelling. *Organization Studies*, online first 25 January, 1–27, doi/10.1177/0170840618815523

 VIDEO

Go online to view video clips related to the key themes discussed in this chapter at

https://study.sagepub.com/sveningsson

THE CRITICAL PERSPECTIVE
OF CHANGE

LEARNING OBJECTIVES

When you have completed your study of this chapter, you should be able to:

- Describe what distinguishes a critical perspective on organizational change.

- Discuss critically and problematize some of the most common assumptions of organizational change that are often implicitly proposed in popular change literature and among many practitioners initiating and recommending change.

- Appraise the conventional and more recent change management models in a critical light.

- Broadly discuss why viewing organizations as political arenas may be productive in understanding and managing organizational change.

- Explain the significance and relevance of considering alternatives stories of change proposals.

- Apply a critical perspective on change processes in order to debunk taken-for-granted dimensions by considering what assumptions the change process is founded on and whose voices and interests are recognized and prioritized.

The premise of this chapter is that organizations are made up of individuals and groups with different interests and motivations who compete with each other for scarce resources, power and influence. This is also one of the premises of the process perspective, although not its main focus, as is the case here. The main difference between a critical perspective and a process perspective is that the underlying ambition is not only to understand change processes, but also to unpack them and question them.

The ambition of critical studies is normally to make visible – to reveal – and question the things that are written between the lines, and to scratch the surface to illuminate what lies below the polish. Above all, critical studies highlight the political dimension of management and control, which means that power and the exercise of that power become a central theme. Another distinctive characteristic of the critical perspective is that it questions assumptions that are taken for granted in much of the conventional literature on managing organizational change. In this context, traditional change management theory is considered more as *one* way of viewing and speaking about organizational change – like a discourse – and less as an absolute truth. In addition, the aim with the critical perspective is to allow more voices to be heard, not just those of senior organizational management whose agenda usually receives the most air time. This chapter does not focus primarily on *how* change should be managed but *if* change should be managed at all. It also brings attention to the mental bubble that we often end up in as we become interested in organizational change management.

A central ambition of this chapter is to inspire reflection and consideration as well as to challenge people to take a critical approach to accounts of organizational change. It also offers recommendations for those pursuing organizational change: What is considered and what is not? Whose interests and whose perspectives are in focus and whose are not? Are there any alternative perspectives? Through this chapter we hope to enhance readers' understanding about existing critiques and encourage them to be inspired by a more reflective and nuanced approach to managing change (see Hughes, 2010).

The chapter begins with a brief background to the critical perspective within the social sciences, followed by a presentation of its underlying assumptions and key concepts. Next, we focus specifically on critical studies of organizational change. This section is structured into two parts. First, we highlight studies that problematize traditional ideas within change management theory and challenge common myths and assumptions. Second, we examine studies that present alternative voices about change programmes and change processes, voices that otherwise tend to be marginalized.

ORIGIN AND EMERGENCE OF THE CRITICAL PERSPECTIVE

Critical theory can be traced back to the founding of what is known as the Frankfurt School in the 1920s. This was a group of German intellectuals trained in the tradition of critical, philosophical and sociological knowledge and included several influential social scientists – Horkheimer,

Adorno, Fromm and Marcuse. They developed critiques of social conditions in order to improve societal order. The German philosopher Habermas then took these ideas further.

The role of the researcher within this tradition is to be an engaged and impartial party that can examine society and how it functions from a critical perspective, instead of viewing the prevailing order as natural and inevitable. Critical theory is described by Prasad (2005, p. 136) as the

> extraordinary intellectual product of despair and disappointment – despair over the frightening ascendancy of European fascism and Nazism; and disappointment with the excesses of Stalinist socialism and the cultural emptiness of prosperous high-consumption societies like the United States.

Instead of looking for conformities and simple causal links, critical studies focus on understanding and questioning social phenomena and established institutions. Why does society function the way it does? What does the historical context look like?

In this chapter we are inclusive and use critical theory in its broadest sense. The purpose is to emphasize an alternative perspective on change that differs in its core elements from the traditional tools-based texts.

Critical thinking is nothing new in organizational change. It has been a part of organization and management studies ever since its infancy and is sometimes referred to as far back as 1776 when Adam Smith highlighted the political dimension of organizational life by pointing out that directors watch over their own interests (Fournier & Grey, 2000). However, it was not until the 1970s that the orientation became more prominent and influential within the organizational field more broadly. In the 1990s a more explicit critical theory as an independent subdiscipline became established within organizational studies, under the umbrella term of *Critical Management Studies* (CMS). It combines various critical traditions, such as Critical Theory, Post-Structuralism and Feminism. A key idea of this broad field is to challenge the status quo by questioning established social orders and to contribute to emancipation (Alvesson & Ashcraft, 2009). The discussion of the critical perspective in this chapter is largely based on this research orientation.

REVIEW QUESTIONS 8.1

Recall	Briefly explain the key idea and fundamental ambition that served as the starting point for Critical Theory.
Explain	Describe the role and focus of the researcher in the critical tradition.
Reflect	All academic studies are supposed to be critical to some extent. Elaborate on various meanings of the word 'critical' and explain what the term refers to in Critical Theory. Put differently, in what ways is Critical Theory distinctly critical compared to other studies?

THE CRITICAL PERSPECTIVE – DEFINING FEATURES

Adopting a critical perspective on management and organizations means essentially starting from the premise that something is problematic with management, whether its practice and/or the knowledge of the practice, and having an ambition to change it. To be more specific, and in order to more clearly distinguish critical studies from non-critical studies, Fournier and Grey (2000) have explained the characteristics of critical studies, and these are set out in Table 8.1.

TABLE 8.1 The characteristics of critical studies (Fournier & Grey, 2000)

Denaturalization	Critical studies are committed to denaturalization – to problematize our understanding and knowledge of organizational life and managerial practice in order to open up and provide room for questioning things that are often otherwise taken for granted and considered 'natural'
Non-performative stance	Critical studies are characterized by an anti-performative intent – a stance that distances critical studies from the idea that knowledge should aim to contribute to improved managerial effectiveness
Reflexivity	Critical studies emphasize and are characterized by a commitment to methodological reflexivity

In terms of *denaturalization*, one of the central lines of thought within the critical perspective is that the existing order – our understanding of organizational reality – is constructed but often not considered as constructed in the sense that it tends to be taken for granted and is 'naturalized' in conventional management literature. For example, a common assumption is that somebody must lead a business and therefore hierarchies are typically seen as natural and inevitable. They are also often supported by arguments such as: 'It has always existed in all historical contexts' and 'There is no alternative'. By referring to the natural order and historical necessities, a typical legitimization of the prevailing order is created that reappears in many assumptions about society and organizations. The point that critical theorists make is that in many cases the social order is created and maintained by people and it is therefore possible to problematize and change the social order. Understanding that organizations are social and temporary creations can enable a standpoint of distance from and a more critical positioning towards claims about 'how things have to be organized', and thus form the basis for potential change. In other words, a key ambition of critical studies is to uncover and identify alternatives, and to unlock narrow and frozen mindsets. Things may not be as they appear at first sight.

EXERCISE 8.1

Look up an academic article that explicitly takes a critical perspective on organizational change, i.e. an article in which you can identify an emancipatory ambition (to critically scrutinize organizational practices and/or theories). You can pick an article listed in the Further Reading section at the end of this chapter.

Can you identify a commitment to denaturalization? If so, what specific assumptions are being questioned? How is this accomplished?

A *non-performative stance* involves questioning the traditional assumption that profit maximization is an obvious doctrine in most of the literature about management and organizations. A critical perspective implies a certain distancing from and problematization of this doctrine, which expresses an instrumental and utility maximization view of social relationships and organizations (Grey & Willmott, 2005). Critical researchers are not against improved effectiveness, but they recognize the importance of questioning and criticizing the idea that organizational knowledge is only valuable if it contributes to increased effectiveness. If one only focuses on results and sees actions in organizations solely as means to an end, other important matters, such as those of an ethical and political nature, tend to be marginalized and overlooked. A key point of departure within critical studies is that evaluation of knowledge creation should not be subjected solely to the criteria of effectiveness.

Mainstream research on management and organizations is built upon assumptions of neutrality and objectivity. Critical studies challenge this position and emphasize that neither the choice of study matter nor the way research is carried out is impartial and completely free of values (Grey & Willmott, 2005). *Reflexivity*, the third feature of critical studies, involves clarifying how knowledge production about management and organizations is influenced by traditions, norms, morals and knowledge interests. Accordingly, there is great value in closely examining the assumptions, objectives and premises on which knowledge production is based (to then be able to problematize these if needed). Both critical and mainstream research is produced in specific contexts with particular conditions, and reflexivity is about highlighting these conditions and reflecting upon how they may have influenced knowledge production. This approach stands in sharp contrast to conventional management studies which claim to be neutral and detached (Taskin & Willmott, 2000).

A critical perspective is primarily directed at established theory rather than at the organizational practice which is the main interest within the tool-based and process orientations. One central line of thought is that organizational literature plays an important role in the social construction of reality, and therefore should be the subject of critical examination. As discussed above, the critical perspective is about challenging and disrupting established understandings rather than confirming and reproducing them. Zooming in on critical studies in organizational change, conventional management theories on change are sometimes referred to as a change management discourse, including concepts, models and assumptions about change. Considering it as a discourse opens up the possibility that this way of framing change is not the only alternative. It is only one way of speaking about and, consequently, relating to the subject.

REVIEW QUESTIONS 8.2

Recall	What are the three defining features of critical studies according to Fournier and Grey (2000)?
Explain	What does denaturalization refer to and why is it an important concept in critical studies?
Reflect	Are critical studies against improved organizational performance?

ESTABLISHED ASSUMPTIONS ABOUT ORGANIZATIONAL CHANGE

In this section we problematize three central assumptions about organizational change that are typically expressed in tool-based but also to some extent in process-oriented literature. These are the claims that:

- Change is inevitable
- Change is in everybody's interest
- Change processes are politically neutral and morally justifiable (in particular those run under the banners of participation and democracy).

'Change is inevitable'

Much of the conventional change literature typically starts by characterizing the business environment as fast-moving and turbulent, leading to a greater need than ever for organizations to change and adapt in order to remain competitive. It is not uncommon that change is presented as inevitable due to forces in the environment that more or less compel organizations to change. Here are just a few examples:

With the rate of change becoming faster and faster and the demands on organizations to adapt and change themselves becoming greater and greater...' (Burke, 2002, p. 9)

The pace of global, economic, and technological development makes change an inevitable feature of organizational life. (Cummings & Worley, 2005, p. 22)

We live in a challenging and dynamic time for organizations. The conventional ways in which companies and other collective endeavors have been organized in the past are increasingly regarded as inadequate for twenty-first-century conditions. (Child, 2005, p. 4)

Where once managing change was the exception, or the vanguard, now it is the norm. (Jick & Peiperl, 2003, p. vi)

Companies have had to adjust from a world in which they only need to make organizational changes from time to time to one where they must be prepared to make them almost continuously. (Child, 2005, p. 277)

Usually, the claims that we live in turbulent times are presented without much reflection. Circumstances such as globalization, technological development, economic turbulence and a changed competitive landscape are raised as support for these statements. But these claims are sometimes challenged by critical authors, not the least the assumption that contemporary society is more changeable than ever. The phenomenon of uncritically advocating a need for change is referred to as a kind of 'change fetishism'. In order to question this conventional understanding, critical researchers point to studies suggesting that globalization and turbulence are hardly anything new or typical for the contemporary society – the international economy was, for example, far more turbulent at the beginning of the 1900s than at the end of the century (Grey, 2003). However, people tend to perceive the present and the future as more changeable than what happened yesterday, since indeed, in retrospect, history tends to feel familiar and stable. Stating that the present is more turbulent than the past can also be seen as an expression of nostalgia and a re-writing of history, of the type 'things were better in the past' (Gabriel, 1995).

One of the problems with many of the change advocates, which is particularly common in the tool-based perspective, is the idea of the environment as objective. Individual interpretations and experiences are omitted, such as, for example, that two people can view the same situation in totally different ways, depending on their backgrounds and experiences. Viewing the environment as something external and essentially distinct from the organization undermines the possibility of understanding how one's own actions, such as formal speeches or informal discussions, contribute to shaping the environment. For example, when making impassioned speeches about the organization's critical situation, change leaders themselves participate in creating and maintaining a certain understanding of the situation. Furthermore, if the calls for change are acted upon, it can become something of a self-fulfilling prophecy that organizations are living in a world of constant change (Grey, 2003).

Within conventional management literature, organizational change is normally presented in a politically neutral light. Accordingly, organizations are simply subject to pressures that require them to change. Rather than take statements about today's unusually high level of pressure to change as the absolute truth, critical authors encourage people to reflect upon and consider them, partly by recognizing their context: Who is calling for change? What agenda do they have? We should also not forget that authors want a market for their books and consultants want a market for their services.

To some extent, this is also true of statements from managers who advocate organizational change. It is not uncommon for them to use the idea of the inevitability of organizational change as an argument for implementing a specific change. By using such terms as 'external drivers', the need for change tends to appear as neutral and unavoidable. However, the need for change, including what is possible and desirable, is not unequivocal; instead, whatever aspects are emphasized can be understood as arguments within a power struggle. Following this line of reasoning, a number of external drivers can be brought forward as strong (and seemingly objective) arguments for a specific development of the organization, even though the key driving force might not be related to the 'need of the organization' as claimed, but rather to the interests of its advocates. As such, there may be good reasons to adopt a reflective and critical approach to any calls for change (Dawson, 2003). For instance, one can ask: Why is this direction the only real one? What are the arguments? Which alternatives have been considered?

EXERCISE 8.2

Review a couple of mainstream, well-established writings on change management, such as articles from the *Harvard Business Review's* 10 must-reads in change. For instance:

- Beer, M., Eisenstat, R. A., & Spector, B. (1990). Why change programs don't produce change. *Harvard Business Review*, 68, 158–166.
- Garvin, D. A., & Roberto, M. A. (2005). Change through persuasion. *Harvard Business Review*, 83, 26–33.
- Kotter, J. P. (2007). Leading change: Why transformational efforts fail: The tests of a leader. *Harvard Business Review*, 85, 96–103.

Consider these writings on organizational change management as a discourse(s) and try to reveal the main assumptions being made about change and change processes:

- Who are the main characters supporting the process?
- Whose interests and perspectives are in focus and whose are not?
- What assumptions are being made about the environment?
- What assumptions are being made about controllability?
- What assumptions are being made about resistance?
- What assumptions are being made about the managerial role?

Also reflect on what is being blanked out in the texts. In other words, what is *not* discussed?

MINI CASE 8.1

Globalization as a change discourse

In the Australian TV company ABC (Australian Broadcasting Corporation), globalization was highlighted as the main reason for extensive organizational changes. The changes could just as easily have been described as an enlarged neoliberal commercialization, but they were legitimized by and described as being a result of adaptations to the new global media environment. It was said that ABC were obliged to change in order to survive amid the competition. Thus, the senior managers used an established discourse about globalization, and in light of this the external pressure to change was depicted as being so strong that change appeared to be inevitable. Under this banner, other changes were pushed through, such as a new internationalization strategy (partly through an Asian TV channel) and additional changes that were strongly influenced by a business logic, including outsourcing, intensified marketing, the use of management consultants and cut-backs in personnel. All these changes were presented and legitimized in an objective frame, and thus were seen as a non-political necessity, due to changes in the environment.

Source: Fleming & Spicer (2007)

'Organizational change is in everybody's interest'

One ramification of the predominant view of change being triggered by external objective forces is that it gives the impression that employees and managers should be equally interested in implementing the changes since it is, as they say, for the best of the organization (and subsequently the people within it) and necessary for its survival. It can be practical, comfortable and convincing to depict organizational change in this way. However, when considered critically, it is not always obvious that change processes are really driven by the intentions stated, such as survival and development. In contrast, it can be a question of less glorious and rational reasons, such as wanting to appear as progressive or to give the impression of being in charge and controlling the development, perhaps in line with modern ideas about standardization and centralization through popular management control systems. Or perhaps it is simply about bored managers who want something exciting to work with, or who have ambitions to bolster their ego in their own or others' eyes.

Critical studies of organizational change emphasize these alternative views and also present the possible (side)effects of organizational change, such as increased control and governance and/or the mechanization and standardization of work tasks. As an example, Ogden and Anderson (1995) highlight that one common change mantra is customer orientation, although it is not always obvious what that actually means or whether it is followed, even if that is what is stated (as in the following example in Mini Case 8.2).

MINI CASE 8.2

Who is the customer and what exactly is customer orientation?

A large technology company attempted to implement a change in its organizational culture. One of the central elements of this was to become more customer-oriented. However, when the managers presented the idea about customer orientation at a meeting, people had difficulties in specifying who the customer actually was. Here is a short interaction that took place in a management meeting discussing the significance of customer orientation. As one of the participating managers, Stevens, answers the HR Manager Alison's claim that the company is not customer-oriented enough, a somewhat intense discussion about who the customer is erupts (the other comments are from different line managers):

Stevens   That is Alison's understanding... I believe we are customer-oriented. We are customer-oriented and always have been. We have always been strong in both our internal and external customer focus. I believe we are customer-focused and I think we are strong here.

Walker   I don't agree with that Stevens. I don't think we are close enough to the customer today.

Weller	What do you mean by the customers?
Walker	External customers, honestly speaking. I mean, the internal customer, I think, 'well, fine, we are all fairly responsible in how we treat the people we deal with'. But externally, I think we are miles away from the customer and have been for many years. So I don't agree.
Weller	I don't agree.
Clark	I suppose that depends on one's point of view.
Allen	But perhaps we mean different things when we speak about 'customers'. As I understand it, you mean end-users when you say customer.
Stevens	I think I do.
Richards	But who is the end-user? Our closest customers are surely our end-users, right?
Stevens	Yes.
Clark	Absolutely. We are a business-to-business organization.
Stevens	We are customer-focused but apparently we have to be better.
Kelly	There is some confusion about who the customer is.
Stuart	Of course. The entire organization needs to know who the customer is. Is it the end-user? The intermediaries? Those we actually sell to?
Weller	Those that actually pay the invoices we send out, in the business-to-business interaction. It's not the man on the street, he is practically their customer.
Frank	I think many people are confused.
Clark	As I see it, we are customer-focused both in terms of internal and external customers. Many people are out speaking to the customers, and their focus is on satisfying the customers' needs. So, depending on who you are, what level you are at, you are focused on customer needs.
Peterson	I think we are customer-focused internally, but that we have some shortcomings in our interactions with our external customers.

We can see here that neither the view of who the customer is nor the extent to which they are customer-oriented is particularly clear for the managers present. Customer orientation sounds good, but this and similar arguments often become standardized and easily trivialized if people do not also try to specify what they actually want to achieve and the substantial relevance this might have for the business. In the example above, customer orientation seems to be a way for the company management to give the impression that they know the market and know what customers want, without having reflected on the concept and its significance at a local level. This may also actually be a matter of trying to push the power in the organization away from those who work with the core technology towards those who work with marketing, something that is probably not in everybody's interest.

Source: Alvesson & Sveningsson (2015)

Occasionally, statements about customer orientation can be a way to hide attempts to increase efficiency through cost reduction. At a call-centre, the implementation of a new self-service system was justified by an increased demand for service from customers, while the focus in the change was more on cost reduction than increased customer service (Grey, 2003). Similarly, business process re-engineering (BPR) can be understood as a tool for cutting costs rather than a way to focus on improved customer service, which it is sometimes described as being about (Knights & McCabe, 1998). A number of researchers liken change programmes such as just in time (JIT) and total quality management (TQM) to disciplinary and surveillance systems aimed at achieving increased managerial control more than anything else (Sewell & Wilkinson, 1992). Critical studies also demonstrate how change initiatives that are run under the banner of participation sometimes even reinforce established power structures, bureaucracy and inequality (McCabe, 1999).

Studies performed in the public sector indicate similar insights, with gaps between rhetoric and reality regarding new managerial practices and organizational forms (McNulty & Ferlie, 2004; Worthington, 2004). The ambition to draw upon managerial ideas originating in the private sector to transform public services (commonly referred to as New Public Management) from centralized, inert, rigid and inefficient organizations to becoming more flexible, high-qualitative and service-oriented ones (more value for the money for the taxpayers) in many cases did not result in the grand solution that was hoped for. Research indicates, for instance, that BPR and TQM programmes have resulted in 'widespread dissatisfaction, discontent and alienation' (Worthington, 2017, p. 421). Studies in healthcare have shown that staff (in various functions) have experienced the new work practices as dis-empowering and with an intensification of work rather than as empowering and work-enriching (Wilson, 2004). Arguably, in some cases, the expressed ambitions did not materialize, and it became clear that the changes were not unequivocally beneficial for all.

The critical perspective also highlights that organizational changes can be an expression of power games, initiated because of a person's or a group's specific interests in terms of power, influence, status and other privileges. Changes based on this can be fairly loosely tied to being in the organization's best interests. For example, it is not uncommon for newly appointed managers to initiate an organizational change in order to demonstrate decisiveness and strength. This is seldom made explicit, though. Instead, other change discourses, in particular arguments about external forces, constitute often powerful support for and legitimization of the actions of leadership. To accentuate that the change is done for the best of the organization then only becomes a way of legitimizing the change and making the suggestions appear neutral. This can be seen as a legitimating strategy – consisting of discursive and rhetorical expressions – that change actors employ in order to portray the change as more plausible in the eyes of those affected by the change (as discussed in Chapter 7).

EXERCISE 8.3

Think of a recent change process that you have knowledge of, either from personal experience or from secondary sources. Apply critical reasoning and address the following issues:

- Discuss the potential interests and motivations of a handful of the people involved. Do you think they shared a common goal or can you identify a diversity of interests?
- Discuss the potential reasons for the homogeneity and/or heterogeneity of their interests.

Taken together, a critical perspective does not assume that organizations are harmonic systems, where people share interests and have a common goal. Rather, organizations are understood as a place where people (and groups and units) with different interests interact and compete for access to various types of scarce resources (see Watson, 1994): as conflict-ridden, complex, political systems where order is negotiated rather than being a natural precondition. The notion that an organizational change is in everybody's interest is therefore fundamentally problematic and misleading.

'Change processes are politically neutral and morally justifiable'

As already mentioned, the need for organizational change is often described in a politically neutral light. In addition, many ideas about how the change process is (and should be) carried out also tend to be presented in a morally justifiable tone, and seldom with references to democracy and broad participation. Organizational change, unless it is not deemed to be urgent, is often presented as something that should be communicated broadly and that employees should be involved and participate in the process, all in line with an inclusive and democratic spirit. Critical authors, however, make us aware that these sentiments may only be an impression that those calling for the change want to give, and that the talk about inclusiveness and democracy actually lacks substance in practice. Employee participation is not necessarily introduced out of democratic and humanistic ideals, such as the ones promoted by Human Relations theory. Instead, other, more rational and political reasons can be in play. For example, decision-makers can involve employees in decision processes solely as an influencing tactic, because they are required to do it (e.g. for legislative reasons) or they need to do it because they lack the necessary knowledge about the specifics of the change content (Grey, 2003). Thus, union representatives are involved because it is required by law, and specialists are involved because their knowledge is needed. For those managing the change, continuous communication and deliberations can be used primarily as a mean to generate and ensure commitment. However, involving employees who are to be made redundant in discussions regarding downsizing decisions is a less likely scenario.

It is therefore naïve to believe that that which at first appears to be participative decision-making is genuinely about exercising company democracy or co-determination. Instead, communication and participation – when one is consulted as an expert – is often about retaining and reinforcing established power structures. However, the rhetoric can have the opposite effect. If it doesn't match the content of the change and the employees see through it, the workforce can become cynical of the change initiative (Dawson, 2003).

A critical perspective also highlights the tendency to classify actors in the process as either for or against the change, and subsequently as good or bad, heroes or villains, although in most cases it is a considerably more complex issue which is also dependent on what the observer interprets about what is going on (Reissner et al., 2011). Consider, for instance, the common role and actions of the change actor – a person who critically questions the current state of affairs, confronts taken-for-granted understandings, and challenges the beliefs of many other people in the organization. Then compare this to someone opposing change at a stage when most others are convinced; in other words, a person who also critically questions the current state of affairs, confronts taken-for-granted understandings and challenges the beliefs of other people in the organization. In mainstream literature on change, the former is often treated as the hero and the latter as the villain, even though it can be very heroic to be the one alerting others to possible and foreseen obstacles with a suggested change. Black-and-white characterizations typically strengthen and reproduce the notion that change processes, including managing in terms of convincing and converting those resisting change, are morally justifiable. Villains should by definition be defeated.

In addition to the morally questionable dimension in this way of stigmatizing dissenting voices, there are also business-related risks. To consider opposing voices as problematic by default, as something that should be overcome, can mean that important change contingencies (such as the existing capital of knowledge, norms and values or structures), other possibilities and alternative actions (which may be more economically beneficial for the organization) are not considered. But in much of the mainstream discourse of change management, it goes without saying that dissenting voices and behaviours need to be managed, especially given the assumption that change is inevitable and in everybody's interest.

EXERCISE 8.4

Consider and examine a change situation that you have experience of or are familiar with.

Identify what you believe are the needs and interests of the key stakeholder groups, such as employees, unions, customers, society, or any other that you find relevant for the situation.

Consider how much attention and recognition you would give to each in order to address their interests in the change process.

Critically appraise you own efforts by asking yourself why you connect certain interests to those involved, i.e. why we assume that certain interests are routinely related to certain actors.

Pluralism, dissent and power struggles

It is sometimes emphasized that traditional change management logic almost invalidates opposing voices by presenting opponents as people who are not only wrong, but also acting irrationally (Symon, 2005). In these contexts, the exercise of instrumental power or political manoeuvring by management is seldom mentioned; instead, the processes are described in more flattering terms, using words such as leadership, empowerment and the mobilization of the core values of work. It might sound paradoxical, but the existence of 'opponents' may well suit a change management ideology in that it legitimizes the need for strong and decisive leaders: if there are people who resist, then there is a need for strong leaders who know how to put their foot down and act decisively (Diefenbach, 2007). Perhaps the expression of KITA (kick in the a**) management is an appropriate concept in that respect. In this way, these two types of statements and standpoints feed each other. By criticizing those who are against – the opponents or blockers – and portraying them as less knowledgeable and presenting those who are for the change – the proponents or conformists – in a more positive light, an argument is built indirectly for a need for strong insightful leaders who understand the need for change and can guide those who don't. The critical perspective goes beyond the conventional managerialist orientation towards change management and questions the idea of organizations as controllable and potential harmonious places. In particular, it embraces pluralism and considers organizations as conflict-ridden places, where competing voices struggle to be heard and gain power.

EXERCISE 8.5

Consider the following statement: 'It is difficult for practising managers to recognize all the interests of the many stakeholders that exist in a particular change project, especially in times of pressing demands to show profitability and accountability and when there is a need to demonstrate progress in the change efforts.'

Work in small groups and select an industry where you can identify the relevant stakeholders. Discuss the statement above and create a brief list of the arguments against recognizing too many interests and a similar list of the arguments for recognizing a broad array of interests.

REVIEW QUESTIONS 8.3

Recall	What does it imply to consider concepts, models and assumptions about change as a 'change management discourse'?
Explain	Consider at least two common, established assumptions about organizational change and denaturalize these understandings.
Reflect	Can you identify and problematize claims made in conventional change management literature in addition to the ones mentioned here?

DOMINANT AND MARGINALIZED VOICES OF ORGANIZATIONAL CHANGE PROCESSES

A critical look at organizational change means reflecting on questions such as: What is included and what is excluded? Whose voices are heard and prioritized? Whose interests govern and drive the change in a particular direction and appear legitimate? If organizations are considered to be harmonious units, then these questions perhaps become less important, but if organizations are seen to comprise people with somewhat different interests, motives and incentives, then these become highly relevant questions. Making potentially marginalized voices visible is one of the things that is believed to be highly important.

Changes at the chain of department stores Sears, Roebuck & Co during the 1990s make us aware of how ambiguous a change process can look if one examines the process closely from the point of view of different voices and interests (see Mini Case 8.3).

MINI CASE 8.3

A heroic story or a tragedy?

The original story about Sears, Roebuck & Co, which has been written about in the *Harvard Business Review* among others journals, is an almost epic story about how the manager and leader, Arthur Martinez, saves the company by exercising strong and inspirational leadership. Martinez is described as a person who does not shy away from making difficult decisions, and his ability to engage younger employees is particularly emphasized. For example, he changed the core of the company's marketing strategy, which in practice meant that more than 100 stores were closed down and the remaining 800 stores were renovated. The company's 100-year-old catalogue was also shut down.

A critical examination reveals, however, that the story could have been written completely differently if other voices had been included and listened to. The point is not to talk about what *actually* happened, but to show that history can be told in more than one way. In the hero story, Martinez inspired the employees, but that is probably not how those employees who worked in the catalogue business saw him, or those who lost their jobs when stores were closed down. Nor is there much mention of all the extra work that the employees had to do when they put his overarching ideas into practice, developing the company's operational strategy in addition to carrying out their ordinary work tasks of running the business. The employees held change meetings every week at seven o'clock in the morning (and sometimes earlier) so that they could take care of both sets of tasks. In this respect, the story can be seen as a tragedy, in which the noble workers were exploited by evil leaders (headed by Martinez) who drove their workers hard with a focus on maximizing short-term profits and their own glory.

Source: Collins & Rainwater (2005)

As the Sears case demonstrates, it is not often possible to unambiguously state whether or not an organizational change has been successful. It all depends on whose perspective is taken. A change programme that appears to be successful from one perspective may involve an increase in workload and stress or unemployment from a different perspective. Accordingly, there is reason to revise the traditional image of opposition as being something that is irrational or even sick (see Symon, 2005).

Richardson (1995) contrasts between 'cultural narratives' and 'voice narratives'. Cultural narratives are comprised of the more or less official stories formulated by management – including norms and values – that are often used as tools for efforts at exercising normative control of thoughts and behaviours, for example, in a change process. Voice narratives express the marginalized voices, or those that are left out due to the legitimacy and strong proliferation of the dominant story, for example, in change processes. More specifically, they embody the experiences and sensemaking of those who are neglected, who often differ from the dominant culture narratives, but who must be considered to gain a deeper and more thorough understanding of what is going on in change processes.

The distinction between dominant and marginalized voices is very useful in change contexts as it makes us attentive to the existence of alternative voices. However, in many contexts, the distinction between dominant and marginalized can be perceived as too simple a dichotomy – between those with resources and those without – so that resembles classic conflicts or battles between managers and other employees. The change course of events does not always follow such a simple division, as it can even be individuals with more resources, such as managers, who express alternative standpoints, despite the risk of the consequences. In addition, it can be difficult to generalize the views of the employees or groups of employees, as there are often considerable individual variations, due to the work situation, workers' educational backgrounds, profession or ambitions, and career interests, for example.

MINI CASE 8.4

Two stories of Amazon

With an increasing number of often informal, community-governed internet forums of opinions about organizations (e.g. Quora, WikiAnswers, Glassdoor, etc.), many formerly marginalized voices have found more opportunities to be heard. Although many of these views are anonymized, and caution about the credibility with which they portray organizations needs to be recognized, they also sometimes receive considerable attention in more established media. For example, in Chapter 1 we discussed how the fascinating growth of Amazon partly relied on their way of managing creativity and continuous innovation. Based on that assessment, Amazon is sometimes characterized as being an ambidextrous organization, i.e. an organization that successfully improves its existing business while also, in parallel, inventing new business opportunities through renewal and innovation. The element facilitating this is often attributed to their organizational culture, which is said to emphasize an atmosphere of experimentation and constant reinvention. As stated by its founder, Jeff Bezos:

> We want to be a large company that's also an invention machine. We want to combine the extraordinary customer-serving capabilities that are enabled by size with the speed of movement, nimbleness, and risk-acceptance mentality normally associated with entrepreneurial start-ups. [...] There are some subtle traps that even high-performing large organizations can fall into as a matter of course, and we'll have to learn as an

institution how to guard against them. One common pitfall for large organizations – one that hurts speed and inventiveness – is 'one-size-fits-all' decision making. [...] We'll work hard to avoid it [...] and any other large organization maladies we can identify.

While this highly experimental and innovative culture sounds good and promising, there are also other, perhaps less authoritative but still many voices surfacing on various internet forums, that tell alternative stories of Amazon and its culture of change. For example, in a renowned story in the *New York Times* from 2015, a former HR director of Amazon talks of the culture as a 'purposeful Darwinism', and others talk about how the company provides no time for employees to recover from illnesses or miscarriages. The culture is said to dehumanize people by instilling fear and unrealistic work demands, creating severe anxiety and stress among many in its workforce. As stated by one former employee: 'You walk out of a conference room and you'll see a grown man covering his face. Nearly every person I worked with, I saw cry at their desk.' Amazon works with an extremely well-developed and technical data-driven management that tries to measure work tasks and performances in specific detail, partly to enable and improve internal competition among employees. Amazon's reputation, which they also are said nurture, is having a high employee burnout rate and a very rough and intense work culture. For example, it was said on one internet forum that 'Bullies thrive and are rewarded, while promotions are given to people taking credit for lower level employees' work' and 'HR is never on your side and can provoke retaliation'.

Some accounts of the work culture of Amazon thus suggest that it is harsh, competitive and very intense in terms of pressure to achieve results and outcomes. While recognizing the remarkable growth and success of Amazon, it can also be argued that the instrumental culture of performance and short-sightedness of how to exploit people for the purpose of radical growth may backfire in different ways. Organizational change, including experimentation and innovation, normally relies on a culture of commitment and certain long-term work security that enables and inspires people to thrive on creativity and feelings of engagement. Ignoring or abandoning such conditions may be quite harmful in the long run, restricting an organization's ability to learn boldly and thus reinvent itself.

Source: Meyer (2019)

Competing stories about organizational change

The critical perspective offers an alternative to the somewhat one-dimensional way of presenting change processes in mainstream change literature. The critical perspective recognizes that multiple stories often exist, in particular stories about the reasons for, impact and outcome of a specific change as well as about the course of events during a change process (Buchanan & Dawson,

2007). The stories can vary depending on the narrator, but also depending on the audience that the narrator is targeting. This is where the usual discrepancy between the official version of what happens and the unofficial version of what is going on that employees within the organization tell each other (which is sometimes perceived as organizational hypocrisy; Brunsson, 2006) can be found. Modern organizations commonly address different audiences, all of which expect to receive tailored messages depending on (their) interests and profiles. The objective for the organization is to achieve legitimacy for the desired changes among the different groups.

This also prompts a reflection about method. If polyvocality is taken seriously when studying change processes, efforts to understand 'what *really* happened' becomes irrelevant (Buchanan, 2003). Thus, instead of trying to get the story straight, through triangulation and other means of reaching what is assumed to be an objective and neutral description, researchers 'should expose competing narratives of organizational phenomena, and not silence views that do not conform to conventional norms' (Buchanan, 2003, p. 7). Critical authors, in other words, encourage researchers who want to understand change processes in more depth to go beyond unequivocal, doctored versions of change events and to pay attention to and analyze several types of stories in order to capture ambiguities and contradictions. By not aiming to give 'the only and correct version' of the course of events, and instead accepting opposing voices and the insight that all stories are written by somebody for a purpose, a significantly more profound and extensive understanding of change processes and their development dynamics can be gained. As we mentioned earlier, stories are central in political games. They can for instance be used for negotiation, persuasion, threats and preaching, and as such are probably narrated with a specific intention. Organizational change, in particular, is typically a value-laden issue, where the political stakes are high and greater political activity can be expected (Buchanan, 2003). In addition to the political dimension, competing narratives can be expected due also to the complexity of and differences in interpretations. Complexity of interpretations, in the sense that organizational change processes can involve layer upon layer of complications, which tend to be too hard to describe and capture in a simple and singular format. And differences, in that people can be expected to provide alternative accounts based on their own interpretations, but also because interpretations can be dependent upon how individuals position themselves in the change process – that is, whether they see themselves as the drivers, victims or audience.

MINI CASE 8.5

Epic and tragic tales in a merger

When describing the change process in which two colleges – Beta and Gamma – merged, the managers in charge of the process told an epic story in which they described themselves as the heroes. The merger subsequently was portrayed as a rescue and the change process as a struggle towards a Golden Age. They saw themselves as guardians of the new college and claimed that the staff not had been helpful enough in working towards the mission. Therefore they, as managers, had to be strong and motivate the staff and make tough decisions.

However, the teachers at the two merging colleges told tragic tales. One of the stories had an undertone of hopelessness and resignation. The ex-Beta staff were proud of what they had accomplished as teachers, but felt that the college was in a downwards spiral of student quality. The managers were described as uncaring, unresponsive and incompetent. Their ex-Gamma colleagues were seen as spoiled. Ex-Gamma staff, on the other hand, told a story of betrayal and stated that they had been forced into this merger. The new organization was described as slow, uncaring and too bureaucratic, and they felt that their previous sense of purpose and community was lost. In both these tragic stories, management was portrayed as hypocritical villains.

Source: Brown & Humphreys (2003)

EXERCISE 8.6

Assume that you are about to design a critical study of an organizational change process. List at least three methodological aspects you would take into consideration.

Insight about the existence of multiple stories can also have practical relevance. During conflicts in change processes, many people probably assume that events can be managed and conflicts reduced through more control and information. Some people may believe that insufficient information is provided to groups that oppose or do not want to accept a new change orientation. A common idea is that more information will make people understand. They believe that some people are obstructive largely because they enjoy being a nuisance and questioning the ideas of others is another possible outlook. Change situations are often tense, and it is not always easy to understand why somebody else may be for or against something that one believes is self-evident. As a change agent, one may try to mobilize others to see obstructive people as the conservative and reluctant-to-change kind, who do not understand the proposal for market orientation, for example. From a critical perspective, this can be described in terms of marginalization and attempts to silence voices. It is not certain, though, that more information or marginalization are successful methods in convincing change sceptics. More information seldom changes underlying beliefs, which also perhaps involve people's identities. In addition, marginalization tends to lead to increased polarization, and thereby makes it more difficult to achieve integration between people or groups as part of coordinating the change work. Furthermore, disregarding and marginalizing opposing voices does not make them disappear. This relates to another common but problematic assumption in many conventional change management theories, that managers are more or less omnipotent and proactive while employees are passive actors who will eventually understand and be persuaded of the necessity and importance of change (Reissner et al., 2011). Although non-compliant voices are excluded from the official and formal conversations of change, they invariably continue to exist underneath the surface and often grow stronger if others join in the conversation (see Gabriel's idea of the unmanaged organization; Gabriel, 1995). It can, in other words, be a lose–lose choice to pursue this strategy.

From a critical perspective, dissent is an inherent part of organizational life, rather than a disruption to the otherwise harmonious and well-aligned state of the organization. Critical writings about change question and problematize the managerial point of view as the superior one, and subsequently make the readers see that in order to uphold a single story of the need for and/or success of change alternative voices are dismissed or even oppressed. An alternative view would be to identify and allow the marginalized voices to be heard, to embrace the pluralism, and subsequently to enable a more in-depth and multifaceted understanding of change work.

REVIEW QUESTIONS 8.4

| Recall | What do the concepts 'cultural narratives' and 'voice narratives' refer to in the context of organizational change? |
| Explain | How can recognizing alternative voices in times of organizational change be of practical use? |

Politics and power – a more realistic view of change

The basic approach of many change management theories is that change is something that can (and should be) controlled and organized by managers. By switching from this perspective and describing the course of events in change attempts from the bottom up, the power of other employees also becomes visible. A different perspective can thus have a sobering effect. By considering conflicts, opposition and politics as part of everyday organizational life, many change ideas no longer appear as realistic as they did before recognizing the complexity of the situation. It becomes clear that it is not sufficient to carry out a comprehensive and exemplary analysis of the company's situation and then create an equally sophisticated and exemplary change plan. If the change initiatives do not align with the interests of other members of the organization, and if they are not accepted, sound plans do not help very much.

Radical organizational changes under the banner of Business Process Re-engineering (BPR), among others, have proven to be difficult to implement, and the concept has been criticized for its over-reliance in powerful leadership and its simplified view of organizations which overlooks conflicts and opposing interests. It has been shown that strong leadership – in the classic sense of command – risks reinforcing organizational politics and inciting resistance, rather than the opposite, in particular if employees experience the change as being enforced. Opposing interests and political power games are part of the everyday life of organizations, and considering them as irrational, marginal or dysfunctional circumstances rather expresses an all too naïve and limited understanding of organizational life. As such, both a tool-based view of BPR and a more processual view are problematic: the former does not deal with politics sufficiently and the latter assumes that such circumstances can actually be led and controlled (Knights & McCabe, 1998).

In particular, ideas about the possibility of managing and controlling cultural change tends to be over-optimistic. Grey (2003, p. 10) suggests that 'nowhere is the fantasy of managerial omnipotence more obvious than in the field of culture management'. Management is supposed to decide upon and formulate suitable core values and then implement them throughout the organization in order to create a cohesive organization where people's values align with each other and the organization. Several studies note the difficulties with changing organizational culture (among others, Alvesson & Sveningsson, 2015). Still, cultural change is brought forward and suggested as a key dimension in change programmes (e.g. in BPR and TQM) and as the most effective means of controlling for and countering organizational fragmentation.

EXERCISE 8.7

Imagine that somebody is trying to change you – what you value and how you reason in a given context. In small groups, discuss to what extent this would be possible and to what extent it would be morally justifiable?

One important ambition of the critical perspective is to highlight the opportunities for employees to prevent them being over-exploited under the banner of productivity. In this context, opposition is seen as positive, something that can be mobilized and even seen as favourable, at least from the employees' point of view. Instead of seeing opposition as destructive and irrational, which is a common view in mainstream change management theory, within the framework of the critical perspective it is seen as completely logical and reasonable. For example, opposition can be understood as a way to secure or strengthen self-esteem as a consequence of a strong identification with an established work situation or practice (Ezzamel et al., 2001). We return to this theme in the next chapter. The point here is that critical studies are interested in and highlight opposition from a fundamental and different perspective than in traditional change literature.

REVIEW QUESTIONS 8.5

Recall	What does it mean to acknowledge organizations as political arenas?
Explain	Why might it be necessary to acknowledge power and politics as relevant to understanding and managing change processes?
Reflect	Why do you think issues of power and politics often tend to be treated rather superficially, if at all, in many conventional change management models and theories?

SUMMARY

The critical perspective of change provides a less romantic and idyllic, although a more realistic, view of organizational change, partly by acknowledging organizations as political arenas and by recognizing the inherent exercise of power, which is often marginalized or completely ignored within some of the established change literature and practice. Its basic approach aligns with Hardy (1996, p. 14), who expresses the point clearly: 'Pretending that power does not exist does not make it go away.' It involves emphasizing the political dimension of management and control and trying to increase awareness about how power is used, which consequently allows more people to gain insight into the dynamics of the change game and increase their possibility to mobilize and defend their interests.

From a managerial perspective, it is obvious to consider those change actors who are good at undermining or blocking resistance to change as competent, effective and smart. However, if one instead considers the managers to be playing political games, is it then as clearly admirable to succeed in stifling change opposition? When do actions go from being effective and appropriate to immoral and unacceptable? When does it become a question of manipulation (Dawson, 2003)? Further, it is not uncommon for traditional change literature to be seductive and enticing in its positive view of the managers' abilities to control and decide in organizations, as well as the value of their efforts. This chapter can be seen as a kind of antidote to that. In the introduction to this chapter we presented and problematized some of the basic beliefs about organizational change, including the assumptions that change is inevitable and is in everybody's interest. People's need and desire for stability is seldom talked about. This is something that has fundamentally been pushed into the background in change literature, in which change is largely depicted as being something desirable. In some cases, there may be greater value in leading stability rather than change, but this is rarely said out loud (Hughes, 2010).

 # KEY PRACTICAL INSIGHTS

What we can say about organizational change following this chapter:

- It is important to adopt a reflective stance towards commonly told claims about the need for and value of organizational change. Appeals to pursue organizational change, made in particular in popular-oriented management literature, is often exaggerated.

- Considering the potential interests of the change actor (e.g. a consultant selling change management services or a newly recruited manager wanting to make a bold first impression) can support a reflective and critical stance and enable a questioning of assertive claims.

- Organizations are seldom harmonious places where people share understandings, drives and interests. Organizations should rather be understood as political arenas in which people and groups of people compete and struggle to pursue their own interests.

- By considering a pluralism of voices, a broader and more practical and useful understanding of organizational life can be achieved.

- Stories told by various groups of people can be understood as being part of the political game which involves negotiation and persuasion. The search for 'the true story' therefore becomes futile, since whatever story is told will depend on the how the narrator understands the situation, his/her identity as well as his/her motives and interests.

- By acknowledging the competing understandings and interests inherent in organizations, the assumption that conflicts and opposing voices in times of change can be reduced by more communication can be critiqued. It might be the case, but alternative standpoints can also have more fundamental underpinnings than the lack of information. Deeper insights into the various interests of the stakeholders can potentially support coordination efforts.

- Managerial exercises of power, such as marginalizing alternative voices and standpoints, can backfire by generating fragmentation, polarization, cynicism and a lack of trust. Excluding deviant voices from official conversations about change does not mean they have disappeared. They often continue to exist, but in more informal and covert versions.

- Considering organizations as arenas of competing interests, ambitions and motives, as proposed by the critical perspective, supports a more realistic view on the ability to implement and accomplish organizational change. It can also act as a counterweight to more optimistic and even romantic ideas of managerial omnipotence, which are often reproduced in the conventional change management literature.

- A critical perspective can aid organizational actors at various hierarchical levels to broaden their perspectives and inspire the questioning of taken-for-granted notions. It can also support a better insight into the political games that take place in organizations (which often are intensified during times of organizational change).

CASE

The implementation of Lean Production

When N-Gineering, a large US-based automotive manufacturing company, opened the Northern Plant in the UK, the plant employed 70 employees and manufactured and supplied a limited product range of high-tech automotive products to only two European companies. Within 10 years the factory had become the flagship of N-Gineering's European operations with 700 employees and worldwide deliveries. The plant was well-known for offering high-quality products, both in terms of design and manufacturing, and had become the market leader with almost 90% of the international market.

During this time of steady growth and strong market demand, Northern Plant experienced delivery problems. Since they couldn't produce the parts fast enough, shipments were not being dispatched in time. Complaints from customers started to come in. In order to deal with the situation, at first line managers made informal agreements with the shop-floor workers. A deal that could be described as a management-by-objectives approach was adopted. The shop-floor workers were free to structure their days as they wanted as long as deadlines were held, daily production levels were maintained and the products were up to standard. This form of self-management, where managers would tolerate almost any shop-floor practice, can be understood as a kind of informal, unplanned responsible autonomy, where the managers trusted the workers to deliver high-quality products on time. The company also offered high wages in order to attract skilled employees. When the workers had finished their daily quota, they were free to undertake leisure activities, such as reading books or newspapers, playing darts, cards or table tennis, or even sleeping or going to the pub; the managers turned a blind eye to what they did. The unwritten agreement included incentives to do the right thing the first time because if the products did not meet the standards, they had to be re-worked during employees' 'free time'. Furthermore, in times of unexpected high delivery levels, the workers agreed to put in the extra time needed to finish the orders as fast as possible. It was, in other words, a give and take relationship. Without these agreements, the targets would not have been reached so readily.

By the time the plant had been up and running for eight years, managers at Northern Plant started to experiment and implement 'new wave' production and employee involvement techniques such as JIT and TQM, and did so for the next 10 years. Since Northern Plant had an extraordinary market position and reputation of delivering high-quality products in a reliable way, there was little pressure from senior managers at N-Gineering to fully implement these techniques on a large-scale. They were simply expected to keep producing what they had always produced.

Motor-Co, a Fortune 500 company, acquired N-Gineering when Northern Plant had been in production for 15 years. Shortly after, N-Gineering went through a major reorganization in which the number of manufacturing plants were reduced and production concentrated. Furthermore, the competition for Northern Plant increased significantly and so did the pressure from the top to change how the work was performed. Productivity was supposed to increase in order to maintain profit levels and the plant needed to comply to world-class standards. It was then that Northern Plant was about to implement Lean Production.

The basic principles of Lean Production were actually not so far removed from the practices already in place at the factory, with its flexible teamworking built on high levels of trust as well as worker responsibility for maintaining high-quality products, doing the job right the first time and ensuring 'total quality control'. So managers thought it would be easy to introduce Lean Production since they already had their own version of it. But this assumption could not have been more wrong.

The key idea with Lean Production is to establish a smooth flow in the manufacturing process by identifying and eliminating all types of waste: waste of time, warehouse space, labour, materials, etc. The ambition is to do more with less, which is accomplished through such things as just-in-time manufacturing and *kaizen* techniques, as well as multi-skilled workers organized in small flexible teams, working in specific production areas ('product-focused cells'). Direct supervision is relaxed in favour for worker empowerment and involvement.

At Northern Plant, the work was reorganized into teams, with each team working in a product-focused cell. Training sessions with the personnel were held, where the workers were educated in the principles of Lean Production. Policy statements were produced, proclaiming that the plant had now invested in Lean Production. And headquarters, customers and suppliers were fed with information about the achievements made. At the shop-floor, performance charts were installed in each cell. From the outside, the production would appear as a fully functioning Lean Production system.

The workers fully agreed to be flexible in order to meet production demands as well as to be strictly attentive to product quality – all to meet the requirements of the customers.

(*Continued*)

However, they only agreed to do so as long as their informal arrangement of getting time off remained untouched. Therefore, in practice, little had changed. The shop-floor workers attended the training seminars and quality circles but saw them primarily as a way to get some time off. Efforts made by the managers to control the free time – what the workers did once the targets were met – were resisted, with threats to expose the window-dressing version of Lean Production upheld by Northern Plant managers to please corporate management.

A senior manager at N-Gineering headquarters in the US, who had come to Northern Plant to support the implementation of Lean Production, tells us about his view of the situation:

> Coming here has been a nightmare [...] Everyone talks about union problems at [Northern Plant], that it's militant [...] but militancy is normally associated with formal union activities, isn't it? [...] Well, it doesn't mean that here. [...] This is one of the most militant shops I've ever seen but none of it is union activity.

According to Motor-Co, the working practices at Northern Plant were way behind the times and they talked about it as the 'factory with a problem'. The senior manager mentioned above was initially enthusiastic about getting the opportunity and challenge of facilitating the implementation of Lean Production and had willingly joined the project team, assuming that this would advance his career. He saw himself as a progressive and effective HRM specialist who now had the chance to apply his stock of knowledge.

The workers were very sceptical about the implementation of Lean Production. For them, it was 'bullshit' and a 'con' – a change that would increase managerial control, rather than reducing direct supervision:

> What they're really saying is that they want you stuck on a machine and never getting a break... working like battery hens.

Job rotation would only mean more boring tasks to perform. The workers accused the middle managers of introducing these changes only to promote their own careers and claimed that they were 'looking after their own interests' by making others work harder. Furthermore, increases in efficiency and productivity were seen as a threat to their opportunities to earn extra by working overtime (and thereby getting a time-and-a-half rate) and risked a reduction in the head-count.

According to the shop-floor workers, Motor-Co's ambition to implement Lean Production had ruined the plant and the cooperative relations between managers and workers. They talked nostalgically about the past as a time when they 'didn't mind' coming to work, and even enjoyed it, as a time when 'it was a laugh' and 'everyone [both workers and managers] got stuck in together'. Above all, they saw themselves as qualified workers who had superior knowledge, who understood and could run high-tech manufacturing with complex production mixes.

Managers, on their side, described the new initiatives as beneficial for all, and thought it was possible to reach a mutual understanding through negotiations. They argued that the workers were being 'ridiculous', 'unreasonable' and 'unrealistic' towards what they saw as 'the need for change' and blamed a group of obstinate employees:

We're a premier company, we've got preferred supplier and even single-source supplier status with a string of customers, and this lot [plant workers] won't talk to us without all kinds of guarantees [...] it's unheard of anywhere else. What annoys me is that we have some really good people who are being held back by the 'they're out to screw us brigade', the cynics, who know what they're doing, who know how to whip up the rest of the skilled men about this kind of thing.

Questions

- Scrutinize the way managers describe Lean Production in the case. Would you say that it is beneficial for all? Empowering?
- Identify the different types of interests and motivations for the people involved in this case.
- How do people in the case struggle for power?

Sources: Ezzamel et al. (2001, 2004); Worthington (2017)

FURTHER READING

Go online to access free and downloadable SAGE Journal articles related to this chapter at **https://study.sagepub.com/sveningsson**

Davies, A. (2000). Change in the UK police service: The costs and dilemmas of restructured managerial roles and identities. *Journal of Change Management*, 1(1), 41–58.

Dawson, P., & Buchanan, D. (2005). The way it really happened: Competing narratives in the political process of technological change. *Human Relations*, 58(7), 845–865.

Gordon, R. D. (2005). An empirical investigation into the power behind empowerment. *Organization Management Journal*, 2(3), 144–165.

Spicer, A., & Fleming, P. (2007). Intervening in the inevitable: Contesting globalization in a public sector organization. *Organization*, 14(4), 517–541.

Sturdy, A., & Grey, C. (2003). Beneath and beyond organizational change management: Exploring alternatives. *Organization*, 10(4), 651–662.

Todnem, R., Hughes, M., & Ford, J. (2016). Change leadership: Oxymoron and myths. *Journal of Change Management*, 16(1), 8–17.

Willmott, H. (1993). Strength is ignorance; slavery is freedom: Managing culture in modern organizations. *Journal of Management Studies*, 30(4), 515–552.

 VIDEO

Go online to view video clips related to the key themes discussed in this chapter at https://study.sagepub.com/sveningsson

THE COMPLEXITY OF RESISTANCE

LEARNING OBJECTIVES

When you have completed your study of this chapter, you should be able to:

- Explain the meaning and implications of psychological resistance to change as well as discuss the limitations of the approach.

- Discuss political and cultural reasons for resistance to change and how these types of resistance can be approached.

- Differentiate between a diffusion and translation model of organizational change.

- Discuss the meaning and implications of viewing resistance as a natural part of change processes.

- Explain the meaning and implications of understanding resistance as identity work.

- From a critical perspective, illuminate how the label 'resistance' can be used as an instrument of power to marginalize alternative voices.

As the tool-based, process and critical perspectives proceed from different assumptions of change, they also vary quite significantly in their view of the respondents' interpretations of and reactions to change. Thus, a key ambition with this chapter is to inspire reflection and encourage multidimensional analyses of a key element in change processes, namely, resistance. We will focus on resistance specifically since understanding reactions to change, such as resistance, in more depth is crucial to manage change successfully. Furthermore, because the term 'resistance to change' is often adopted too hastily as a description of (negative) reactions to change, it is particularly important to demonstrate the many varieties of resistance.

In conventional change literature, resistance is usually regarded as a troublesome element, as something undesirable that slows down change processes or causes them to end in the worst-case scenario. Resistance is in those cases considered as obstructive friction to be avoided at all costs and counteracted through, for example, leadership and communication.

Resistance is normally attributed to employees and it is seen as the management's task to deal with it. However, this is only one way to relate to resistance. Resistance can also be understood as a potentially productive force in change processes, especially if the negative reactions are taken seriously and used as a valuable resource in the change work. In addition, that which at a first glance appears to be resistance to change may not actually have anything to do with the change. Thus, understanding the meaning of negative reactions to change and what these are about for the employees becomes an important management task.

This chapter is organized according to the three perspectives adopted in the book. Initially, we discuss resistance from the tool-based perspective and explain different types of resistance. This is a classic way of approaching the issue of resistance within the conventional change literature. We then look at an account of resistance from the process perspective. We highlight the necessity of being attentive to how people relate to proposals for change and what the change means for people in terms of matters like identity. We close with the critical perspective, and discuss how a focus on resistance can also involve clarifying the political game for resources and how proposals for change often mean a strengthening of the prevalent hierarchical circumstances in organizations.

RESISTANCE AS A TROUBLESOME ELEMENT: A TOOL-BASED PERSPECTIVE

From a tool-based perspective, resistance is seen as a troublesome but common element that change actors must attempt to understand in order to avoid it or deal with it if it arises (Erwin & Garman, 2010). Accordingly, resistance constitutes a central theme, both in the planning and implementation phases of change projects.

The types of resistance discussed comprise explicit resistance, such as strikes, material sabotage and non-compliance with rules, as well as passive resistance, such as dragging one's feet and making the least possible effort. The over-zealous following of rules is also often seen as a form of resistance as it can put a spanner in the works and hamper progress. Following instructions and procedures to the letter often creates a rigidity that impedes flexibility and adaptation to local work situations. In short, everything that in some way thwarts the implementation of change is considered to be resistance.

From this perspective, resistance is consistently regarded as something negative, and sometimes something irrational, that must be dealt with in one way or another. The premise is to understand why employees are resisting in order to identify suitable countermeasures. Various reasons exist to explain why employees resists. Various reasons exist to explain why employees resist change attempts. Palmer et al. (2017) suggest and discuss one of the more extensive lists of common causes for resistance. These causes are listed in Table 9.1 in which we have related them to broader categories of resistance discussed in this book, i.e. psychological, political, cultural and sensemaking-related resistance. In addition, Palmer et al. (2017) point out that employees not only resist the substance of change, they can also resist the process of change – how change is managed – which is a reminder to change actors to scrutinize their own actions and not only blame others for poor results. This topic will be discussed under the heading 'Resistance as a valuable contribution'.

TABLE 9.1   Common causes of resistance

Innate dislike of change	Psychological reasons	Resistance towards the substance of change
Low tolerance of uncertainty		
This is not in my interests	Political reasons	
Perceived breach of psychological contract		
Perceived ethical conflict		
Attachment to organization culture and identity	Cultural reasons	
Lack of conviction that change is necessary	Lack of sensemaking or readiness for change	
Lack of clarity as to what is expected		
Belief that the proposed changes are inappropriate		
Perception that the timing is wrong		
Too much change		
The cumulative effects of other life changes		
The legacy of past changes		
Disagreement with how the change is managed	Resistance towards the process	

We have touched upon several of the dimensions of resistance listed in Table 9.1 in previous chapters. In particular, we have discussed the importance of 'unfreezing' in order to overcome restraining forces and to create readiness for change (in Chapter 4) and highlighted cultural and political dimensions of change management (in Chapter 5). We have also emphasized the importance of understanding the local context, including people's understandings and sensemaking (in Chapters 6 and 7). The ambition with this chapter is to go more in depth in some areas as well as further the discussion by demonstrating the value of regarding resistance in a multidimensional manner.

Psychological resistance

An idea with a vast impact in the change management literature and among practitioners is that negative reactions to change have psychological causes, i.e. that people have a natural aversion to change (Grey, 2003). However, this is a line of reasoning that has also been problematized to a great extent (Dent & Goldberg, 1999; Grey, 2003; Palmer et al., 2017). Here we discuss both its popularity and its limitations.

The approach originates from the idea that people like to have control and since change always involves some degree of uncertainty and occasionally a loss of control, established routines and familiar organizational contingencies are preferred rather than change (Jick & Peiperl, 2003). It's a case of better the devil you know than the one you don't. People can also react negatively to change attempts as they are scared to lose control and lose face. It may also be that they experience concern and feel confused ahead of new circumstances.

From this perspective, resistance to change is not regarded as anything strange, but as something that is natural and to some extent inevitable. It is a common idea, both in theory and in practice, that people tend to react to extensive changes in a similar way, through a number of transitory phases (Jick & Peiperl, 2003):

1. Shock (perceived threat and denial).
2. Defensive retreat (anger and holding on to the past).
3. Acknowledgement (mourning and letting go).
4. Adaptation and change.

The contents of the various phases vary somewhat, but the basic idea is the same, namely that extensive changes will be met with some form of strong negative reaction, but that it is transitory (provided that the change process is managed correctly). It is worth noting that these phases were originally created to describe how people deal with trauma, such as bereavement or serious illnesses, i.e. radical, life-changing events (Kübler-Ross, 1969).

This emotional roller-coaster ride is often cited by management consultants and is illustrated in what is known as a *change curve* (see Figure 9.1). There are different versions of the curve, even if the basics are the same, and it is primarily phase four that usually varies. According to Kübler-Ross (1969), this phase is distinguished by depression and dejection, but the change models usually adopt a more positive tone and speak of adaptation or processing instead, or the phase is omitted completely, such as in Jick and Pieperl's (2003) model above.

According to this logic, the experience of uncertainty is an important source of resistance to change. By extension, this means that the less people understand about the logic behind a proposed change and what it entails for their own work situation, the greater their resistance will be. To deal with psychological change, the main advice is thus to inform and involve the employees in the change process. By giving detailed information to those concerned, one can prevent their feeling doubt, concern and uncertainty, and thereby avoid resistance to change. Managers and others who lead change initiatives are encouraged to be prepared for that because change processes are often lengthy, and it is natural for employees to apply the brakes to begin with. This natural reaction will gradually pass, although it can take more time with different people (see the example in Mini Case 9.1).

MINI CASE 9.1

The change process as a journey

During change work within a global charity organization (studied by one of the authors), the process was likened to a boat journey in which it took different lengths of time for people to jump into the boat and travel from one coast to another. The change consultant encouraged the managers to identify where their respective employees were along that journey so that they could respond to them in the best way. This included exhibiting an understanding for those people who had not yet reached the destination, giving them extra support and encouragement, and further explaining the content of and need for the change.

This activity, as well as the chosen metaphor (a boat journey), indicates the underlying logic described above. Resistance is seen as natural, but will eventually pass away; everybody will gradually reach the other side. It also implies that everybody has the same final goal, travelling to the other shore; it just takes a different amount of time for some people because it is an individual process.

The concept of psychological resistance places the primary focus on the individual – resistance is based on individual circumstances. However, the same reasoning has been used to explain group reactions and behaviours. People collectively may perceive the future of the group to be uncertain, and feel concerned and suspicious about the new situation and jointly oppose managerial attempts to change. One extreme example of this is groups that have developed a culture characterized by paranoia and anguish, which is expressed as resistance to anything they do not recognize and that they believe is a threat to the group. In this kind of situation, concern about the unknown is reinforced in a collective process, in which people together reinforce the significance of protecting

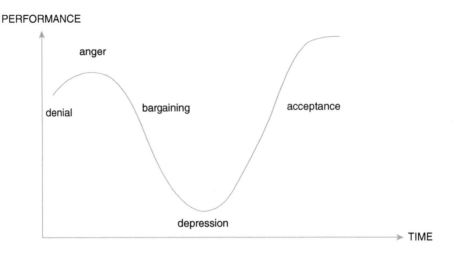

FIGURE 9.1 The change curve – emotional reactions to change (by kind permission of Elisabeth Kübler-Ross Family Limited Partnership)

what they have and being suspicious of everything from outsiders, including new ideas and organizational models (Baum, 2002). Normally, however, resistance is attributed to single individuals.

Explaining resistance as a psychological and individual phenomenon has been heavily criticized (Dent & Goldberg, 1999). One criticism is the assumption that employees automatically resist changes because uncertainty is always seen as a threat. In contrast, it is said that what employees mostly react to in change processes is the worsening of their work conditions, such as a lower status, a reduced income or a heavier workload. Criticism has also been directed at the individualization of resistance. When resistance is largely seen to be based on individual people, this overshadows the social change dynamic and the significance of relationships and group dynamics as a basis for resistance.

In other words, there is a strong argument against limiting resistance to change to psychological explanations. In the next section we discuss alternative ways to understand and relate to resistance to change.

REVIEW QUESTIONS 9.1

Recall	Briefly describe the change curve and its various phases.
Explain	What are the key roots of resistance to change from a psychological perspective?
Reflect	Is it reasonable to compare an organizational change process with a serious illness? Can we assume that the coping processes would be similar? Why or why not?

Political resistance

According to a political perspective, an organization is not assumed to be a coherent unit by default. It is rather understood as a number of more or less loosely connected coalitions of people with different interests and goals. In this context, resistance is a matter of people reacting to changes that they perceive to threaten their interests in some way.

From this perspective, resistance to change can be understood as employees (individually or in groups) fighting to protect their interests, power and influence, which they perceive to be under threat (e.g. Cummings & Worley, 2009). In practice, this can mean that the work situation worsens to some degree. It can involve people being at risk of losing their jobs, or that their workload increases, or that people can no longer work with their preferred colleagues, or that they are given less interesting and rewarding tasks, or that they are forced to do things (such as administration) that does not match their professional experience, and so on. It can also mean that the change is managed in a way that undermines individuals' or groups' abilities to exert influence, informally and/or formally. In other words, this perspective goes beyond the idea that resistance is primarily about uncertainty of the unknown. Even if the organizational members had known the very finest details of the change plans, this would not have been any guarantee that they would have accepted them. Rather, knowledge about the changes creates resistance because people then know they stand to lose something, in one way or another, if the changes are implemented (Pfeffer, 1992).

Another way of expressing this is that the individual's 'implicit contract' changes for the worse (Watson, 2006). This means that the employee perceives that the tacit agreement about what efforts s/he is supposed to put into work, in relation to the rewards and benefits given in return (see Figure 9.2), has been broken or is unbalanced. This does not necessarily mean that only their job or specific work duties are threatened, but also that the individual's identity is challenged or

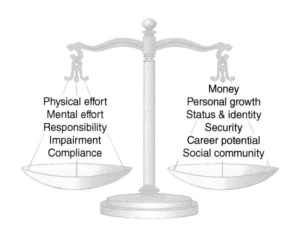

Physical effort
Mental effort
Responsibility
Impairment
Compliance

Money
Personal growth
Status & identity
Security
Career potential
Social community

FIGURE 9.2　The implicit contract (based on Watson, 2006)

questioned, as individuals' identities are often closely associated with their working life (Sveningsson & Alvesson, 2016). For example, threats to people's perceived status as well as threats to their conception of a coherent and distinct identity can be stressful, and constitute a basis for resistance (Eilam & Shamir, 2005). We develop this below in conjunction with our discussion of resistance from a process perspective.

To deal with this type of resistance, a key managerial advice (from a tool-based perspective) is to master organizational politics through strong leadership. This may involve identifying the power structure in an organization and trying to mobilize the key people in power in the direction of the attempted change (Bateman, 1980). It can also involve trying to bring about greater trust in management (which is a long-term effort) or creating a strong feeling that the organization really needs to change and that it is the best outcome for all employees. Some authors advise managers and other change agents specifically to take the implications for identity into account (Eilam & Shamir, 2005). This can imply framing change efforts – by symbolic means, if possible – in line with the existing organizational identity. For instance, when businesses are relocating offices, key artefacts from an old location can be transferred to the new one. In situations when people's identities are threatened, managers can support alternative ways for individuals and groups to express themselves and communicate the potentially positive effects of the change for self-expression and self-enhancement (Eilam & Shamir, 2005).

Cultural resistance

From a cultural perspective, resistance to change means that (groups of) employees oppose the change attempt because they believe that it counters important – or even sacred – values (Gagliardi, 1986). Increased formalization and new rigid routines for reporting and approvals for travel and business matters may, for example, clash with an earlier approach that involved flexibility, trust and confidence between co-workers. In the same way, the implementation of detailed time reporting may conflict with an ethos of helpfulness and an accepted norm of always giving a colleague a hand, even if the person works in another part of the company. To avoid this kind of resistance, the tool-based perspective underlines the importance of symbolic leadership. Managers should *walk the talk*, and create effective and clear communication to change the views of the members of the organization. The ambition should be to make the employees understand the value of the change (Rosenfeld & Wilson, 1998).

Resistance may also have its origins in poor communication and misunderstandings. As an example, different professional groups can have specific forms of expression which can complicate communication and subsequently undermine and counteract efforts to create a shared understanding of a change. In schools and healthcare, for example, this situation is probably common when administrators and professionals speak to each other about change plans (Norbäck & Targama, 2009). Different language use and a lack of understanding can also add to confusion and trigger negative feelings and even distancing from the ideas of others (Pieterse et al., 2012). A classic example in this context is when poor communication between production and marketing personnel obstructs overall organizational changes due to one group's incomprehension of the other's view. The best advice in this instance is to allow the different groups to specify their interpretations and their basic assumptions and expectations of each other, and the future change, with the objective of trying to reduce misunderstandings.

A similar line of thought is referred to as 'clashing grammar'. This recognizes that resistance can arise – even though people are initially favourable – because those involved speak different languages and thus do not understand each other. It is the classic Tower of Babel scenario, which P. C. Jersild describes in his book, *House of Babel* (1978), in the context of large-scale transformations in healthcare in Sweden. The most problematic issue is when the parties involved lack a shared image or understanding of what is supposed to change and they are unaware that this is the case. Terms and concepts that have different meanings for people easily create confusion, which subsequently can develop into extensive conflicts without participants even realizing what is happening. Based on this, change agents are advised to acknowledge the risk of clashing grammar, and thus avoid being in too much of a rush. They need to familiarize themselves with the organizational culture and the language spoken in the organization so as to facilitate shared understanding (Vann, 2004).

A multidimensional perspective

So far we have mainly discussed resistance from a one-dimensional perspective. Resistance has been regarded as either individual or collective and has been attributed to either psychological, political or cultural causes. It has also been described as somewhat static; resistance that lasts for an extended period of time has not been addressed (with the exception of the 'it will eventually pass' reasoning). There is a purpose in not having too narrow a view of resistance and instead being aware of how individual and collective resistance interact, and how resistance can change focus and nature over time, as shown in the example in Mini Case 9.2.

MINI CASE 9.2

Resistance that intensified over time

During the implementation of a new IT system in three different hospitals, resistance was initially related to different individuals and understood as primarily directed towards the new system itself. However, this changed during the course of the process. As the change process progressed, the employees' resistance fused together and transitioned from individual resistance to collective resistance. In all three cases, the resistance behaviour

(Continued)

varied initially, but converged in later stages when physicians formed coalitions. For instance, a physician who at first was indifferent towards the change, later on became a key advocate for its withdrawal.

The object of resistance also altered from the system itself to the significance of the system and finally towards the advocates of the change. The shifting direction and shape of the resistance led to it becoming increasingly political and consequently more difficult to manage. In all cases, the resistance intensified over time from apathy, passive resistance to active resistance. In two of the cases, it even developed into aggressive resistance, where doctors resigned or gave the managers an ultimatum, demanding that the new system be withdrawn. In the end, this led to significant problems in the overall function of the organization as well as financial difficulties.

Source: Lapointe & Rivard (2005)

These cases of resistance stand in stark contrast to the 'it will pass' reasoning presented in the section on psychological resistance earlier in this chapter. It is therefore not recommended that change agents wait for the employees' resistance to fade, but rather that they manage it at an early stage to avoid it escalating (Lapointe & Rivard, 2005). The illustration in Mini Case 9.2 also demonstrates the value of paying attention to the object of the opposition, and not simply assuming that it is about the change as such. The reactions may concern the advocates of the change process or the way in which the change is being implemented, and this may shift over time.

To add to the complexity, it needs to be taken into account that resistance to a change is rarely an either/or position. People can be both for and against a certain change. Piderit (2000) suggests adopting a multidimensional view of resistance and claims that most people's response to organizational change is *ambivalent* to some degree. If cognitive, emotional and behavioural responses are studied separately, ambivalence can be noted more easily: a cognitive response can range from strong positive to strong negative beliefs (the change is essential versus it will ruin the business); an emotional response can be everything from excitement to anger and fear; behavioural responses can range from intentions to support or to oppose a change. These three responses do not necessarily align. For example, a person's emotional reaction (shock and frustration) to a suggested change can differ from his/her cognitive response (a belief that the change will have positive effects). Ambivalence can also occur within a single dimension, which is the case when an individual experiences, for instance, both excitement and fear towards change plans (Piderit, 2000).

EXERCISE 9.1

Consider the case at the end of Chapter 8, entitled 'The implementation of Lean Production', and analyze the reactions of the employees as

a.   Psychological resistance

b.   Political resistance

c.   Cultural resistance

Do you think some explanations are more plausible than others in this case? Explain why or why not.

Based on your analysis, what recommendations would you give to the senior managers and the line managers?

REVIEW QUESTIONS 9.2

Recall	What does an ambivalent attitude towards a change proposal imply?
Explain	Describe and contrast psychological, political and cultural resistance to organizational change by discussing their respective explanations regarding (a) why resistance arises and (b) suggestions about how it can be managed.
Explain	Discuss why it can be problematic to treat resistance to organizational change as primarily psychologically rooted. What dimensions are overlooked?
Reflect	It is common to treat resistance to change as being psychologically rooted. Why do you think it is so common?

RESISTANCE AS A VALUABLE CONTRIBUTION: A TOOL-BASED PERSPECTIVE

Irrespective of the assumed cause of the resistance, the basic approach in the tool-based perspective is often the same, i.e. that resistance is negative and undesirable. Resistance is attributed antagonistic undertones and the change dynamic is often understood to be a battle or schism between two parties.

Problems related to resistance are often connected to the employees affected by the change: recipients are described as worried and uncertain ahead of new circumstances, as eager to defend their positions of power and as people lacking the right mindset. It is the role of the management to deal with this. It is not uncommon for resistance to be described in pathological terms, as something irrational that individuals 'should get help' to deal with, while change is more or less explicitly described as unequivocally good. In this case, practical guidance for the managers driving the change is: 'Help those people who are in a defensive position and who project and act up [...] help them to understand the need and the conditions for change' (Erwin & Garman, 2010, p. 51).

However, this is an image that is increasingly being questioned as many emphasize that resistance can be a positive force and a valuable input into the change process (e.g. Perren & Megginson, 1996). Reactions against a proposed change can in fact initiate and stimulate sensible reflection about the extent to which an organization really needs to change. In a world in which organizational change is often uncritically acclaimed, questioning from people who cherish the organization's original mission, and who are strong enough to resist modern fads, can be very valuable. It is also possible that resistance to change can make management aware of shortcomings in the change plans, which is why it is important that resistant voices are not automatically rejected. Those who react negatively to a change attempt are often committed to and identify themselves with the organization, otherwise they would not care so much (Lapointe & Rivard, 2005).

Resistance is thus not necessarily the major cause for concern. 'Blind acceptance' may be more problematic as it can undermine the change plans in the long term (Ford et al., 2008). An absence of reaction actually means an absence of potentially valuable contributions. If employees do not involve themselves in a change process and fail to provide their opinions on matters that concern their knowledge and business area, important modifications may be neglected. When employees contribute with critical opinions, it enables a tailored implementation of the change. At the same time, support for the change increases within the organization as the 'opponents' participate in the process. Along this line of reasoning, managers should not to be too hasty in dismissing resistance or alternative opinions and voices. Instead, these voices can be seen as valuable contributions – in the shape of knowledge and commitment – to the change process.

In this way, resistance can be understood as a resource: it can access understanding and learning from employees – how they view the business – and can be utilized as input in the process. In other words, this is a view that stands in sharp contrast to the understanding of resistance as something bad and problematic that needs to be conquered (Wadell & Sohal, 1998). Managers can thus benefit from being attentive to and embracing other opinions and positions, instead of automatically regarding people who resist as egotists causing problems.

Courpasson et al. (2011) introduce the concept *productive resistance* and describes how people resisting change can influence and contribute to the shaping of management decisions and initiatives. They thereby suggest a far less antagonistic picture of resistance. The idea that resisters solely oppose change – that they represent a dysfunctional freezing of the change project – is toned down. Instead, their viewpoints are regarded as a positive contribution to the organization's development, and their efforts to mobilize and exercise resistance are highlighted and examined as politically useful acts. Courpasson et al. (2011) describe how resisters create forums where alternative opinions can be explored and discussed. They also explain how 'objects of resistance' can be used, i.e. tangible expressions of an alternative position, such as written reports specifying the group's ambitions.

Within a tool-based perspective, it is assumed that managers are for change while other employees – subordinates – are against it. As mentioned previously, this is a rather problematic assumption, as subordinates may well initiate a change process just as managers may resist change (Cooke, 2002). Middle managers are most often those who are expected to implement formulated changes at a higher level, and this can mean they develop a critical view of the change. Interestingly, it is often the middle managers, who are considered to have high potential in an organization, that often neglect to implement radical changes. Speitzer and Quinn (1996) suggest that it can simply be that they have more to lose than those who are in a weaker position in the organization. Even senior managers can resist change, not necessarily in conjunction with its implementation, but rather during the formulation phase when different strategic alternatives are discussed. Above all, there is a large risk that managers in successful organizations miss signals that they themselves need to change since they can be stuck in their conception that they do everything right and, as such, are not as receptive to alternative messages (Palmer et al., 2017).

EXERCISE 9.2

Think of a change experience or a change process that you have knowledge of personally or that you find in secondary sources. Note and reflect upon how opposing voices (and actions) were described. Were they primarily regarded as negative or positive? Can the same opposing voices be understood differently?

REVIEW QUESTIONS 9.3

Explain	Explain in what ways resistance to change can be productive and valuable.
Reflect	Does the term 'resistance to change' have a negative, positive or neutral connotation for you? Why do you think this is the case?

RESISTANCE AS A NATURAL OCCURRENCE: A PROCESS PERSPECTIVE

Resistance is also central according to a process perspective, although for different reasons from those in the tool-based perspective. Within the process perspective, resistance is a matter of interpretation and builds upon the idea of change as a translation. In short, it emphasizes that the outcome of a change attempt depends on how involved employees receive, reinterpret, engage with and pass on change initiatives (Latour, 1986, 1998).

In change processes, it is common to wonder why proposals and ideas meet opposition. In contrast, one can instead ask what it is that makes proposals and ideas take root and stick – what is it that makes other people seize upon a certain idea? To clarify the distinction between these approaches and to answer the question of what it is that makes people seize upon certain ideas, one can compare a diffusion model with a translation model of change (Latour, 1986). These two models provide different explanations for how an idea or an objective can circulate and spread in time and space.

In the *diffusion model* it is assumed that an objective (e.g. a change idea or a command, order or desire) possesses some kind of inner force that will make the objective continue to move in the same direction as long as there are not any obstacles. If the objective slows down or even stops, it is due to some kind of friction (resistance). This model can be compared to the tool-based perspective, which puts significant emphasis on the initial actions – to formulate a change and mobilize resources – and less emphasis on how ideas are interpreted and carried out. It is assumed that when the change-button is pressed but nothing happens, it is due to oppositional forces. In line with this model, employees are considered as passive receivers of the change initiative. They are expected to follow orders or the desires of the manager through mechanically carrying out predetermined tasks. Resistance, in turn, constitutes unfortunate friction that can be rationally addressed if one simply spends enough time formulating and designing plans and change ideas. If the initial force is significant enough in terms of resources, instructions, persuasion and reward, resistance can be overcome.

In the *translation model* an objective (an order, a desire or a change attempt) will change through the meaning that people attach to it. An objective's or an idea's circulation is determined by people and their sensemaking, interests and identity work. In line with this reasoning, people are regarded as messengers who convert, translate, distort or modify the content of the objective (Latour, 2005). The movement of a change idea depends on how people work with it, how they take ownership of it, modify and adapt it and try to make it comprehensible, based on their own experiences, cultures, interests and ambitions. According to the translation model, it is essential to understand the local interpretation, sensemaking and identity creation that form the foundation for change dynamics. Here, strategies, plans and ideas are considered as sources of inspiration – rather than given inputs – for a series of re-interpretations of the process. Whatever happens with planned change attempts or ideas is thus primarily a result of renewed energy that comes from people doing something with the attempt or the idea, and not due to the original force: '...as in the case of rugby players and a rugby ball. The initial force of the first in the chain is no more important than that of the force of the second or the fortieth, or the four hundredth person' (Latour, 1986, p. 267).

During change work one should therefore ask what it is that interests employees of an organization and encourages them to take the ideas further. For instance, could it be factors like increased job security, salary rises, promotion, prestigious assignments, an improved physical environment, a wider job specification, a greater sense of challenge, new contacts (with influential people) and operational efficiencies. Any factors that employees believe will benefit them can encourage support for change plans (Palmer et al., 2017). If there are strong incentives, the process can become more or less self-managing, as the example in Mini Case 9.3 shows.

MINI CASE 9.3

The change that was accepted with open arms

When a new IT system within a Health Maintenance Organization in the United States was implemented, nurses and physician assistants perceived that the technological change in question would bring about a significant upgrade to their own status, both as individuals and as an organization. The new technology helped them to secure their professional identities – by working with professional technology, they too could consider themselves as professionals. As such, the change was something they welcomed and looked forward to. Since it was in their interests to ensure that the change was implemented, they were committed and motivated to maintain the change process in line with the ideas of management.

So the reason that the change went so well was not because there was no reason to resist, but because there was every reason for the employees to seize upon the idea.

Source: Prasad & Prasad (1994)

The distinction between diffusion and translation models may be seen as splitting hairs, but the questions asked in a change process normally indicate which perspective of change is being embraced by management. From a process perspective, it is important to highlight the views and behaviour of the members of the organization, and not solely those of the change agent, in order to understand the change course of events. What a management-driven change initiative means for the recipient is closely connected to the recipient's self-image – in other words, their identity.

Consequently, from a process perspective, organizational changes are not expected to spread by themselves, more or less automatically, as in the diffusion model. The fact that the process *is not* developing according to plan is almost self-evident. It is rather the interaction between the change agents and the presumed targets, and their respective interpretation of the interaction and the processes, that are critical and necessary to understand. The tool-oriented and antagonistic picture of two separate parties – one that is for and the other that is against – does not, according to the process perspective, provide a sufficient enough understanding of how change processes unfold.

In contrast, organizational change should be regarded as a process in which many people are actively interpreting events. Recipients of change can be seen as co-producers of change, and the managers who refuse to engage in alternative discussions are as big a part of the cause of unsuccessful change attempts as those who initially oppose them (Thomas et al., 2011).

Also, from a process perspective, resistance to change is not regarded as some undesirable (or unexpected) appendix, but more as a natural part of the process. From a process perspective, it is unreasonable to assume that a change attempt will go exactly according to plan. It is more important to understand the reactions to the change, partly to be able to have an active part in the continued shaping of the process. Rather than regarding resistance as an undesirable anomaly, and the resistant employees as troublesome or short-sighted egotists and therefore something that must be resolved or eradicated, the managerial challenge is to listen to their reactions and use them for deepening understanding and learning (Wadell & Sohal, 1998).

Furthermore, the process perspective does not regard people's interpretations as static but as meanings that are continuously shaped in dialogue with others, as the example in Mini Case 9.4 demonstrates.

MINI CASE 9.4

Interacting processes of interpretation

The implementation of a cultural change project at a telecom company revealed two types of dialogue: one constructive and one oppositional. The middle managers of the company were initially positive about the cultural change and engaged in discussions about the content of the change. At the same time, they challenged the leadership's view by proposing a different content. This could have been seen as resistance to change because the middle managers opposed the management's original suggestion. It could also be understood as engaged participation in the change process.

How the position of the middle managers then developed was partly due to how their initial position and behaviour was interpreted and met by the more senior managers. During the implementation workshops, two kinds of development were noted. In one of the working groups, a constructive dialogue emerged in which both parties took shared responsibility for the task and willingly engaged in and tried to understand the views of the other. Ultimately, a shared approach was developed and consensus was reached on what the task required and what needed to be done. In another working group, the relationship between the middle managers and senior managers developed into oppositional standpoints, and the dialogue was marked by calculated engagement which primarily involved maximizing the outcome for the managers' own interests. Rather than coming together, this type of dialogue created a distancing from each other and a refusal to see things from the other's perspective.

The interpretation and conception of the change shifted in both cases. In the latter case, the view of the change shifted radically – from meaningful to meaningless – during the course of just one workshop.

Source: Thomas et al. (2011)

Ideas on changes are not static but can transform and also subsequently settle down. By understanding change processes as interacting processes of interpretation, the value of listening and participating in constructive dialogue becomes apparent.

This reasoning illustrates that it can be disadvantageous to assume that alternative – and occasionally opposing – perspectives and ideas are not productive. Apparently opposing standpoints and ideas can be used to create greater value, and thereby achieve more effective change processes. Constructive dialogue can contribute significantly to the final design of the change process and its implementation. However, this requires that employees, who may not be directly involved in the change proposal, are allowed to suggest counter-proposals and can expect that the managers pay them due attention and are open for mediation and compromise. This kind of constructive dialogue implies a range of counter-proposals and a mediation process. If managers are less open to considering alternative perspectives, the dialogue is likely to invite frictions and clashes, with a lower expectation of achieving any benefits from cooperation. Ironically, by rejecting an act of resistance in this way, managers may inflame the very resistance they wish to avoid. Opposing the opinions of others and counter-ideas can contribute to more systematic resistance in practice (Thomas et al., 2011).

When the significance of the interaction between change-oriented managers and other employees is pointed out, the value of questioning the traditional terms that are used to label and evaluate the different parties involved also becomes more visible. It is conventional to refer to change agents and change recipients, but this labelling categorizes people in terms of opposing parties – some that are for and some that are against change. An alternative could be to see those participating in change as *co-producers*. When people use this label, they are obliged to consider the views of the other side, because who knowingly aims to belittle their co-players?

An example can also be used to illustrate how the concept of resistance is socially constructed (Hollander & Einwohner, 2004; Prasad & Prasad, 1998). What is considered to be resistance versus engaged participation is in the eyes of the beholder. The same type of behaviour can be interpreted differently in the sense that what is understood as resistance from a top management perspective is not necessarily intentional resistance from a middle management point of view (and vice versa).

EXERCISE 9.3

Based on the suggestion that employees should be considered as co-producers of change:

a. Make a list of advice that managers aiming to implement organizational change need to consider.

b. What specific advice would you give to the line managers at Northern Plant in the case entitled 'The implementation of Lean Production' at the end of Chapter 8?

REVIEW QUESTIONS 9.4

Recall	What do the concepts 'diffusion' and 'translation' refer to in the context of organizational change?
Explain	Contrast how resistance is approached in the tool-based perspective with the process perspective on change. What are the key differences?
Explain	From a process perspective, resistance to change tends to be understood as natural and inevitable. Explain the logic behind this claim (i.e. what makes it inevitable?).
Reflect	In what way(s) can the logic of the diffusion model be appealing for managers?

RESISTANCE IN THE FORM OF IDENTITY WORK: A PROCESS PERSPECTIVE

Adopting an identity perspective can be useful for understanding reactions to change initiatives (Alvesson & Sveningsson, 2015). The premise for this perspective is that people often make sense of situations based on how they understand themselves, their self-image or identity

(Weick, 1995). When linked to change work, identity can be described according to the following four principles (Eilam & Shamir, 2005). An individual normally aspires to:

- have a feeling of control over themselves and their situation
- create a distinct self (that is separate from others)
- develop a positive self-image (status and prestige)
- attempt to bring about a continuous and somewhat coherent self.

In times of change these conditions are sometimes challenged, which can trigger identity work – in other words, reflections about the self with the purpose of maintaining and possibly reinforcing a distinct, positive and coherent self. Identity work refers to how people more or less constantly form, repair, maintain and revise beliefs that help them create and maintain a coherent image of who they are and what they can do. People often engage in identity work during times of uncertainty, worry, questioning or doubt, conditions that tend to become accentuated in times of turbulence and change. In more stable contexts, it is often easier to maintain a stable view of oneself and one's capabilities. But organizational change can often involve anxiety and uncertainty, triggering people to reflect upon who they are and what capabilities they have. If a change entails a certain loss in status, or that people are forced to compromise greatly about their ideals and identity, there is a high risk that people will be sceptical towards change, perhaps ignoring it or even mobilizing active resistance (Sveningsson & Alvesson, 2016). If, on the other hand, the change aligns with the employee's self-view, and if the change provides an opportunity to reinforce this view, then the person is likely to support the change, as the example in Mini Case 9.5 highlights (Eilam & Shamir, 2005).

EXERCISE 9.4

Consider a change process you have experienced yourself (it can be a minor or major change at work, in school or elsewhere). Recall your reactions to the change proposal and analyze them from an identity perspective. Were you positive or negative towards the change plans? Could this reaction be related to the four principles of individual aspirations as described by Eilam and Shamir (2005)? What conclusions do you draw from this exercise?

MINI CASE 9.5

Change as a reinforcement of or threat to the identity

At Intermotors (pseudonym), which is a large UK-based car manufacturing company, team-work was implemented as a key organizational principle. The reactions to these changes were very diverse.

One group of employees reacted very positively to the change and believed that the new way of working better utilized their capabilities. The change also meant that they saw increased opportunities to advance in their careers. Those reacting very negatively, on the other hand, perceived the change as a threat to their existing way of working and an insult to them as individuals. The management message about doing the work 'right first time' and following the principle of 'zero mistakes' was something the employees perceived they already did. They regarded themselves as competent and dedicated workers, but the change terminology questioned their self-image and therefore their identity.

This case illustrates how changes that are perceived as providing opportunities to positively reinforce the identity of the people involved have a greater chance of gaining support.

Source: Knights & McCabe (2000).

Other studies have also investigated the impact of the introduction of new ways of working on people's self-image. For example, Ezzamel et al. (2001) describe how the implementation of Lean Production at Motor Co (pseudonym) caused more concern for the employees' self-image and identity than the fear of losing their jobs. Components of a corporate culture can in some cases be directly linked to how employees view themselves, which in turn can affect reactions to cultural change attempts, as in the next example in Mini Case 9.6.

MINI CASE 9.6

From service people to sales people?

In a change process moving towards a more sales-oriented culture at two federal banks in Canada, the employees' responses varied between early, later and partial adopters. This mainly related to how the employees viewed themselves and their work. The changes being made required employees to establish 'total relationships' with customers, to more proactively sell services and to set and work towards sales targets.

For the early adopters, a sales culture was not something new to them. As they saw it, it had always been present at the bank and would therefore not change their work in any fundamental way. As an investment representative commented, they have 'always basically been salespeople' (Chreim, 2006, p. 1275), continuing:

> You can change the way of doing it with goal-setting and changing titles and all that, but the sales culture hasn't changed. (An investments representative)

For this group of employees, a sales culture was in line with how they perceived that great bankers worked and what they strived for. Selling was presented as something positive, in contrast to the opposite identity of the 'stuffy old banker' (Chreim, 2006, p. 1275):

> Rather than sitting back as a stuffy old banker behind a desk waiting for a customer to approach you, [you] recognize the business opportunity to go out there and go after the business. (An account manager)

A second group of employees told initially resistant accounts that over time transformed to acceptance. For instance, an investment representative explained that the word 'sales' had triggered associations of 'product pushes and flavors of the month' and caused worries (Chreim, 2006, p. 1276):

> [...] that the bank [...] would be more focused on us making the profits and not so much focused on what the clients really need. [...] We weren't sales-type people; we were customer-service-oriented people. (An investments representative)

Over time these employees reframed their previous way of working in a negative stance – as order-taking – and presented their new practices as praiseworthy – as helping the customers – which in turn facilitated the cultural transition (Chreim, 2006, p. 1276):

> We don't just want to be order-takers. We now want to make sure we're helping our customer. (An account manager)

An investment representative described how they had previously just taken a 'responsive role' and served the customers what they had asked for – no more and no less. In contrast, they described their new role as more professional and supportive (Chreim, 2006, p. 1276):

> [The customers] come in and say, 'This is what we want', and then we say, 'Well, let's just talk about that. [...] What are your goals, what are your dreams? [...] What other advice can we give you?' [...] 'Cause a lot of times we're in the profession that this is what we do, we can see things that these clients may not be aware of, or are aware of but haven't acted on, and we just help them realize what they're really looking for in life. (An investments representative)

(Continued)

A third group of employees considered the suggested sales culture as unacceptable since it diluted the service given to the customers, which was what these people defined as their key role. For instance, an investment representative talked about the risk that the bank would 'forget about the service' (Chreim, 2006, p. 1277) and blamed board members for being too far away from the business and the customers of the bank. For another investment representative, the new requirement to phone people at work seemed to be a key issue (Chreim, 2006, p. 1277):

> I've had to really work on my comfort level of phoning people. I don't like to phone people at work, but I'm told I should phone people at work. A big part of me says I would be just ticked off if somebody phoned me at work, I don't have time for this crap, you know. [...] What you're trying to do is solicit [the customers'] business over and it's a comfort level. [...] Some people are fabulous at it, it's not my strong point [...] I'm just not a salesman. (An investments representative)

The way they talked about the new business orientation implied that sales did not mean service. It implied generating revenue, which in turn would lead to lower quality service.

Source: Chreim (2006)

Van Dijk and Van Dick (2009) argue that a significant aspect of resistance can be related to threats to employees' identities and the *management* of the change, rather than the change plan as such, which the following example shows.

MINI CASE 9.7

We should have been involved

At the IT company AlphaTec, developers reacted very strongly to the way the managers managed a reorganization process. In their minds, *they* were the ones that should have been involved, not the managers, no matter how experienced they were. The developers perceived themselves as a proficient and qualified group with a high status and did not accept that technology matters became secondary to anything else. In their minds, the planned change was just another step in a line of negative developments, away from the company's original technology focus. In particular, they disliked being outmanoeuvred by the managers, whom they saw as insignificant administrative personnel with mixed-up priorities. As they had not been consulted on matters that they truly believed they were experts in, they felt completely by-passed and accused the managers of being unprofessional hypocrites. It did not seem to matter how much the managers explained the rationale for the reorganization or made concessions in line with their suggestions, their strong opposition lingered.

Generally, resistance in the form of identity work involves individuals resisting because they experience that their identities are under threat as a result of the change. In these cases, the resistance is not primarily directed at the change as such; instead the opposition is a matter of warding off the threat to the self-image of those involved. The developers' reaction in the example in Mini Case 9.7 can be understood as a form of organizational identity work – as a defence of the entire company's identity as the change was driven in a way that made the company's overarching technological orientation lose ground. It can also be understood as collective identity work of the developers, primarily concerning how the changes were driven. More specifically, that they, as developers, were not consulted or involved in the change work. The fact that they were not asked to participate – when they had been in previous situations – was understood as a marginalization of them as developers and their viewpoints. One can argue that the developers resisted against a lowering of their status and a perceived degradation. In other words, what appeared to be resistance to change on the surface may actually involve resistance to perceived identity violations.

EXERCISE 9.5

Consider the case entitled 'The implementation of Lean Production' at the end of Chapter 8.

Would it be relevant and appropriate to view some of the employee reactions to the change proposal as identity work? Explain why or why not.

Based on your analysis, what recommendations would you give the line managers?

In summary, from a process perspective, it is suggested that employees should be regarded as co-producers (rather than primarily as recipients and potential opponents) to change. In practice, this necessitates understanding and taking into account how people perceive and react to change initiatives, including how they see themselves and their role in the organization and what the change would mean for them.

REVIEW QUESTIONS 9.5

Recall	What does it mean to acknowledge resistance as identity work?
Explain	How can recognizing resistance as identity work be of practical use?
Explain	Why can intensified identity work be expected in times of organizational change?

THE TERMINOLOGY OF RESISTANCE AS AN INSTRUMENT OF POWER: A CRITICAL PERSPECTIVE

While resistance is usually regarded as something to be identified, explained and dealt with from a tool-based perspective, a critical perspective makes us aware that the terminology can be used as an instrument of power. One of the basic aims of critical theory is to reveal and prevent oppression, and one of the ways to do that is to highlight and problematize assumptions and language use that are taken for granted and that reproduce a distorted sense of dominance through their usage and acceptance. The critical perspective takes the idea of resistance as being socially constructed one step further, by emphasizing how certain voices can be oppressed and marginalized through the choice of terminology.

For example, critical studies highlight that resistance and resistant employees are often depicted as reactionary and troublesome – as people destroying and counteracting the organization's development (which is depicted as inevitable and positive). The predominant perspective in the change management literature is the one of the change agents assuming that they are doing the right thing while change recipients are the ones putting it all at risk. As a result, 'change agents are portrayed as undeserving victims of the irrational and dysfunctional responses of change recipients' (Ford et al., 2008, p. 362). As we have discussed previously, though, a change is not obviously necessary or suitable. Nevertheless, it is not unusual for management to blame opponents for the collapse of a change project. This often serves as a legitimate excuse and explanation as to why the plans could not be implemented, which gives managers an easy retreat (cf. Ford & Ford, 2009).

Describing resistance as something irrational, and those resisting it as weak and scared, even as sick and in need of help and support, upholds the image of the leaders as heroes – the ones who drive the organization forward. Employees are depicted as having a natural reluctance to change as well as a tendency to cling to the familiar. However, an overlooked element that is not often discussed is the fact that negative reactions to change can actually originate from negative consequences for individuals. As Dent and Goldberg (1999) argue: People do not resist change as such – they resist the expected effects of the change, such as loss of status, pay or work satisfaction. Instead, changes are depicted as unequivocally good, as being in the interest of the organization and thus in everybody's interest, and that employees simply need to realize this first. Divergences in interests are seldom discussed.

EXERCISE 9.6

Imagine that management proposes a change in the form of an increase in salary for all personnel. Can we then expect the stages of denial, anger, bargaining, depression and acceptance? What conclusions do you draw from this exercise?

The assumption that people have an inherent aversion to change has been problematized (see Grey, 2003). This is supported by research that suggests that the extent to which employees are for or against a change is based on whether they gain from the change or not. How the change process is managed then becomes irrelevant for individuals who gain from the change (see Gaertner, 1989).

An alternative way to relate to the term 'resistance' is to see it as part of a change management discourse and therefore as being strongly influenced by the management agenda (Piderit, 2000). Rather than assume that resistance exists and must be countered, the critical perspective encourages us to reflect on the practical consequences of the usage of the terminology (resistance, resistant). For example, employing the word 'resistant' may create an image of the people who are against change plans as troublemakers and as being psychologically unstable. By explaining away critical and questioning voices as being psychologically-based change resistance – something that is completely natural but transitory – change initiatives can be legitimized, even in situations when alternative solutions would have been more productive for the organization.

In addition, since the term 'resistance' is often associated with something negative, and occasionally pathological, it can be exploited to legitimize the exercise of power. Pathologization implies treating people and their actions as psychologically abnormal, which in turn delegitimizes them by dismissing them as unreasonable, unhealthy and potentially destructive (Theodossopoulos, 2014). Change agents challenged by opposition can be tempted to engage in undermining resistance by dismissing it as illogical or as something resulting from impulsive behaviour (Theodossopoulos, 2014). Pathologization, as expressed in some of the change literature and practice, can thus be understood as attempts to silence opposing voices.

MINI CASE 9.8

Classification as an instrument of power

In a technological change process in a public sector organization located in the UK, the managers described the resistant workers as 'fanatics' and 'die-hards'. The professional staff, who had graduate degrees and long-term organizational experience, worked in evaluating complex technical documents. These are the words of the head of the organization (Symon, 2005, p. 1650):

> MR: Those that don't like it are basically just a little frightened. They have a nice image of themselves – they've been doing the job for 25–30 years, they feel that they've got no cause for concern – they know they can handle it. You put something like this on their desk and they're reduced to the most raw recruits' status.

(Continued)

The die-hards will have to recognize that they are being die-hards and not protecting the grade as a whole. I think what we'll find is that a half to 2/3rds [of users] have actively had a hand in shaping the system. And will want it. It would be silly to throw that away on the basis of the die-hard pushing the Union along.

In other words, the manager legitimizes the opinions of some of the staff – the ones who agree with the change plans. Those who do not agree are identified as foolish 'die-hards' who are being too emotional. It is important to note here how their opposing reactions are ascribed to their personalities rather than to an alternative, collective and legitimate standpoint. In the choice of words, the behaviour of the opponents is framed as pathological as they are presented as scared and unreasonable fanatics. This makes their opinions less legitimate, and consequently undermines their counter-arguments.

Source: Symon (2005)

Theodossopoulos (2014) discusses how pathologizing narratives rely on a decontextualization of the opposing action, which makes the behaviour appear to be fanatical and even irrational. By taking away the context and logic (i.e. the perspective and reasoning of the opponent), the acts can be presented as abnormal and in turn illegitimate. However, in the case above, some background to the resistance is provided by the head of the organization, but it too is presented as illegitimate: as something of an egocentric act performed by people who have an overrated image of themselves.

EXERCISE 9.7

Consider how managers in the case 'The implementation of Lean Production' (at the end of Chapter 8) labelled the opposing reactions of the employees and discuss from a critical perspective how this can be understood as oppression.

REVIEW QUESTIONS 9.6

Explain	From a critical perspective, discuss how the label 'resistance' can be used as an instrument of power.
Reflect	In what way(s) does the conventional change management literature reproduce the image of resistance as pathological?

COMPLIANCE AS RESISTANCE: A CRITICAL PERSPECTIVE

It is not obvious what actually constitutes resistance or not. Rather than regarding certain actions as acts of resistance, the critical perspective makes us aware that resistance is a term that is used – more or less consciously and actively – to understand and describe certain behaviour. As such, one cannot equate perceived resistance with intentional resistance. Managers can perceive and label a certain kind of behaviour as resistance, irrespective of whether the parties intend to resist.

A management perspective dominates the change literature, and with slight exaggeration it can be said that resistance has almost become a collective name for 'anything and everything that workers do which managers do not want them to do, and that workers do not do that managers wish them to do' (Davidson, quoted in Piderit, 2000, p. 785). This is the case even if the people involved do not intend to counteract the ambitions of management. In the previous section we discussed how management can draw upon the term 'resistance' to try to dethrone certain people and their actions by labelling them as resistant. However, it is not only management that more or less consciously exploits the term. Other employees can also allude to the term, but in a reverse sense; in other words, they can act in a way that suggests that the term *cannot* be used to classify their behaviour. Employees can thus actively counteract the ambitions of management and at the same time try to guard themselves against being accused of resistance by appearing to act completely in accordance with the instructions of management. In other words, by cleverly crafted resistance it is possible to achieve destructive results without the actions being unequivocally classified as resistance by management (cf. Fleming & Sewell, 2002; Kondo, 1990). A classic example of this is, as mentioned at the beginning of the chapter, following instructions to the letter.

There may also be identity-related reasons that suggest that employees want to avoid being labelled as someone resisting change, such as the stigma and the associations that often come with the term. It is easy to perceive resistant employees as being primarily people of scarce resources, in relatively subordinate positions, with little opportunity to manage and control their work, and many would probably rather regard themselves in more positive terms, which the example in Mini Case 9.9 highlights.

MINI CASE 9.9

Compliant pilots...?

In a study of US commercial airline pilots, the pilots expressed the view that the pilot's role and its popular image had long since been in decline. The 1960s and 1970s was identified as the 'heyday' of the pilots, when being an 'airline captain was one of the best jobs you could

(Continued)

possibly have'. Since then, the prestige of being a pilot had been undermined by factors such as automation, a decreasing hierarchy and an increase in numbers of both passengers and air crew. In addition, the pilots emphasized their eroding power, primarily due to an industry-wide change that introduced cockpit or crew resource management (CRM), which was largely about allowing flight attendants and service people greater influence and participation.

During this industry-wide change process, the pilots – traditionally a privileged professional group – were subjected to changes that challenged their identities. It is notable, however, that the pilots did not show any open resistance to the changes, despite the fact that they perceived them as a threat to their professional prestige (as the changes risked demasculinizing their professional role).

Since the pilots viewed themselves as high status, autonomous and professional people, they did not consider themselves as people who resisted. Resistance was something the weaker people did, people who lacked control. Instead, the pilots explicitly expressed their consent to the change project. At the same time, they exerted subtle but persistent resistance towards the intended change in the power balance (where their formal power would decrease). This was primarily done through how they talked – their choice of words, expressions and jargon. In particular they made an effort to give the impression that they themselves had introduced CRM as 'a generous gift from the captain to his subordinates'.

In this way, the pilots managed to retain and even reinforce the impression of themselves as autonomous and professional with influence and control over the flight business. In fact, they were able to turn the change in allowing the crew more influence to their own advantage by stating that they were modern and safety-conscious pilots who showed consideration for their crew. Therefore, they succeeded in counteracting a shift in power in the business while appearing to embrace the change.

Source: Ashcraft (2005)

This case shows that resistance can sometimes be hidden and even masked as consent. In addition to the beneficial effect of the pilots' identity work, it is likely that their behaviour considerably reduced the risk of their being questioned and blamed for counteracting the change – they were (on the surface) compliant and embraced the changes. The case also illustrates that resistance can come from seemingly privileged groups. It provides another example of the value of investigating the local context and the sensemaking of those involved in order to get past the superficial, and in this case fundamentally misleading, image of a situation, and thereby gain a deeper understanding of change dynamics.

REVIEW QUESTION 9.7

| Explain | Discuss the potential reasons for employees to conceal their resistance to change as compliance. |

SUMMARY

One of the most common concepts within the change literature is resistance. We have touched upon resistance earlier in the book, but this chapter provides a focused discussion of the theme, and approaches it from all three perspectives of change. According to a tool-based perspective, resistance was viewed as both a troublesome element and a valuable contribution. Thereafter, resistance was discussed from a process perspective as a natural occurrence and in the form of identity work. Finally, a critical perspective was applied, and the terminology of resistance was discussed as an instrument of power. At the very end we dealt with a perhaps more unexpected expression of resistance, namely, compliance.

The purpose of the breadth in this chapter is to inspire reflection and encourage consideration when using well-established terms in order to avoid becoming stuck in too much of a one-sided understanding of the phenomenon. In this chapter we have moved between a number of positions.

To begin with, we moved from a traditional image of resistance as a problematic element in organizations that must be counteracted at all costs, to a more embracing and welcoming position: resistance as making a valuable contribution. Rather than seeing employees as recipients of change, it can be preferable to understand them as co-producers of change.

We have also moved from resistance as an individual and psychological phenomenon to illustrating its social dimensions. We argued that people's perceptions of a proposed change are dynamic – they are shaped and maintained in conversations with other people. In conjunction with this, we also suggested that attitudes can change and quickly become embedded. During the course of one workshop people can go from perceiving the change as meaningful and being engaged in the process to regarding the change as meaningless and placing themselves in opposition to those driving the change.

We challenged the traditional view of who the 'resistant' employees are – more specifically, that they are primarily individuals in subordinate positions, furthest down in the hierarchy – by showing that privileged professional groups can also engage in change resistance. However, the forms of expression differ somewhat. To understand change processes in depth, it is therefore important not to be too quick to define certain actions as resistance and others as consent, and instead to take an interest in the (different) perspectives of those involved.

Finally, we have provided new angles to the idea that resistance is problematic by introducing a critical perspective and considering resistance as an instrument of power that is exploited to stifle divergent voices. From this angle, resistance, or, more correctly, the term 'resistance' is understood as a part of the change management discourse – as a term that depicts leaders and their behaviour in a positive light by casting a shadow over and marginalizing alternative voices and opinions.

 # KEY PRACTICAL INSIGHTS

What we can say about organizational change following this chapter:

- It is important to consider alternative explanations for resistance to change. It is common to assume that resistance to change has psychological roots and that employees therefore primarily need more information and time to overcome it. However, there are alternative explanations too, such as resistance being related to political and cultural dimensions of organizational life, and subsequently alternative suggestions on how to approach it.

- Resistance to change can be understood as positive for several reasons. First, it indicates that employees are interested and engaged in the organization. Second, employees defending the origins of the organization can be a valuable opposing force against fashionable ideas that might not necessarily be suitable for the organization. Third, input from organizational members with extensive knowledge and a thorough understanding of the daily practices can assist the adaptation and thus the implementation of the new ideas. In addition, employee participation can ensure that the organizational change becomes rooted in the organization.

- The implementation of organizational change can be compared to a ball game in the sense that a change idea needs a continous supply of new energy in order to spread. An initial kick of the ball (such as top managers introducing a change process) is insufficient; it is what happens afterwards that is crucial. How is the change idea received? Is it passed on and in what way? Do the actors involved have a shared understanding of the game they are playing? Are they interested in spreading the ideas? To assume that a change process will spread by itself can deflate or even ruin a change initiative.

CASE

Reorganization at AlphaTec

The Scandinavian IT company AlphaTec's roots could be traced back to a youth centre, where Rolf Petersson (the founder) was responsible for computer activities. Among other things, they created music with the help of computers, and there were also courses in form and design. Quite soon, an interest in making webpages began to dominate. Little by little, services were offered to companies at a small scale, in order to fund the purchase of new computers. This proved to be a happy venture because soon there were a number of clients, including an international business group. When the activities started to bring in revenues, it no longer corresponded to the municipality's definition of a municipal youth centre, at which point Rolf decided to found AlphaTec (pseudonym).

The company initially consisted of the three people who had been running the activities at the youth centre and one new recruit. All four were more or less involved in all projects. Work was carried out under quite simple conditions: an old kitchen table became one workplace and an empty cupboard another. Clients were enlisted through personal contacts and word of mouth. In the early years, the business was driven by enthusiasm rather than financial profit motives and it was run in a non-authoritarian way with a specific emphasis on having fun. It was a genuinely technically-oriented company, where the best technical argument always won and employees saw themselves as proud craftsmen who put a lot of effort into delivering software with as few bugs as possible. The business idea was successful in the sense that the company received a number of awards for different websites it had developed, and the company was known in the industry for solving technical issues that others could not. According to Rolf, the initial employees were 'full-time nerds – the kind of people who both work with computers and go home and have computers as a hobby'. Many of the developers explained that they applied to work at AlphaTec due to its technical orientation and the exceptionally high competence level of the employees.

The organization grew fast organically and the business and workforce gradually diversified. A little more than four years later, three new offices had been opened, and sales representatives, project leaders as well as marketing people had been employed, expanding the total workforce to 170 employees. The company had moved from producing primarily web-shops to making complex business systems for large multinational companies. The scope of the projects could range from a few days to several years, and the number of project members from one to 25.

The founder resigned from his position as managing director four years after it started in order to work in human resources. He explained that the MD role did not suit him anymore since it now included tasks he did not enjoy, such as leading people he did not know, giving 'pompous speeches' and working with business plans. Instead, the sales manager, Lennart Svensson, took over the role.

The atmosphere at the company was very familiar. Employees could have breakfast at work, there were soft drinks in the fridge and offices were personalized with plants, posters, sofas and paintings. There was a music room, a photo lab, a work-out room, a sauna and shower in the basement, and on the top floor a bar area and a big open space with a disco ball in the ceiling, sofas, armchairs and a flipper game in a corner. A number of evening activities

(Continued)

were arranged, such as movie and pizza nights, poker games and table-hockey tournaments, which were well attended. Among most employees there was an optimistic and positive spirit, and people were proud of working at AlphaTec. The chaos and unstructured way of working were joked about, although some newly recruited project leaders were of a different opinion. Some of the more senior developers complained about the increased top-down control and lack of information, though.

Top management had a different opinion of the state of the company. Both Lennart and the newly recruited production manager Ove believed that it was too unstructured and chaotic. In their minds, the organization needed to be fundamentally restructured. Their plan was to divide the employees in smaller units, appoint experienced managers, clarify areas of responsibility and introduce an accounting system in order to allow follow-ups. To them, these changes were obvious and inevitable, something that was needed in all companies that had expanded. For AlphaTec it had become urgent due to a revelation of major shortcomings in the financial control systems.

The reorganization plans were introduced in a meeting with all employees (described further on pp. 192–193). First, the company was presented as a leader in its field, then the MD stressed the importance of financial awareness. While talking about the need to change, he assured the audience that there was no plan for radical change or some kind of 'musical chairs'. Ove was introduced as the person who would lead the restructuring work. Lennart also pointed out that since Ove had worked at a large international technology company with responsibility for 800 people and managed a similar change process, he would be the right person for the job.

Shortly after the meeting, Ove gathered the managers at Operations to plan the organizational changes. This reorganization team met once a week and had meetings with their respective employees in between. Early on, the team decided to divide Operations into separate divisions with a number of projects in each. However, this idea was met with severe resistance.

It was primarily a group of 20 developers who had worked at the company for a long time that opposed the proposed change. Ove and the reorganization team were quick to classify these developers as being resistant to change and referred to them as 'old-timers', despite the fact that most of them were no older than 30. According to Ove, they had no self-awareness and only cared for what they as developers needed, not what was best for the company. His efforts to explain why the company needed to change had been in vain.

Many developers, and not only the group of 20 experienced senior workers, expressed a striking incomprehension and disapproval of the upcoming reorganization. For them, it was 'a very stupid idea' which they did not buy into either 'emotionally' or 'rationally'. A division into units would, as they saw it, be confining and limit the opportunity to work with exciting and cool projects. The developers particularly expressed a worry that they would only be allowed to work with what they already knew, and therefore not get the opportunity to develop their skills. They were afraid of being stuck in a unit 'forever', and not being able to choose to join interesting projects or get the chance to work with and learn from other experienced people. Furthermore, they feared that divisions would create segregation and rivalry between groups, which in turn would undermine knowledge-sharing. According to the developers, the change primarily satisfied the needs of the managers, i.e. it aimed to provide an organization that was easy to handle and administer.

Gradually, the arguments altered. From initially being against the proposed change, the developers began to attack 'the Management'[1] as a group. The Management was portrayed as a group of false people who misled others and hid information. The whole change process was described in terms of 'fake democracy' and that 'they said they listened but surely...'. Furthermore, the managers were talked about as being immoral, unreliable types who did not keep their promises. In particular, they told a story about a promised trip to London[2] that never took place as evidence for why Management could not be trusted.

Due to this strong reaction, the reorganization team abandoned substantial parts of their plans in order to appease the developers. Among other things, they accepted that projects could be run across unit lines, even if that was not the original intention. They also promised that it would be possible for the developers to sign up for future projects that they were interested in. However, the developers still expressed resistance to the proposal with equal force.

The change agents never succeeded in convincing the developers about the need for a reorganization. The explicit opposition did though decline but rather as a result of apathy. As one of the developers described it, he finally gave in, not because he was convinced about the advantages of the change, but because he realized that it was useless to oppose it: 'You realized that they don't listen to us anyhow. Maybe they listened, but they didn't care.'

The new organizational structure was implemented a couple of months later. Several developers, including some who had been against the division into units, seemed to appreciate them once they were in place. In particular, many valued having a unit manager who could raise their interests to top management. Others were indifferent and said that the new organization was not that different from before, given that the projects – as a key organizing principle – continued as usual. However, the reorganization was not implemented without costs. The negative attitude towards the Management (in particular the top-management) had been reinforced and widely spread.

Questions

- Discuss alternative explanations for the developers' resistance.

- Why do you think the resistance grew to such proportions?

- From a critical perspective, analyze the use of the label 'old-timers' applied by Ove and the reorganization group. What do you think this label signifies? What effects do you think the use of the label has? Can you think of alternative labels?

---

[1]The Management (with a capital M) is a concept used by the developers. The management is not confined to the people in the company's management group, but can include managers in general. 'The Management' is usually pronounced with a tinge of disdain in the voice and includes people who are not on their side but decide things above their head.

[2]The trip was to be offered when certain production targets were met, which they were.

FURTHER READING

Beech, N., Kajzer-Mitchell, I., Oswick, C., & Saren, M. (2011). Barriers to change and identity work in the swampy lowland. *Journal of Change Management*, 11(3), 289–304.

Cooke, F. L. (2002). The important role of the maintenance workforce in technological change: A much neglected aspect. *Human Relations*, 55(8), 963–988.

Dent, E. B., & Goldberg, S. G. (1999). Challenging 'resistance to change'. *The Journal of Applied Behavioral Science*, 35(1), 25–41.

Fleming, P., & Spicer, A. (2007). *Contesting the corporation: Struggle, power and resistance in organizations*. Cambridge: Cambridge University Press.

Ford, J. D., Ford, L. W., & D'Amelio, A. (2008). Resistance to change: The rest of the story. *Academy of Management Review*, 33(2), 362–377.

Kondo, D. K. (1990). *Crafting selves: Power, gender, and discourses of identity in a Japanese workplace*. Chicago, IL: The University of Chicago Press.

Piderit, S. K. (2000). Rethinking resistance and recognizing ambivalence: A multidimensional view of attitudes toward an organizational change. *Academy of Management Review*, 25(4), 783–794.

Worthington, F. (2004). Management, change and culture in the NHS: Rhetoric and reality. *Clinician in Management*, 12(2).

MANAGING ORGANIZATIONAL CHANGE: PRACTICAL LESSONS AND KEY INSIGHTS

LEARNING OBJECTIVES

When you have completed your study of this chapter, you should be able to:

- Explain what elements are particularly important to consider when trying to manage organizational change.

- Demonstrate understanding about what challenges an organizational change attempt typically entails for managers and others responsible for setting it in motion.

- Explain what it means to be thoughtful and reflective when managing organizational change in practice.

We have presented three perspectives and ways of relating to managing organizational change: the tool-based, process and critical perspectives. The tool-based orientation is the most ambitious when it comes to giving advice and instruction on *how* to explicitly manage organizational change – how to go about it in practice. In this respect, organizational change is primarily regarded as controllable and desirable. The focus is on the change programme, as conceived by management. This is the spirit in which most literature on the subject is written. However, our general stance is that this approach to organizational change is not without its challenges and that it has had a too big an impact in *how* many have come to view change.

From a process perspective, organizational change is seen as more dynamic, complex and ambiguous. As organizational change from this perspective normally involves the thinking and acting of numerous members of the organization, the central role of the management in the change process is sometimes questioned. The idea behind the process perspective is to emphasize sensemaking and encourage questions on *what* happens in change processes: How do people view themselves? How do they view the business and the need for change? How do they perceive the management's change plans? What are the implications of this understanding of people's sense-making for managing change?

Finally, the critical perspective questions all naïve and romantic notions that change is (or should be) in everybody's interest. The central questions are *why* change is important and whose interests does it serve to make the change. From the critical perspective, organizational life is seen to be full of conflicts and struggles between the diverse interests of individuals and groups. It is something that also needs to be considered when managing change.

The three perspectives offer different advice on how to approach the issue of managing change. We have tried to capture the extent of this in the different chapters in the book, but would like to widen and deepen the discussion in this last chapter by approaching the issue of managing change from a more general angle. Here we ask what practical lessons can someone who works with change or who is subject to change draw from these different perspectives? This final chapter is dedicated to trying to answer this question by extracting some more general and central insights and lessons from the different chapters. Taken from the lessons call for a conscious and thoughtful approach to organizational change work. The discussion is structured by revisiting some of the key themes in the different chapters of the book.

MANAGING ORGANIZATIONAL CHANGE: PRACTICAL LESSONS

The practical lessons of organizational change will in total revolve around eight themes. These themes are listed in Table 10.1. Each theme relates to a chapter of the book (Chapters 2–9).

TABLE 10.1   Summary of the practical lessons of organizational change

Realism and identity

Is there a need for change?

Scepticism – old wine in new bottles?

The parts and the context

Interpretation and sensemaking

Convincing and engaging stories

Reflection and pause for thought

Resistance as a constructive dialogue

Realism and identity

In Chapter 2 a conceptual structure for different types of change was introduced. We contrasted the different extents of change – radical versus minor and less pervasive change – and the different extents and paces of change – fast and in big steps (revolutionary) versus gradual and in small steps (evolutionary).

It is very common in popular scientific literature or in mass media to present heroic tales of how one or a few leaders drive radical and fast-paced change; for example, stories of how the management miraculously turned around an organization on the brink of bankruptcy to become an undisputed success in a short space of time (see Iacocca, 1984; Warren, 2015). However, it is important not to be swept away and blinded by such mass-media heroic portrayals, and instead to remain level-headed and critical regarding these types of narratives. The simplification of complex organizational contexts in the tool-based perspective – as in these heroic stories – incites a kind of romantic faith in the ability of leaders to steer a change course of events. *Instead, it is essential to develop a realistic view of the possibilities of achieving the planned change and a sensible view of one's own capacity and power to manage change.* A more critical and nuanced view of the ability to control a change course of events may reduce unnecessary stress on one's sense of identity and even a clash of identities (Sveningsson & Alvesson, 2015). In the long run, this entails working with change in a manageable way and placing realistic demands on oneself as a manager and leader.

The majority of successful organizational changes are evolutionary (Collins, 2001). Radical change proposals can of course occasionally mobilize major efforts and large-scale engagement among employees, especially if the organization is in serious crisis and change is longed for and awaited by large groups of employees. Typically, however, change proposals generate anxiety and people will question their identity with queries such as: 'Am I not doing a good job?' or 'Will I no longer be needed?' Incremental or evolutionary changes will often be perceived as less threatening for people's self-image or identities. Rather than coming up with radical change actions, which imply the management's absolute power, it is often better from a change perspective to work towards long-term change in incremental steps, even if this means that a manager doesn't come across as the grandiose strategist or paramount change leader (in their own eyes or the eyes of others). In other words, issues related to people's identity are often important when working with change. *Managers who push for change must therefore be attentive to their own identity or self-image. It is also particularly important to consider and follow up on how change proposals are perceived by the recipients of the change.* Do they perceive the change as a threat to their belonging and identity? Do they feel that their status and privileges are at stake?

One way to try to understand how people understand a change is to pay attention to the choice of words being used. What metaphors are used when they talk about the change? Is change described in terms of repairing a machine, a building project, a journey or as something innovative? *It is essential in a change process to try to create and maintain a shared idea of what the change means.* Contradictory interpretations easily encourage fragmentation and confusion about what is to be accomplished and subsequently undermine engagement.

Is there a need for change?

An important subject discussed in Chapter 3 is what triggers change. There is a central divide here between whether the changes are a result of internal driving forces (such as company expansion that requires restructuring or simply a change inspired by the management's intentions and desires) or whether they are mainly the result of external factors, what we refer to as external triggers. Another question concerns whether to view change at an organizational level or rather as part of a larger perspective.

Observing external factors that can initiate change can help managers to be observant and attentive to threats and opportunities so that they react in time. It is not unusual to become stuck in historical success stories and fail to observe changes occurring in the world around an organization. Invisible but strong and dominating ideas of one's own excellence often prevail in organizations. This can partially be counteracted with the help of models that enable broader analyses of the organization and its relationships with its external environment. *Consequently, it can be worthwhile to consider one's own organization as part of a larger context, and to adapt and align actions to the specific and local context of the organization rather than regarding the organization as an isolated and malleable entity.* On a personal level, the realization that change cannot simply be explained as the result of appropriate plans – regardless of the competency of the management – reduces managers' self-reproach and/or search for scapegoats when facing setbacks.

In connection with this, we also highlighted that change can be initiated by and gain momentum from ideas that are in conflict with one another. *The practical insight is therefore not to be too hasty in regarding tension and clashes as purely negative*, as they can be productive breeding grounds for organizational development and, in other words, contribute positive energy.

One last important insight from this chapter is that changes in the external environment should not be considered as objective and unambiguous. People interpret situations differently. Consequently, an important activity in change work includes trying to influence other people's opinions about the need for change. At the same time, reflecting on one's own ideas can be beneficial, so as to avoid allowing oneself to be swept along by ideas that over-glorify the need for and manageability of change. *It is valuable to critically examine change ideas that are 'trendy' and 'hot'. They are easy to adopt in terms of fashionable expressions, but may only have vague relevance to one's own reality.* Following trends may create legitimacy *per se*, as this signals ambition and being contemporary. However, following fashion may also produce outcomes that are somewhat unoriginal, as 'everybody wants the same kind of different clothes'. Above all, change suggestions built on trends, and with only a loose connection to the organizational reality, risk being met with mistrust, cynicism and irritation from employees.

Scepticism: Old wine in new bottles?

Chapter 4 undertook a historical review of how attitudes towards change work have developed in different schools of thought. The purpose of Taylorism was to address issues of control, motivation and efficiency in the new factories at the start of the 20th century. At that time, focus was placed on the division of labour, rationality and instrumental motivation. The Human Relations school was established in response to the negative side effects of Taylorism – alienation and conflict. The focus here was on people, and the approach underlined the value of paying attention to and involving employees in change work and taking their inner motivations into account. Kurt Lewin then developed the line of reasoning around group dynamics and the importance of identifying norms, roles and values in work groups.

A knowledge of history can highlight when 'old wine is being sold in new bottles', that is, when classic management ideas are revitalized and reused having being given a fresh new appearance. For example, many ideas in the broad category of 'change management', such as Business Process Re-engineering (BPR), actually have great similarities with classic Taylorism. It involves radical changes in the work design, a focus on making operations more efficient through streamlined work processes as well as designing and driving organizational change from the top down, based on a rational method. *It is therefore valuable to highlight the lessons from Taylorism, that an all too strict focus on efficiency supported by assumptions of the existence of powerful vertical control and a disregard of the human aspect can backfire on change attempts. Instead of increased efficiency, this approach can result in alienation and contempt for the work and the organization.* Given the popularity of many 'change management' ideas, this is a very relevant lesson.

In a society that strives for efficiency and performance measurement with a primary focus on economic gains, efficiency and consolidation of organizations, the contributions of Lewin and Organizational Development (OD) can provide valuable reminders and a counterforce. A central practical lesson from these schools is that knowledge and engaged participation in change work often reduces resistance. Within the field of OD, these ideas are developed through a focus on different forms of learning based on the underlying idea that organizations develop if individuals and groups develop. *One of their practical conclusions is that participation and potential for growth breeds commitment and creativity.*

These ideas are, however, not unproblematic as they are founded on a harmonious view of organizations, which suggests that people's motives can easily be aligned with those of the organization, and that conflicts and disagreements can therefore be reduced. From a critical perspective, assuming such harmony is seen as problematic and naïve since diverse factions, power and asymmetries of authority are a natural occurrence in organizations that cannot simply be ignored during a change process. Calls for openness, participation and consensus are important, but they need to be understood within the framework of politics and power structures. *Power, hierarchies, discipline, obedience and other central political circumstances always constitute an important dimension in the change process.*

Lewin's ice-cube metaphor has provided a basis for many n-step change models that are prevalent in much of the existing literature on change. Criticism of these models primarily targets the assumption that change takes place in defined episodes and that organizations are normally stable. This means disregarding the fact that organizations are also constantly changing. For example, it is not uncommon that organizational culture changes as an organization grows. *In practical change work, therefore, it is sensible to consider the underlying assumptions for the models or guidelines that are used to support the change work.* If these assume that an organization is normally constant – as the ice-cube metaphor suggests – then it is worthwhile questioning whether this is a meaningful way to understand organizational development. It may indeed be meaningful, but there is a risk that the significance of evolutionary change, and how current change work is affected by historical circumstances, is ignored.

The parts and the context

The integrated organizational models in Chapter 5 were developed as practical guidelines for how change should be diagnosed and implemented. At the same time, many of them are somewhat clichéd and banal. Universal advice that applies to everybody easily becomes abstract or meaningless – for instance, when managers are told to do 'good' things and avoid doing 'bad' things. The practical usefulness of such advice sounds rather hollow. It is, however, quite possible that many of the models can help leaders, during the initial phase, to structure diagnoses and analyses of the current situation of the organization, especially if the models are meaningfully translated into the local situation. *It is important to consistently avoid allowing the change work to develop into an abstract desktop project, far from the reality of the managers and other employees; rather, the project needs to be set in its context.* Even if many of these models can give managers a sense of control over change processes, the change course of events often turns out to be unique in its characteristics and thus follows its own complex and difficult-to-control dynamics.

The premise of the presented models – to view organizations as open systems – can provide valuable insights for change leaders. Above all, this perspective highlights that *the different subparts of an organization are linked to each other, and that a seemingly limited change in one part of the organization can have repercussions in other parts.* Thus, even small projects can prove to be complex and difficult to manage. Certain models highlight dependencies between so-called soft and hard subsystems of an organization. A seemingly hard change (technology) may end up having consequences on softer aspects that affect human resource issues and organizational culture.

One last important insight from Chapter 5 is the significance of considering the cultural dimension in change work, even if there is no ambition to change the culture. It is important not to be satisfied with a superficial understanding of the general culture of the organization or to be swept away in the potentially appealing idea that culture is something that managers can control to suit the intentions of the change work. People's values and perceptions should instead be taken very seriously and investigated rather than assumed. Making assumptions about one's own organization and its competencies is often inflated by fantasies and dreams about what one is capable of – creating hyperrealities (Alvesson & Sveningsson, 2015) – that have little do to with the existing reality. Investigating the existing reality implies paying attention to questions such as: How do the organizational members view the organization today? How do they view the change plans? How do they react to a specific attempt at implementation? What could be the reasons for their reactions? *One should therefore avoid viewing culture as something the organization has and instead view it as something the organization is (just as an organization can be viewed as a machine or an organism).* This latter approach means that the organizational culture expresses itself in other organizational subsystems or relationships, such as in structures, control systems, leadership, incentive systems and strategies.

Interpretation and sensemaking

In Chapter 6 we emphasized the value of observing and considering how individuals and groups in organizations interpret and position themselves *vis-à-vis* change work. Leaders may formulate plans and ideas for change, but if they do not encounter understanding and some level of acceptance from those affected by the change and those who carry out the change work, the plans seldom result in the desired effect. To understand change one needs to understand the sensemaking of the people involved. *Practically, this means that all those involved should be considered as active sensemakers, irrespective of whether they inflame, resist or remain passive to the change work.*

In line with this, practical change work involves supporting and influencing the interpretations of the people involved in order to create and evoke images of what the change will mean. This often demands that managers participate in tangible change work to gain insight into and influence the people involved in productive dialogue. *In other words, an all too strict division between those who plan and those who implement should be avoided.* Maintaining mutual trust between the parties involved is essential to the quality of communication.

Based on this, it is reasonable to assume that change occurs constantly as people interpret events and communicate their experiences with others. For example, the implications of a new organizational structure or new working methods are formed when people talk and interact with each other. These processes continuously influence how people view what is urgent and how to act. Two practical conclusions in particular can be drawn from this. *First, reactions to change initiatives should be attended to and followed up: how are ideas received and what happens to them when they are processed by people?* Change work needs to gain momentum rather than fade away after all those affected by it have been informed. *Second, change processes from more informal origins should be attended to and even be encouraged and supported if appropriate.* This can be particularly pertinent for organizations in turbulent and complex environments where it is considered especially important to capture current information broadly, and make the most of grass-roots initiatives and developments to ensure progress and growth.

Management-initiated change proposals often have unintended consequences. For example, change initiatives can lead to considerable employee stress and spark rumours, which in turn demand the attention of management to be quelled. The change can then be described in terms of reduced productivity. Another common outcome from change initiated by management is a deterioration in relations between management and other employees. A high pace of change often leads to cynicism and contempt towards the changes and those who initiate them. *The practical lesson from this is that change does not always produce positive outcomes; instead, there is a considerable risk of producing undesired consequences, such as cynicism and frustration among large groups of employees.*

From a political dimension, we also emphasize that conflicts and political games are part of daily life in organizations. Organizational change does not only take place as a result of rational motives and well-functioning communications from leaders in an officially more senior position. Further, change is rarely in everybody's interest. Broadly, this means that there are always individuals and groups that benefit and others that lose out. *Thus, organizational change from this perspective involves negotiations, building alliances, persuasion and creating legitimacy.*

Convincing and engaging stories

In Chapter 7 we discussed the value of listening to stories as a way to increase understanding of how employees interpret ideas of change. Stories normally provide local and situational knowledge on how favourable the conditions are for implementing different types of change. Are the ideas consistent with 'how things are done around here?' The very act of listening can also have positive effects. *Paying attention to and including employees in the change process by letting their voices be heard can create commitment and a more favourable attitude to new ideas.*

Practical change work involves creating and spreading stories that are in line with the desired goals. Stories about past successful changes, for example, can increase openness towards and acceptance of the new ideas. When working with storytelling, it is important to pay attention to the established usage of language in the organization in order to make sure that the message seems meaningful, engaging and compelling locally and the stories in turn are received well, adopted and retold. The stories do not need to be new; breathing life into existing stories and refuting the myths of other narratives may be sufficient. As management does not have a monopoly on story-telling, counter-stories often emerge. This may involve stories about historical mistakes or betrayal from top management that perpetuate the idea that management cannot be trusted. Just like the willingness to change, resistance can also be mobilized through storytelling. *An important lesson in this context is that interesting and genuine stories that are presented in line with established use of language and from trusted narrators have a greater chance of having a broader impact on people's perceptions.* For stories to have an impact, it can therefore be useful to identify key people and to try to influence them first. This also points to the value of maintaining mutual trust and trust in the employees.

If change leaders primarily use one-way communication, it can give the impression that con-sensus prevails as people do not want to disrupt the social order or risk being perceived as whining and stubborn. Alternative opinions may not be voiced until the changes are about to go live, either through employees avoiding changing their behaviour or through actively sabotaging the change. *A practical lesson from this is to be present as a change agent and enable dialogue, so that more shared perceptions can be established in the interaction between people.* In practice this requires, in addition to being actively present, an understanding and feeling for the people involved and their use of language.

Reflection and pause for thought

As discussed in Chapter 8, organizational change from a critical perspective involves stimulating reflection and pause for thought during change work. Among other things, the critical perspective problematizes traditional change management theories in terms of both the assumptions they are based on and the methods advocated.

An important lesson that is presented in this chapter involves embracing a reflective and criti-cal approach to calls for change, for example, the slogan 'change or die', which is often expressed in both popular literature and academic texts. *It may seem obvious, but it is worth repeating: change does not unequivocally lead to something favourable or good. Furthermore, change is seldom in everybody's interest.* In contrast, the eager change advocate certainly perceives that he/she has something to gain from the change, just as change authors – such as ourselves – have an interest in selling books and change consultants want to sell their services. Occasionally, however, maintaining an organiza-tion in a certain state, such as retaining a widespread positive and motivated spirit, can be just as important.

A critical view includes examining what popular change programmes mean locally. Changes that are pushed for under fancy banners, such as BPR, resilience or agile change management, often mean increased control and a mechanization of tasks for the staff, but this is something that is rarely brought up. A successful change programme from a management perspective can mean an increased workload or unemployment for others. The fact that employees resist such a change project is therefore unsurprising. Instead, the mantra 'It is for the good of the organization' is often repeated, despite the fact that there is rarely a harmony of interests. Above all, the idea that resistance is irrational and something that can be reduced through more information is an expression of a narrow and limited understanding of complex everyday organizational life.

A focus on conflicts of interest and power games can balance over-romantic ideas of change as being something primarily driven by management, well governed and controlled. *In short, it is about promoting thoughtful and realistic beliefs about what is possible and even morally reasonable to achieve.* Is it always good to succeed in overcoming resistance to change? But when does strong management or leadership become more a matter of discrimination and manipulation? What actions are morally justifiable?

In addition to strong management sometimes being morally questionable, there is also a risk that employees become obstructive simply because the proposals for change have been initiated by the management or a specific manager whose leadership is not liked. If a change is perceived as forced or if the rhetoric regarding participation and democracy is not exercised in practice, change proposals can be met with vigorous resistance and cynicism. *Silent alternative voices can be effective in the short term, but in the longer term, confidence in the management and the possibility for productive cooperation are undermined.*

Resistance as a constructive dialogue

In Chapter 9, one of the central practical messages is not to restrict oneself to a one-sided understanding of resistance, because this risks undermining change projects. Above all, this involves not restricting oneself to the classic standard perception that resistance is due to recipients being uncertain and afraid of the unknown, that is, that resistance is psychologically founded. Resentment towards new circumstances may also be the result of employees experiencing a deterioration of the work situation or that important values are being eroded. *The lesson here is therefore to pay attention to and reflect upon the political and cultural aspects of the change process that can form the basis of the resistance for change.*

It is also important not to be too hasty in perceiving challenging voices as irrational and problematic. Critical studies emphasize that it is not uncommon for management to blame opponents for the failure of a change project. This often provides a legitimate excuse and leaves the management free from blame. Apart from this behaviour being morally questionable, it can also have negative consequences for future change work.

A stalled change project is often seen as a result of opposing forces, that is, a person or several people have actively thwarted the chances of implementing the project. Thus, all resistance appears as something undesirable that should be stopped. However, ideas of change do not in themselves contain any power; their strength depends on the extent to which people regard them as meaningful. *In change work, one should therefore ask what would give the employees a reason and willingness to adopt and move the ideas forward.* If there are strong incentives for the members of the organization to identify with the new situation, the process can become virtually self-sustaining.

In that spirit, conflicting views should not automatically be dismissed as pointless resistance. The fact that people react at all can be seen as an expression of engagement and desire to contribute. If this is dismissed as irrelevant and attributed to psychological instability – fear or egotism – it instead causes unnecessary deadlock between parties who distance themselves clearly from one another, further aggravating coordination issues. *To dismiss an act as resistance can, ironically, fuel the very resistance one seeks to avoid.*

The practical message for change leaders is that they should take an interest in opposing ideas as these may provide valuable contributions to the organization's progress. *Responding to alternative opinions with constructive dialogue can enable the emergence of shared views on the direction of change and facilitate the spreading of the change.* To enable this, it may be beneficial to avoid thinking and talking in terms of change actors and change recipients, and instead to consider everyone involved as co-producers.

Another important lesson is that people can react particularly strongly to suggestions that they perceive threaten their self-image, their identity. Resistance to change is not always about the proposal for change in itself, but can also be about identity, self-esteem, image, status and the personal prestige of many of the people involved. If a change is perceived to strengthen the identity of those who are affected by it, it is likely that it will be accepted. *An awareness of whether change proposals may challenge and undermine people's identity can increase the chances of change ideas being accepted.* If there is powerful backlash, it is important for management to try to understand what the change proposal means for employees.

SUMMARY: KEY POINTS TO CONSIDER IN MANAGING CHANGE

The main message of this book can be summarized in the following eight points:

- Organizational change is about *people*, more than anything else. Those involved in change processes are all *co-producers* in one way or another, and should be recognized and treated as such. Local sensemaking is essential.

- Change work largely involves paying attention to and shaping the *understandings and interpretations* of the organization's members. It concerns views of the need for change, organizational identity, ideas for change and the self-images – identities – of those involved.

- Influencing and shaping people's interpretations usually requires active *presence* and constructive dialogue throughout the entire change process. The strict division of work between those who formulate and those who implement creates unnecessary fragmentation and counteracts the possibilities of influencing people's beliefs.

- Active involvement by many of the people involved throughout the entire change process can also contribute to increased *trust* and *confidence* in those who are driving the change.

This is also something that can be beneficial for the emergence of a common view of what needs to be changed.

- Change processes are facilitated if they are supported by rich and engaging *stories*. Confidence and faith in the narrators facilitate the acceptance and spread of change ideas in organizations. This involves working with *symbols* and rich language, not only to convince people of the need for change, but also to encourage perseverance throughout the change process.

- There is an inevitable political dimension in working with change. Attention should be paid to conflicts of interest and the exercise of power, and these should balance the all too idyllic and romantic images, which are common in the popular literature, of the ability to control change processes. Being visionary is not a bad thing, but it is important to remain *realistic* as to what can be achieved.

- Change processes are governed by the context in which they take place. Change actors do not act in a social vacuum but are affected by external circumstances. For example, it may come down to what is financially justifiable and politically legitimate to achieve. One should develop an awareness of and a feeling for the significance of different forces in *the local organizational context*. Not all management trends and ideas about governance and leadership have the same relevance, and they often require nuanced local interpretation.

- Reflection and development of a *critical approach* to organizational change is generally important. This includes not accepting cheerful calls for change too easily, or accepting a change model as comprehensive, even when this is asserted by a consultant or an author. That also, quite naturally, includes the authors of this book.

REFERENCES

Abrahamsson, E. (1996). Management fashion. *Academy of Management Review*, 1, 254–285.

Akhtar, O. (2013). The hatred and bitterness behind two of the world's most popular brands, *Fortune*, 22 March, http://fortune.com/2013/03/22/the-hatred-and-bitterness-behind-two-of-the-worlds-most-popular-brands/?# (accessed 2 January 2018).

Alvesson, M. (2004). *Knowledge work and knowledge-intensive firms*. Oxford: Oxford University Press.

Alvesson, M. (2012). *Understanding organizational culture*. London: Sage.

Alvesson, M., & Ashcraft, K. L. (2009). Critical methodology in management and organization research. In D. Buchanan & A. Bryman (eds.), *The SAGE handbook of organizational research methods* (pp. 61–77). London: Sage.

Alvesson, M., & Kärreman, D. (2000). Varieties of discourse: On the study of organizations through discourse analysis. *Human Relations*, 53(9), 1125–1149.

Alvesson, M., & Lundholm, S. (2014). *Personalchefers arbete och identitet: Strategi och strul*. Lund: Studentlitteratur.

Alvesson, M., & Spicer, A. (2010). *Metaphors we lead by: Understanding leadership in the real world*. London: Routledge.

Alvesson, M., & Sveningsson, S. (2003). The good visions, the bad micro-management and the ugly ambiguity: Contradictions of (non-)leadership in a knowledge-intensive company. *Organization Studies*, 24(6), 961–988.

Alvesson, M., & Sveningsson, S. (2011a). Management is the solution: Now what was the problem? On the fragile basis for managerialism. *Scandinavian Journal of Management*, 27(4), 349–361.

Alvesson, M., & Sveningsson, S. (2011b). Identity work in consultancy projects: Ambiguity and distribution of credit and blame. In C. Candlin & J. Crichton (eds.), *Discourses of deficit*. London: Palgrave.

Alvesson, M., & Sveningsson, S. (2015). *Changing organizational culture: Cultural change work in progress* (2nd ed.) London: Routledge.

Alvesson, M., & Thompson, P. (2005). Post-bureaucracy? In S. Ackroyd, R. Batt, P. Thompson & P. S. Tolbert (eds.), *The Oxford handbook of work and organization*. Oxford: Oxford University Press.

Andrews, K. R. (1971). *The concept of corporate strategy*. Homewood, IL: Dow Jones Irwin.

Ansoff, H. I. (1965). *Corporate strategy*. Harmondsworth: Penguin Books.

Arthur, C. (2011). Nokia's chief executive to staff: 'We are standing on a burning platform', *The Guardian*, 9 February, www.theguardian.com/technology/blog/2011/feb/09/nokia-burning-platform-memo-elop (accessed 10 January 2019).

Ashcraft, K. L. (2005). Resistance through consent? Occupational identity, organizational form, and the maintenance of masculinity among commercial airline pilots. *Management Communication Quarterly*, 19(1), 67–90.

Balogun, J. (2006). Managing change: Steering a course between intended strategies and unanticipated outcomes. *Long Range Planning*, 39, 29–49.

Balogun, J., & Johnson, G. (2005). From intended strategies to unintended outcomes: The impact of change recipient sensemaking. *Organization Studies*, 26(11), 1573–1601.

Bamford, D., & Daniel, S. (2005). A case study of change management effectiveness within the NHS. *Journal of Change Management*, 5(4), 391–406.

Barnard, C. (1938). *The functions of the executive*. Cambridge, MA: Harvard University Press.

Bartunek, J. M. (1984). Changing interpretive schemes and organizational restructuring: The example of a religious order. *Administrative Science Quarterly*, 29, 355–372.

Bartunek, J. M., & Reid, R. D. (1992). The role of conflict in second order change attempt. In D. M. Kolb & J. M. Bartunek (eds.), *Hidden conflict in organizations: Uncovering behind-the-scenes disputes*. Newbury Park, CA: Sage.

Bateman, T. S. (1980). Organizational change and the politics of success. *Group & Organization Studies*, 5(2), 198–209.

Baum, H. S. (2002). Why school systems resist reform: A psychoanalytic perspective. *Human Relations*, 55(2), 173–198.

BBC News (2018). Netflix's history: From DVD rentals to streaming success. *Newsbeat*, 23 January, www.bbc.com/news/newsbeat-42788099 (accessed 28 May 2019).

Beech, N., & Johnson, P. (2005). Discourses of disrupted identities in the practice of strategic change: The mayor, the street-fighter and the insider-out. *Journal of Organizational Change Management*, 18(1), 31–47.

Beech, N., & McIntosh, R. (2012). *Managing change: Enquiry and action*. Cambridge: Cambridge University Press.

Beer, M., & Eisenstat, R. A. (1996). Developing and organization capable of implementing strategy and learning. *Human Relations*, 49(5), 597–619.

Beer, M., & Nohria, N. (2000). Cracking the code of change. *Harvard Business Review*, 78(3), 133–141.

Beer, M., Spector, B., & Eisenstat, R. A. (1990). *Critical path to corporate renewal*. Cambridge, MA: Harvard Business School Press.

Berger, P., & Luckmann, T. (1966). *The social construction of reality*. London: Penguin.

Bies, R. S., & Sitkin, S. B. (1992). Explanation as legitimation: Excuse-making in organizations. In M. L. McLaughlin, M. J. Cody & S. J. Read (eds.), *Explaining one's self to others: Reason-giving in a social context*. Hillsdale, NJ: Lawrence Erlbaum Associates, pp. 183–198.

Bigelow, B., & Arndt, M. (2000). The more things change, the more they stay the same. *Health Care Management Review*, 25(1), 65–72.

Blegen, H. M. (1968). The system approach to the study of organizations. *Acta Sociologica*, 11(1–2), 12–30.

Boje, D. M., & Winsor, R. D. (1993). The resurrection of Taylorism: Total quality management's hidden agenda. *Journal of Organizational Change Management*, 6(4), 57–70.

Borak, B. (2018). How Meituan Dianping became China's super-platform for services, *Technode*, 27 June, https://technode.com/2018/06/27/how-meituan-dianping-became-chinas-super-platform-for-services/ (accessed 19 December 2018).

Boulding, K. (1956). *The image: Knowledge in life and society.* Ann Arbour, MI: University of Michigan Press.

Brown, A. (1998). Narrative, politics, and legitimacy in an IT implementation. *Journal of Management Studies*, 3571, 45–75.

Brown, A., Gabriel, Y., & Gherardi, S. (2009). Storytelling and change: An unfolding story. *Organization*, 16(3), 323–333.

Brown, A., & Humphreys, M. (2003). Epic and tragic tales making sense of change. *Journal of Applied Behavioral Science*, 39(2), 121–144.

Brown, A., Humphreys, M., & Gurney, P. (2005). Narrative, identity and change: A case study of Laskarina Holidays. *Journal of Organizational Change Management*, 18(4), 312–326.

Brunsson, N. (2006). *The organization of hypocrisy: Talk, decisions and actions in organizations* (2nd ed.). Copenhagen: Copenhagen Business School Press.

Buchanan, D. (2003). Getting the story straight: Illusions and delusions in the organizational change process. *Tamara: Journal of Critical Postmodern Organizational Science*, 2(4), 7–21.

Buchanan, D., & Badham, R. (1999). Politics and organizational change: The lived experience. *Human Relations*, 52(5), 609–629.

Buchanan, D., & Dawson, P. (2007). Discourses and audience: Organizational change as multi-story process. *Journal of Management Studies*, 44(5), 669–686.

Bullock, R., & Batten, D. (1985). It's just a phase we're going through: A review and synthesis of OD phase analysis. *Group & Organization Management*, 10(4), 383–412.

Burke, W. W. (2002). *Organization change.* Thousand Oaks, CA: Sage.

Burke, W. W., & Bradford, D. L. (2005). The crisis in OD. In D. L. Bradford & W. W. Burke (eds.), *Reinventing organization development: New approaches to change in organizations.* San Francisco, CA: Pfeiffer/Wiley.

Burnes, B. (2004). *Managing change: A strategic approach to organizational dynamics.* Harlow: Prentice Hall.

Burns, T. E., & Stalker, G. M. (1961). *The management of innovation.* London: Tavistock.

Bushe, G. R., & Marshak, R. (2009). Revisioning organization development: Diagnostic and dialogic premises and patterns of practice. *Journal of Applied Behavioral Science*, 45(3), 348–368.

Casey, C. (1999). Come, join our family: Discipline and integration on corporate organizational culture. *Human Relations*, 52, 155–178.

Chandler, A. D. (1962). *Strategy and structure: Chapters in the history of the American industrial enterprise.* Washington, DC: Beard Books.

Child, J. (1972). Organizational structure, environment and performance: The role of strategic choice. *Sociology*, 6, 1–22.

Child, J. (2005). *Organization: Contemporary principles and practice.* Oxford: Blackwell.

Chreim, S. (2006). Managerial frames and institutional discourses of change: Employee appropriation and resistance. *Organization Studies*, 27(9), 1261–1287.

Clark, A. (2002). Tail of woe. *The Guardian*, 10 September, www.theguardian.com/business/2002/sep/10/ftse.theairlineindustry (accessed 25 March 2019).

Collins, D. (1998). *Organizational change: Sociological perspectives*. London: Routledge.

Collins, D. (2018). *Stories for management success: The power of talk in organizations*. London: Routledge.

Collins, D., & Rainwater, K. (2005). Managing change at Sears: A sideways look at a tale of corporate transformation. *Journal of Organizational Change Management*, 18(1), 16–30.

Collins, J. (2001). *From good to great*. New York: Harper-Collins.

Comtois, E., Denis, J. L., & Langley, A. (2004). Rhetorics of efficiency, fashion and politics: Hospital mergers in Quebec. *Management Learning*, 35(3), 303–320.

Cooke, F. L. (2002). The important role of the maintenance workforce in technological change: A much neglected aspect. *Human Relations*, 55(8), 963–988.

Courpasson, D., Dany, F., & Clegg, S. R. (2011). Resisters at work: Generating productive resistance in the workplace. *Organization Science*, 23(3), 801–819.

Cummings, T. G., & Worley, C. G. (2005). *Organization development and change* (8th ed.) Mason, OH: South-Western.

Cummings, T. G., & Worley, C. G. (2009). *Organization development and change* (9th ed.) Mason, OH: South-Western.

Czarniawska, B. (1998). *A narrative approach to organization studies*. London: Sage.

Czarniawska, B., & Joerges, B. (1996). Travels of ideas. In B. Czarniawska & G. Sevón (eds.), *Translating organizational change*. Berlin: de Gruyter.

Dawson, P. (2003). *Understanding organizational change*. London: Sage.

Dawson, P. (2014). Reflections: On time, temporality and change in organizations. *Journal of Change Management*, 14(3), 285–308.

Dawson, P., & Buchanan, D. (2005). The way it really happened: Competing narratives in the political process of technological change. *Human Relations*, 58(7), 845–865.

Dawson, P., & McLean, P. (2013). Miners' tales: Stories and the storying process for understanding the collective sensemaking of employees during contested change. *Group & Organization Management*, 38(2), 198–229.

Degn, L. (2016). Academic sensemaking and behavioural responses: Exploring how academics perceive and respond to identity threats in times of turmoil. *Studies in Higher Education*, 43(2), 305–321.

Dent, E. B., & Goldberg, S. G. (1999). Challenging 'resistance to change'. *Journal of Applied Behavioral Science*, 35(1), 25–41.

Diefenbach, T. (2007). The managerialistic ideology of organizational change management. *Journal of Organizational Change Management*, 20(1), 126–144.

Döjback, D., & Söndegaard, M. (2004). The Spaghetti that became revolutionary. Cases for OrgCon. Oticon. Available at: http://extras.springer.com/2004/978-1-4020-7685-5/Cases/Spaghetti2.pdf (accessed 16 July 2019).

Doolin, B. (2003). Narratives of change: Discourse, technology and organization. *Organization*, 10, 751–770.

Dunford, R., & Jones, D. (2000). Narrative in strategic change. *Human Relations*, 53(9), 1207–1226.

Dunphy, D. C., & Stace, D. A. (1988). Transformational and coercive strategies for planned organizational change: Beyond the O.D. model. *Organization Studies*, 9(3), 317–334.

Dunphy, D. C., & Stace, D. A. (1993). The strategic management of corporate change. *Human Relations*, 46(8), 905–920.

Eilam, G., & Shamir, B. (2005). Organizational change and self-concept threats: A theoretical perspective and a case study. *Journal of Applied Behavioral Science*, 41(4), 399–421.

Erwin, E., & Garman, A. (2010). Resistance to organizational change: Linking research and practice. *Leadership & Organization Development Journal*, 31(1), 39–56.

Ewing, J. (2015). Volkswagen's Chairman, Ferdinand Piëch, is ousted in power struggle. *The New York Times*, 25 April, www.nytimes.com/2015/04/26/business/international/volkswagens-chairman-ferdinand-piech-is-ousted-in-power-struggle.html (accessed 8 January 2019).

Ewing, J. (2018). Ex-Volkswagen CEO charged with fraud over diesel emissions. *The New York Times*, 3 May, www.nytimes.com/2018/05/03/business/volkswagen-ceo-diesel-fraud.html (accessed 8 January 2019).

Ezzamel, M., Willmott, H., & Worthington, F. (2001). Power, control and resistance in 'The factory that time forgot'. *Journal of Management Studies*, 38(8), 1053–1079.

Ezzamel, M., Willmott, H., & Worthington, F. (2004). Accounting and management–labour relations: The politics of production in the 'factory with a problem'. *Accounting, Organizations and Society*, 29(3–4), 269–302.

Fairclough, N., & Thomas, P. (2004). The globalization of discourse and the discourse of globalization. In D. Grant, C. Hardy, C. Oswick & L. Putman (eds.), *The Sage handbook of organizational discourse*. London: Sage, pp. 379–396.

Fassin, Y. (2009). The stakeholder model refined. *Journal of Business Ethics*, 84(1), 113–135.

Fleming, P., & Sewell, G. (2002). Looking for the good soldier, Svejk: Alternative modalities of resistance in the contemporary workplace. *Sociology*, 36(4), 857–873.

Fleming, P., & Spicer, A. (2007). *Contesting the corporation*. Cambridge: Cambridge University Press.

Forbes (2018). How Japan is harnessing IoT technology to support its aging population. *Forbes (online)*, 4 December, https://www.forbes.com/sites/japan/2018/12/04/how-japan-is-harnessing-iot-technology-to-support-its-aging-population/#550200cb3589 (accessed 6 December 2018).

Ford, J. D., & Ford, L. W. (1994). Logics of identity, contradiction, and attraction in change. *Academy of Management Review*, 19(4), 756–785.

Ford, J. D., & Ford, L. W. (1995). The role of conversations in producing intentional change in organizations. *Academy of Management Review*, 20(3), 541–570.

Ford, J. D., & Ford, L. W. (2009). Stop blaming resistance to change and start using it. *Organizational Dynamics*, 39 (1), p. 24–36.

Ford, J. D., Ford, L. W., & D'Amelio, A. (2008). Resistance to change: The rest of the story. *Academy of Management Review*, 33(2), 362–377.

Foucault, M. (1976). *The history of sexuality*, Vol. 1. London: Penguin.

Fournier, V., & Grey, C. (2000). At the critical moment: Conditions and prospects for critical management studies. *Human Relations*, 53(1), 7–32.

Freeman, E. (1984). *Strategic management: A stakeholder approach*. Boston, MA: Pitman.

Gabriel, Y. (1993). Organizational nostalgia: Reflections on 'the golden age'. In S. Fineman (ed.), *Emotion in organizations*. Thousand Oaks, CA: Sage, pp. 118–141.

Gabriel, Y. (1995). The unmanaged organization: Stories, fantasies and subjectivity. *Organization Studies*, 16(3), 477–501.

Gabriel, Y. (2000). *Storytelling in organizations: Facts, fictions, and fantasies*. Oxford: Oxford University Press.

Gaertner, K. (1989). Winning and losing: Understanding managers' reactions to strategic change. *Human Relations*, 42(June), 527–546.

Gagliardi, P. (1986). The creation and change of organizational cultures: A conceptual framework. *Organization Studies*, 7(2), 117–134.

Garrety, K., Badham, R., Morrigan, V., Rifkin, W., & Zanko, M. (2003). The use of personality typing in organizational change: Discourse, emotions and the reflexive subject. *Human Relations*, 56(2), 211–235.

Giddens, A. (1979). *Central problems in social theory: Action, structure, and contradiction in social analysis*. Berkeley, CA: University of California Press.

Gollan, D. (2017). Did British Airways make one cut too many? *Forbes*, 18 January, www.forbes.com/sites/douggollan/2017/01/18/did-british-airways-make-one-cut-too-many/#698f09484713 (accessed 25 March 2019).

Goodstein, L. D., & Burke, W. W. (1993). Creating successful organizational change. In C. Maybe & B. Mayon-White (eds.), *Managing change* (2nd ed.). London: Paul Chapman, pp. 164–172.

Grant, D., Hardy, C., Oswick, C., & Putman, L. (2004). *The Sage handbook of organizational discourse*. London: Sage.

Grant, D., & Marshak, R. (2011). Towards a discourse-centered understanding of organizational change. *Journal of Applied Behavioral Science*, 47(2), 204–235.

Greiner, L. (1972). Evolution and revolution as organizations grow. *Harvard Business Review*, 50(4), 37–46.

Greiner, L., & Cummings, T. (2005). OD: Wanted dead or alive. In D. L. Bradford & W. W. Burke (eds.), *Reinventing organization development: New approaches to change in organizations*. San Francisco, CA: Pfeiffer/Wiley.

Grey, C. (2003). The fetish of change. *Tamara: Journal of Critical Postmodern Organizational Science*, 2(2), 1–19.

Grey, C., & Willmott, H. (2005). *Critical management studies: A reader*. Oxford: Oxford University Press.

Gruley, B., & Butters, J. (2018). How China's 36th-best car company saved Volvo. *Bloomberg Businessweek*, 24 May, www.bloomberg.com/news/features/2018-05-24/volvo-is-better-than-ever-thanks-to-this-chinese-billionaire (accessed 28 May 2019).

Guo, O. (2018). Behind the rise of Meituan-Dianping, China's food-delivery giant. *Tech in Asia*, 13 July, https://www.techinasia.com/rise-of-meituan-dianping (accessed 19 December 2018).

Habermas, J. (1972). *Knowledge and human interests*. Trans. Jeremy J. Shapiro. London: Heinemann.

Hannan, M. T., & Freeman, J. (1977). The population ecology of organizations. *American Journal of Sociology*, 82(5), 929–964.

Hardy, C. (1996). Understanding power: Bringing about strategic change. *British Journal of Management*, 7, 3–16.

Hardy, C. (2001). Researching organizational discourse. *International Studies of Management and Organization*, 31(3), 25–47.

Hardy, C., & Phillips, N. (2004). Discourses and power. In D. Grant, C. Hardy, C. Oswick & L. Putman (eds.), *The Sage handbook of organizational discourse*. London: Sage.

Heath, M., & Porter, T. (2019). Sensemaking through a storytelling lens: Physician perspectives of health information exchange. *Qualitative Research in Organizations and Management: An International Journal*, February (no pages available).

Helms-Mills, J. (2003). *Making sense of organizational change*. New York: Routledge.

Henderson, B. (1989). The origin of strategy. *Harvard Business Review*, November, 139–143.

Heracleous, L. (2001). An ethnographic study of culture in the context of organizational change. *Journal of Applied Behavioral Science*, 37(4), 426–446.

Heracleous, L., & Langham, B. (1996). Strategic change and organizational culture at Hay Management Consultants. *Long Range Planning*, 29(4), 485–494.

Hollander, J. A., & Einwohner, R. L. (2004). Conceptualizing resistance. *Sociological Forum*, 19(4), 533–554.

Horwitz, J. (2018). China's latest multibillion-dollar IPO is an app offering everything from hot pot to haircuts. *Quartz*, 25 June, https://qz.com/1313308/chinas-meituan-whose-app-offers-everything-from-hot-pot-to-haircuts-has-filed-for-an-ipo/ (accessed 19 December 2018).

Hughes, M. (2010). *Managing change: A critical perspective*. London: Chartered Institute of Personnel and Development.

Hughes, M. (2016). Leading changes: Why transformation explanations fail. *Leadership*, 12(4), 449–469.

HUI Research Council (The Swedish Retail and Wholesale Council) (2018). *What Happens when Amazon Arrives?* Report. Stockholm: HUI Press. http://handelsradet.se/press/2018-2/det-hander-nar-amazon-kommer/ (accessed 28 May 2019).

Huy, Q. (2002). Emotional balancing of organizational continuity and radical change: The contribution of middle managers. *Administrative Science Quarterly*, 47, 31–69.

Huzzard, T. (n.d.). System-wide change in cancer care – a teaching case. (Teaching material).

Huzzard, T., Hellström, A., & Lifvergren, S. (2014). System-wide change in cancer care: Exploring sensemaking, sensegiving, and consent. *In Research in Organizational Change and Development* (Vol. 22, pp. 191–218). Bingley, UK: Emerald.

Iacocca, L. A. (1984). *Iacocca: An autobiography*. New York: Bantam Books.

Isaacson, W. (2011). *Steve Jobs*. New York: Simon & Schuster.

Jabri, M. (2012). *Managing organizational change: Process, social construction and dialogue*. Basingstoke: Palgrave Macmillan.

Jabri, M., Adrian, A. D., & Boje, D. (2008). Reconsidering the role of conversations in change communication: A contribution based on Bakhtin. *Journal of Organizational Change Management*, 21(6), 667–685.

Jacobs, G., Van Witteloostuijn, A., & Christe-Zeyse, J. (2013). A theoretical framework of organizational change. *Journal of Organizational Change Management*, 26(5), 772–792.

Jersild, P. C. (1978). *Babels hus* [*House of Babel*]. Stockholm: Bonniers.

Jian, G. (2007). Unpacking unintended consequences in planned organizational change: A process model. *Management Communication Quarterly*, 21(1), 5–28.

Jian, G. (2011). Articulating circumstance, identity and practice: Toward a discursive framework of organizational changing. *Organization*, 18(1), 45–64.

Jick, T. D., & Peiperl, M. A. (eds.) (2003). *Managing change: Cases and concepts*. New York: McGraw-Hill.

Johnson, G., Whittington, R., & Scholes, K. (2011). *Exploring strategy: Text and cases* (9th ed.). New York: Prentice-Hall.

Joost & Pim (2017). How Lars Kolind created immense success by abolishing hierarchy (20 times!). *Corporate Rebels*, 18 January, https://corporate-rebels.com/lars-kolind/ (accessed 28 May 2019).

Kanter, R. M. (1999). *The change masters*. London: International Thomson Business Press.

Kärreman, D., Sveningsson, S., & Alvesson, M. (2002). The return of the machine bureaucracy? Management control in the work settings of professionals. *International Studies of Management and Organizations*, 32(2), 70–92.

Katz, D., & Kahn, R. L. (1966). *The social psychology of organization*. New York: Wiley.

Kavadias, S., Ladas, K., & Loch, C. (2016). The transformative business model. *Harvard Business Review*, 94(10), 91–98.

Kjærgaard, A., Morsing, M., & Ravasi, D. (2011). Mediating identity: A study of media influence on organizational identity construction in a celebrity firm. *Journal of Management Studies*, 48(3), 514–543.

Kleppestø, S. (1993). *Kultur och identitet*. Stockholm: Nerenius & Santérus.

Klich, T. (2018). The other power women: Women banding together to create change. *Forbes*, 4 December, www.forbes.com/sites/tanyaklich/2018/12/04/the-worlds-most-powerful-women-changing-the-world-together-from-2-journalists-to-20000-tech-workers/#4b2c f3ad2290 (accessed 19 December 2018).

Knights, D., & McCabe, D. (1998). When 'life is but a dream': Obliterating politics through business process reengineering? *Human Relations*, 51(6), 761–798.

Knights, D., & McCabe, D. (2000). 'Ain't misbehavin'? Opportunities for resistance under new forms of 'quality' management. *Sociology*, 34(3), 421–436.

Knights, D., & Morgan, G. (1991). Corporate strategy, organizations, and subjectivity: A critique. *Organization Studies*, 12(2), 251–273.

Kondo, D. K. (1990). *Crafting selves: Power, gender, and discourses of identity in a Japanese workplace.* Chicago, IL: The University of Chicago Press.

Kotter, J. P. (1995). Leading change: Why transformation efforts fail. *Harvard Business Review*, 73, 259–267.

Kotter, J. P. ([1996] 2012a). *Leading change.* Boston, MA: Harvard Business School Press.

Kotter, J. P. (2012b). Accelerate! How the most innovative companies capitalize on today's rapid-fire strategic challenges. *Harvard Business Review*, 90, 43–58.

Kotter, J. P. (2014). *Accelerate.* Boston, MA: Harvard Business Review Press.

KPMG (2008). Stop the presses! Newspapers are struggling: Can an all-digital strategy be the path to profitability, 17 January, https://home.kpmg.com/content/dam/kpmg/co/pdf/co-17-01-08-tmt-stop-the-presses.pdf (accessed 30 May 2019).

Kübler-Ross, E. (1969). *On death and dying.* New York: Taylor & Francis.

Kunda, G. (1992). *Engineering culture: Control and commitment in a high-tech corporation.* Philadelphia, PA: Temple University Press.

Labianca, G., Gray, B., & Brass, D. (2000). A grounded model organizational schema change during empowerment. *Organization Science*, 11(2), 235–257.

Lapointe, L., & Rivard, S. (2005). A multilevel model of resistance to information technology implementation. *MIS Quarterly*, 29(3), 461–491.

Larsen, H. (1996). Oticon. Thinking the unthinkable: Radical (and successful) organizational change. In J. Storey (ed.), *Blackwell cases in human resource management.* Oxford: Blackwell.

Latour, B. (1986). The powers of association. In J. Law (ed.), *Power, action and belief: A new sociology of knowledge?* London: Routledge & Kegan Paul.

Latour, B. (1998). *Artefaktens återkomst: Ett möte mellan organizationsteori och tingens sociologi.* Övers. E. Wennerholm. Stockholm: Nerenius & Santérus.

Latour, B. (2005). *Reassembling the social.* Oxford: Oxford University Press.

Lawrence, B. (2018). Netflix is as successful as ever in early 2018, here's the latest. *Cinema Blend*, https://www.cinemablend.com/television/2403992/netflix-is-as-successful-as-ever-in-early-2018-heres-the-latest (accessed 28 May 2019).

Lewin, K. (1947). Frontiers in group dynamics: Concept, method and reality in social science: Social equilibria and social change. *Human Relations*, 1(1), 5–41.

Lewin, K. (1951). *Field theory in social science.* New York: Harper & Row.

Lozano, R. (2015). A holistic perspective on corporate sustainability drivers. *Corporate Social Responsibility and Environmental Management*, 22, 32–44.

Luthans, F., Luthans, B., & Luthans, K. (2015). *Organizational Behavior: An evidence-based approach* (13th ed.). New York: McGraw-Hill.

Lutz, A. (2013). Nordstrom will use Pinterest to decide what merchandise to display in stores. *Business Insider*, 22 November, www.businessinsider.com/nordstroms-pinterest-in-stores-plan-2013-11?r=US&IR=T

Maclean, M., Harvey, C., & Chia, R. (2012). Sensemaking, storytelling and the legitimization of elite business careers. *Human Relations*, 65(1), 17–40.

Mainardes, E. W., Alves, H., & Raposo, M. (2011). Stakeholder theory: Issues to resolve. *Management Decision*, 49(2), 226–252.

Maitlis, S., & Sonenshein, S. (2010). Sensemaking in crisis and change: Inspiration and insights from Weick (1988). *Journal of Management Studies*, 47(3), 551–580.

March, J. G., & Simon, H. A. (1958). *Organizations*. New York: Wiley.

Marr, B. (2018). The digital transformation to keep IKEA relevant: virtual reality, apps and self-driving cars, *Forbes*, 19 October, www.forbes.com/sites/bernardmarr/2018/10/19/the-amazing-digital-transformation-of-ikea-virtual-reality-apps-self-driving-cars/#4e3a 307476be (accessed 26 June 2019).

Marshak, R. (2005). Contemporary challenges to the philosophy and practice of organizational development. In D. L. Bradford & W. W. Burke (eds.), *Reinventing organization development: New approaches to change in organizations*. San Francisco, CA: Pfeiffer/Wiley.

Marshak, R. (2009). *Organizational change: Views from the edge*. Bethel, ME: Lewin Center.

Marshak, R., & Grant, D. (2011). Organizational discourse and new organization development practices. *British Journal of Management*, 19(1), 7–19.

Marwan, S. (2018). #GoogleWalkout: 'Don't Be Evil,' 'Not OK Google,' protest workers in fallout to sexual harassment charges, *Forbes*, 1 November, https://www.forbes.com/sites/samarmarwan/2018/11/01/google-walkout-dont-be-evil-not-ok-google-protest-workers-in-fallout-to-sexual-harassment-charges/#1bb84ce4502b (accessed 19 December 2018).

Maslow, A. (1954). *Motivation and personality*. New York: Harper Collins.

Mayo, E. (1933). *The human problems of industrial civilization*. New York: Macmillan.

McCabe, D. (1999). Total quality management: Anti-union Trojan horse or management albatross? *Work, Employment & Society*, 13(4), 665–691.

McCord, P. (2014). How Netflix reinvented HR. *Harvard Business Review*, 92(1), 70–76.

McGee, T. (2017). How millennials are changing retail patterns, *Forbes*, 23 January, www.forbes.com/sites/tommcgee/2017/01/23/the-rise-of-the-millennial/ (accessed 28 May 2019).

McGregor, D. (1960). *The human side of enterprise*. New York: McGraw-Hill.

McMenemy, L. (2018). What is a chief storyteller? Five business leaders share their stories. *Skyword*, 22 March, www.skyword.com/contentstandard/marketing/what-is-a-chief-storyteller-five-business-leaders-share-their-stories/ (accessed 13 January 2019).

McNulty, T., & Ferlie, E. (2004). Process transformation: Limitations to radical organizational change within public service organizations. *Organization Studies*, 25(8), 1389–1412.

McSweeney, B. (2006). Are we living in a post-bureaucratic epoch? *Journal of Organizational Change Management*, 19(1), 22–37.

Meyer, J., & Rowan, B. (1977). Institutionalized organizations: Formal structure as myth and ceremony. *American Journal of Sociology*, 83(2), 340–363.

Meyer, P. (2019). Amazon.com Inc.'s organizational structure characteristics (an analysis). *Panmore Institute, Business & Management*, 16 February 2019, http://panmore.com/amazon-com-inc-organizational-culture-characteristics-analysis (accessed 30 May 2019).

Milne, R. (2018). Ikea to turn big stores into delivery hubs. *Financial Times*, 11 October.

Mintzberg, H. (2005). The magic number seven – plus or minus a couple of managers. *Academy of Management Learning & Education*, 4(2), 244–247.

Mintzberg, H., & McHugh, A. (1985). Strategy formation in an adhocracy. *Administrative Science Quarterly*, 30, 160–197.

Mirfakhar, A., Trullen, J., & Valverde, M. (2018). Easier said than done: A review of antecedents influencing effective HR implementation. *The International Journal of Human Resource Management*, 29(22), 3001–3025.

Mitchell, A., Jurkowitz, M., & Guskin, E. (2013). What's behind the Washington Post sale: The newspaper industry overall, *Pew Research Center, Journalism & Media*, 7 August, http://www.journalism.org/2013/08/07/the-newspaper-industry-overall/ (accessed 30 May 2019).

Montano, D. (2018). A systemic organizational change model in the occupational health management. *Journal of Change Management*, 10, 1–18.

Morgan, G. (2006). *Images of organization*. Thousand Oaks, CA: Sage.

Morrison, P. (1981). Evaluation in OD: A review and an assessment. *Group & Organization Studies*, 3(1), 42–70.

Nadler, D. A., & Tushman, M. L. (1980). A model for diagnosing organizational behavior. *Organizational Dynamics*, 9(2), 35–51.

Nadolny, A., & Ryan, S. (2015). McUniversities revisited: A comparison of university and McDonald's casual employee experiences in Australia. *Studies in Higher Education*, 40(1), 142–157.

Newton, T. (1998). Theorizing subjectivity in organizations: The failure of Foucauldian studies. *Organization Studies*, 19, 415–447.

Ng, W., & De Cock, C. (2002). Battle in the boardroom: A discursive perspective. *Journal of Management Studies*, 39(1), 23–49.

Norbäck, L.-E., & Targama, A. (2009). *Det komplexa sjukhuset: Att leda djupgående förändringar i en multiprofessionell verksamhet*. Lund: Studentlitteratur.

Nyberg, S. (2018). Därför floppar Homepod – fem saker Apple måste fixa innan högtalaren kommer till Sverige. *MacWorld*, 24 April.

Ogden, S. G., & Anderson, F. (1995). Representing customer interests: The case of the UK privatised water industry. *Public Administration*, 73, 535–559.

O'Leary, M. (2003). From paternalism to cynicism: Narratives of a newspaper company. *Human Relations*, 56(6), 685–704.

Palmer, I., Dunford, R., & Buchanan D. A. (2017). *Managing organizational change* (3rd ed.). New York: McGraw-Hill.

Parker, L. D. (2012). From privatised to hybrid corporatised higher education: A global financial management discourse. *Financial Accountability & Management*, 28(3), 247–268.

Perez, M. (2018). Nintendo ends its comeback year with over $9 billion in revenue. *Forbes*, 26 April, www.forbes.com/sites/mattperez/2018/04/26/nintendo-ends-its-comeback-year-with-over-9-billion-in-revenue

Perren, L., & Megginson, D. (1996). Resistance to change as a positive force: Its dynamics and issues for management development. *The Career Development International*, 1(4), 24–28.

Peters, T. J. (1992). *Liberation management*. New York: Alfred A. Knopf.

Peters, T. J., & Waterman, R. (1982). *In search of excellence*. New York: Harper Row.

Pettigrew, A. (1985). *The awakening giant: Continuity and change in Imperial Chemical Industries*. Oxford: Basil Blackwell.

Pettigrew, A. (1997). What is a processual analysis? *Scandinavian Journal of Management*, 13(4), 337–348.

Pettigrew, A. (2012). Context and action in the transformation of the firm: A reprise. *Journal of Management Studies*, 49(7), 1304–1328.

Pew Research Center (2018). Newsroom employment dropped nearly a quarter in less than 10 years, with greatest decline at newspapers. *Pew Research Center*, 30 July. http://www.pewre search.org/fact-tank/2018/07/30/newsroom-employment-dropped-nearly-a-quarter-in-less-than-10-years-with-greatest-decline-at-newspapers/ (accessed 30 May 2019).

Pfeffer, J. (1992). *Managing with power: Politics and influence in organizations*. Boston, MA: Harvard Business School Press.

Piderit, S. K. (2000). Rethinking resistance and recognizing ambivalence: A multidimensional view of attitudes toward an organizational change. *Academy of Management Review*, 25(4), 783–794.

Pieterse, J., Caniëls, M., & Homan, T. (2012). Professional discourses and resistance to change. *Journal of Organizational Change Management*, 25(6), 798–818.

Prasad, P. (2005). *Crafting qualitative research: Working in the post-positivist traditions*. Armonk, NY: M.E. Sharpe.

Prasad, P., & Prasad, P. (1994). The ideology of professionalism and work computerization: An institutionalist study of technological change. *Human Relations*, 47(12), 1433–1458.

Prasad, P., & Prasad, P. (1998). Everyday struggles at the workplace: The nature and implications of routine resistance in contemporary organizations. *Research in the Sociology of Organizations*, 15(2), 225–257.

PwC (2018). SDG Reporting Challenge 2018. From promise to reality: Does business really care about SDGs? *PwC Global Study*, www.pwc.com/gx/en/services/sustainability/sustainable-development-goals/sdg-reporting-challenge-2018.html (accessed 28 May 2019).

Reissner, S. C. (2011). Patterns of stories of organizational change. *Journal of Organizational Change Management*, 24(5), 593–609.

Reissner, S. C., Pagan, V., & Smith, C. (2011) 'Our iceberg is melting': Story, metaphor and the management of organisational change. *Culture and Organization*, 17(5), 417–33.

Rhenman, E. (1974). *Organizationsproblem och långsiktsplanering*. Stockholm: Bonniers.

Richardson, L. (1995). Narrative and sociology. *Journal of Contemporary Ethnography*, 19(1), 116–135.

Ritzer, G. (2002). Enchanting McUniversity: Toward a spectacularly irrational university quotidian. In D. Hayes & R. Wynyard (eds.), *McDonaldization of higher education*. Westport, CT: Bergin & Garvey, pp. 19–32.

Ritzer, G. (2018). *The McDonaldization of society* (9th ed.). Thousand Oaks, CA: Sage.

Roethlisberger, F., & Dickson, W. (1950). *Management and the worker: An account of a research program conducted by the Western Electric Company, Hawthorne Works, Chicago*. Cambridge, MA: Harvard University Press.

Rose, M. (1988). *Industrial behaviour*. Harmondsworth: Penguin.

Rosenfeld, R., & Wilson, D. (1998). *Managing organizations*. London: McGraw-Hill.

Sahlin-Andersson, K. (1996). Imitating by editing success: The construction of organizational field. In B. Czarniawska & G. Sevón (eds.), *Translating organizational change*. Berlin: de Gruyter.

Schein, E. H. (1987). *Organizational culture and leadership*. San Francisco, CA: Jossey-Bass.

Schmitt, B. (2017). Report: Piech throws Winterkorn under Volkswagen bus, *Forbes*, 4 February, www.forbes.com/sites/bertelschmitt/2017/02/04/report-piech-throws-winterkorn-under-volkswagen-bus/#c488a7a41bb6 (accessed 8 January 2019).

Schwabel, D. (2012). How to use storytelling as a leadership tool, *Forbes*, 13 August, www.forbes.com/sites/danschawbel/2012/08/13/how-to-use-storytelling-as-a-leadership-tool/#6281e4f45e8e (accessed 13 January 2019).

Schwär, H. (2018). Puma and Adidas' rivalry has divided a small German town for 70 years – here's what it looks like now. *Business Insider Germany*, 1 October, www.businessinsider.com/how-puma-and-adidas-rivalry-divided-their-founding-town-for-70-years-2018-10?r=US&IR=T (accessed 2 January 2018).

Sevón, G. (1996). Organizational imitation in identity transformation. In B. Czarniawska & G. Sevón (eds.), *Translating organizational change*. Berlin: de Gruyter.

Sewell, G., & Wilkinson, B. (1992). 'Someone to watch over me': Surveillance, discipline and the just-in-time labour process. *Sociology*, 26(2), 271–289.

Sminia, H. (2016). Pioneering process research: Andrew Pettigrew's contribution to management scholarship, 1962–2014. *International Journal of Management Reviews*, 18, 111–132.

Smircich, L. (1983). Concepts of culture and organizational analysis. *Administrative Science Quarterly*, 28(3), 339–358.

Smircich, L., & Morgan, G. (1982). Leadership: The management of meaning. *Journal of Applied Behavioral Science*, 18(3), 257–273.

Smyth, N. (2018). What is a chief storyteller and do you need one? *Techmarsec*, 24 October, https://www.techmarsec.com/what-is-a-chief-storyteller-and-do-you-need-one/ (accessed 2 January 2019).

Sörgärde, N. (2006). *Förändringsförsök och identitetsdramatisering: En studie bland nördar och slipsbärare i ett IT-företag*. Lund: Lund Business Press.

Speitzer, G., & Quinn, R. (1996). Empowering middle managers to be transformational leaders. *Journal of Applied Behavioral Science*, 32(3), 237–261.

Spicer, A., & Sewell, G. (2010). From national service to global player: Transforming the organizational logic of a public broadcaster. *Journal of Management Studies*, 47(6), 913–943.

Statista (2019). Number of Netflix paying streaming subscribers worldwide from 3rd quarter 2011 to 1st quarter 2019 (in millions). *Statista, Media & Advertising*, www.statista.com/statistics/250934/quarterly-number-of-netflix-streaming-subscribers-worldwide/ (accessed 28 May 2019).

Sveningsson, S. (1999). *Strategisk förändring, makt och kunskap: Om disciplinering och motstånd i tidningsföretag*. Lund: Lund University Press.

Sveningsson, S., & Alvesson, M. (2014). *Det ska fan vara chef: Om chefsliv i moderna organizationer.* Lund: Studentlitteratur.

Sveningsson, S., & Alvesson, M. (2016). *Managerial lives: Leadership and identity in an imperfect world.* Cambridge: Cambridge University Press.

Sveningsson, S., & Larsson, M. (2006). Fantasies of leadership: Identity work. *Leadership*, 2(2), 203–224.

Symon, G. (2005). Exploring resistance from a rhetorical perspective. *Organization Studies*, 26(11), 1641–1663.

Taskin, L., & Willmott, H. (2000). Introducing critical management studies: Key dimensions. *Gestion*, 25(6), 27–38.

Taylor, B. (2018). To see the future of competition, look at Netflix. *Harvard Business Review*, 18 July, https://hbr.org/2018/07/to-see-the-future-of-competition-look-at-netflix (accessed 28 May 2019).

Taylor, C. (2015). How Netflix reinvented HR. *Human Resources Director Australia*, 26 June, www.hcamag.com/au/specialisation/change-management/how-netflix-reinvented-hr/143109 (accessed 7 December 2018).

Taylor, F. W. (1911). *The principles of scientific management.* Harper: New York.

Tengblad, S. (2003). *Den myndige medarbetaren: Strategier för konstruktivt medarbetarskap.* Malmö: Liber ekonomi.

Theodossopoulos, D. (2014). On de-pathologizing resistance. *History and Anthropology*, 25(4), 415–430.

Thomas, R., Sargent, L. D., & Hardy, C. (2011). Managing organizational change: Negotiating meaning and power-resistance relations. *Organization Science*, 22(1), 22–41.

Thompson, P., & McHugh, D. (2009). *Work organizations: A critical introduction* (4th ed.). Basingstoke: Palgrave Macmillan.

Thurlow, A., & Helms-Mills, J. (2015). Telling tales out of school: Sensemaking and narratives of legitimacy in an organizational change process. *Scandinavian Journal of Management*, 31(2), 246–254.

Tichy, N. M. (1983). Managing organizational transformations. *Human Resource Management*, 22(1–2), 45–61.

Todnem, R., Kuipers, B., & Procter, S. (2018). Understanding teams in order to understand organizational change. *Journal of Change Management*, 18(1), 1–9.

Tsoukas, H. (2005). Afterword: Why language matters in the analysis of organizational change. *Journal of Organizational Change Management*, 18(1), 96–104.

Tsoukas, H., & Chia, R. (2002). On organizational becoming: Rethinking organizational change. *Organizational Science*, 13(5), 567–682.

Van de Ven, A. H., & Poole, M. P. (1995). Explaining development and change in organizations. *Academy of Management Review*, 20(3), 510–540.

Van Dijk, R., & Van Dick, R. (2009). Navigating organizational change: Change leaders, employee resistance, and work-based identities. *Journal of Change Management*, 9(2), 143–163.

van Hulst, M., & Ybema, S. (2019). From what to where: A setting-sensitive approach to organizational storytelling. *Organization Studies*, online first 25 January, 1–27, doi/10.1177/0170840618815523

Vann, J. L. (2004). Resistance to change and the language of public organizations: A look at 'clashing grammars' in large-scale information technology projects. *Public Organization Review*, 4(1), 47–73.

Wadell, D., & Sohal, A. (1998). Resistance: A constructive tool for change management. *Management Decision*, 36(8), 543–548.

Wallander, J. (2002). *Med den mänskliga naturen – inte mot! Att organisera och leda företag.* Stockholm: SNS.

Warren, P. (2015). *Big change, best path: Successfully managing organizational change with wisdom, analytics and insight.* London: Kogan Page.

Waterman, Jr, R. H., Peters, T. J., & Phillips, J. R. (1980). Structure is not organization. *Business Horizons*, 23(3), 14–26.

Watson, T. J. (1994). *In search of management: Culture, chaos and control in managerial work.* London: Routledge.

Watson, T. J. (2006). *Organising and managing work: Organizational, managerial and strategic behaviour in theory and practice* (2nd ed.). Harlow, UK: Pearson.

Weick, K. E. (1993). The collapse of sensemaking in organizations: The Mann Gulch disaster. *Administrative Science Quarterly*, 38, 628–652.

Weick, K. E. (1995). *Sensemaking in organizations.* Thousand Oaks, CA: Sage.

Weick, K. E., & Quinn, R. E. (1999). Organizational change and development. *Annual Review of Psychology*, 50, 361–386.

Weick, K. E., Sutcliffe, K. M., & Obstfeld, D. (2005). Organizing and the process of sensemaking. *Organization Science*, 16(4), 409–421.

Willmott, H. (1993). Strength is ignorance, slavery is freedom: Managing culture in modern organizations. *Journal of Management Studies*, 30, 515–552.

Willmott, H. (1994). Business process re-engineering and human resource management. *Personnel Review*, 23(3), 34–46.

Woodward, J. (1958). *Management and technology: Problems and progress in technology 3.* London: HMSO.

Wooten, K. C., & White, L. P. (1999). Linking OD's philosophy with justice theory: Postmodern implications. *Journal of Organizational Change Management*, 12(1), 7–21.

Worthington, F. (2004). Management, change and culture in the NHS: Rhetoric and reality. *Clinician in Management*, 12(2).

Worthington, F. (2017). Change and innovation: New organizational forms. In D. Knights & H. Willmott (eds.), *Introducing organizational behaviour and management* (3rd ed.). Andover, UK: Cengage Learning EMEA.

Ybema, S. (2004). Managerial postalgia: Projecting a golden future. *Journal of Managerial Psychology*, 19(8), 825–841.

Zaleski, A. (2017). 7 businesses that cloned others and made millions. *CNBC*, 4 October, www.cnbc.com/2017/10/03/7-businesses-that-cloned-others-and-made-millions.html (accessed 28 May 2019).

Ziegler, C. (2011). Nokia CEO Stephen Elop rallies troops in brutally honest 'burning platform' memo? (update: it's real!), *Engadget*, 2 August, www.engadget.com/2011/02/08/nokia-ceo-stephen-elop-rallies-troops-in-brutally-honest-burnin/ (accessed 10 January 2019).

INDEX

Note: Page numbers in *italics* refer to tables and figures.